The Manual of Ideas

*The Proven Framework
for Finding the Best
Value Investments*

JOHN MIHALJEVIC

WILEY

Published by John Wiley & Sons, Inc., Hoboken, New Jersey.
Published simultaneously in Canada.

For general information on our other products and services or for technical
support, please contact our Customer Care Department within the United States at
(800) 762-2974, outside the United States at (317) 572-3993 or fax (317) 572-4002.

Wiley publishes in a variety of print and electronic formats and by print-on-demand.
Some material included with standard print versions of this book may not be included
in e-books or in print-on-demand. If this book refers to media such as a CD or DVD
that is not included in the version you purchased, you may download this material at
http://booksupport.wiley.com. For more information about Wiley products, visit www
.wiley.com.

Library of Congress Cataloging-in-Publication Data

Mihaljevic, John, 1976-
    The manual of ideas : the proven framework for finding the best value
investments/John Mihaljevic.
        pages cm.
        Includes bibliographical references and index.
        ISBN 978-1-118-08365-9 (cloth); ISBN 978-1-118-41889-5 (ebk);
        ISBN 978-1-118-41609-9 (ebk)
            1. Investment analysis.   2. Value investing.   3. Corporations—Valuation.
    4. Portfolio management.   I. Title.
    HG4529.M54 2013
    332.6—dc23

2013012718

To Mark,
whose courage humbles me

Contents

Foreword

When John asked me to write the foreword to his book, I was flattered and honored and immediately agreed to do so. I agreed because I respect John's work and deeply appreciate the intellectual interchange and things I have learned from reading his *Manual of Ideas* periodicals over the years.

John brings a spirit of inquiry to his work and displays a true thirst for knowledge and understanding in his quest to be a better investor. More importantly, and very graciously, he doesn't keep it all to himself. He shares his thoughts and acts as a wonderful role model by showing us how he learns by interacting with other intelligent and dedicated investors.

As John shows us how he learns, we can figure out how to become better learners ourselves.

He also shares some of his life story and how he came to be in his present circumstances. After you read that section, I think you will agree that the quest for learning and knowledge, and creativity, defines much of what we are (and should be) as human beings.

There is a true spirit of humility in John's work. He understands that there are multiple ways to think about investing and many different approaches to gaining understanding about what a business is worth and how that might change in the future. He also understands that those answers may be different in different environments and for different amounts to invest.

As an investor, I find the single most valuable thing that I do is to read. I've been a lifelong reader and I thank my parents for instilling that into me from my earliest memories. As Charlie Munger once noted, one of the best investments you can make is buying a book. He went on to note that for just a few dollars, you get man-years of an author's life that went into producing that book for you. I couldn't agree more.

I recommend John's book as it provides insights and models and methods to systematically think about the craft of investing. While all of us seeking to be good value based investors have different tools and approaches we bring to the task, we can and should, always continue to learn and adapt and improve our work.

This book helps you do just that. Each chapter provides specific examples and discussions of the ways that successful investors approach their work. Successful investing is hard and lonely work. All of the evidence and documentation you can find and demonstrate relates to the past. Your returns though, come in the future, and the future is a paradox of things that are similar to what they were in the past, and different at the same time.

Our challenge as investors is to sort out which is which. Reading, studying, and thinking about the concepts that John lays out in this book will help you with that task.

I hope that you enjoy the challenge!

Thomas S. Gayner
President and Chief Investment Officer
Markel Corporation

Preface

For the solitary endeavor that value investing can be at times, it has also enriched my life with many friendships and new experiences borne out of those friendships. The value investing community is diverse, vibrant, and global. I am grateful to have been deeply involved with VALUEx Zurich/Klosters, the annual gathering of value investors; ValueConferences, the series of online idea conferences for value investors; and *The Manual of Ideas*, the idea-oriented monthly research publication.

Warren Buffett's spectacularly successful investment philosophy has found devoted followers on every continent and in virtually every country. Many of them have used their special talents, cultural sensibilities, and unique circumstances to succeed at their own distinct brands of value investing, including Mohnish Pabrai in the United States, Prem Watsa in Canada, Massimo Fuggetta in the United Kingdom, Guy Spier in Switzerland, François Badelon in France, Francisco García Paramés in Spain, Ciccio Azzollini in Italy, Jochen Wermuth in Russia, Rahul Saraogi in India, Christopher Swasbrook in New Zealand, and Shuhei Abe in Japan.

We have interviewed more than 100 fund managers across the globe in preparation for this book, seeking their wisdom on the topic of idea generation. As such, the following pages feature what I've learned as managing editor of *The Manual of Ideas* and provide a glimpse into the idea-generation process of some of the most successful investors of our times. We have interviewed heavyweights like Chuck Akre, Charles de Vaulx, Jean-Marie Eveillard, Tom Gayner, Joel Greenblatt, Howard Marks, Mohnish Pabrai, Tom Russo, and Guy Spier. We have also gained insights from speaking with up-and-coming fund managers poised to comprise the next generation of value superinvestors. Many of these in-depth interviews are available as free videos on the YouTube channels manualofideas and valueconferences.

In Chapter 1, we focus on the mind-set of a value investor, distinguishing it from that of market participants who too often view stocks as squiggly lines on a computer screen and who cannot help but indulge in Keynes's beauty contest. In Chapters 2 through 10, we dissect the value investment idea-generation process, structuring the discussion around nine categories of value ideas: Graham-style deep value, Greenblatt-style magic formula, small-cap value, sum-of-the-parts or hidden value, superinvestor favorites, jockey stocks, special situations, equity stubs, and international value investments. While quite a bit of overlap exists between some of these categories, we approach ideas in each bucket slightly differently. We examine the uses and misuses of each approach to idea generation, provide insights into the screening process, look beyond quantitative screening methods, and lay out the key points of inquiry in each case. The result is both a practical guide to idea generation and an examination of core value investing principles.

It would be impossible to cite everyone who has influenced my thinking on the subject of investing. A few mentors stand out, however, starting with the late professor James Tobin, Nobel laureate in economics, who was incredibly generous in letting me access his thinking on risk and asset allocation during my time as his research assistant at Yale. David Swensen, Yale's chief investment officer, helped me advance along the path of value-oriented investing, as his seminar brought together students and fund managers in a unique setting. Guy Spier, chief executive officer of Aquamarine Capital, has shared his considerable wisdom on investing and life with me. Warren Buffett, Charlie Munger, Joel Greenblatt, Tom Gayner, and Mohnish Pabrai are role models from whom I have learned mostly through their writings or interactions via *The Manual of Ideas* and ValueConferences. I consider them key influences and thank them for sharing their wisdom with the value investing community.

On a personal note, I'd like to thank my brother and partner at *The Manual of Ideas*, Oliver Mihaljevic, who not only is a great investor in his own right but also displays a unique commitment to value investing as a discipline that deserves a more prominent place in finance curricula. Oliver constantly seeks new insights into the art of investing, and I have been fortunate to benefit from his inquiries. My wife, Branka, has been tremendously supportive throughout the process of writing this book, alleviating me of many duties that might have interfered with its publication. My kids, Mark, Mia, and Mateo, have provided not only a reason for persisting in this endeavor but also much-needed (sometimes too much!) distraction. Enjoy!

John Mihaljevic

CHAPTER 1

A Highly Personal Endeavor

What Do You Want to Own?

Man the living creature, the creating individual, is always more important than any established style or system.
—Bruce Lee

The stock market is a curious place because everyone participating in it is loosely interested in the same thing—making money. Still, there is no uniform path to achieving this rather uniform goal. You may be only a few mouse clicks away from purchasing the popular book *The Warren Buffett Way*,[1] but only one man has ever truly followed the path of Warren Buffett. In investing, it is hard enough to succeed as an original; as a copycat, it is virtually impossible. Each of us must carve out a *personal* way to investment success, even if you are a *professional* investor.

That said, great investors like Ben Graham, Seth Klarman, and Warren Buffett have much to teach us, and we have much to gain by learning from them. One of the masters' key teachings is as important as it is simple: A share of stock represents a share in the ownership of a business. A stock exchange simply provides a convenient means of exchanging your ownership for cash. Without an exchange, your ownership of a business would not change. The ability to sell your stake would be negatively affected, but you would still be able to do it, just as you can sell your car or house if you decide to do so.

Unfortunately, when we actually start investing, we are inevitably bombarded with distractions that make it easy to forget the essence of stock ownership. These titillations include the fast-moving ticker tape on CNBC, the seemingly omniscient talking heads, the polished corporate press releases, stock price charts that are consolidating or breaking out, analyst estimates being beaten, and stock prices hitting new highs. It feels a little like living in the world of Curious George, the lovable monkey for whom it is "easy to forget" the well-intentioned advice of his friend. My son loves Curious George stories, because as surely as George gets into trouble, he finds a way out of trouble. The latter doesn't always hold true for investors in the stock market.

Give Your Money to Warren Buffett, or Invest It Yourself?

I still remember the day I had saved the princely sum of $100,000. I had worked as a research analyst for San Francisco investment bank Thomas Weisel Partners for a couple of years and in 2003 had managed to put aside what I considered to be an amount that made me a free man. Freedom, I reasoned, was only possible if one did not have to work to survive; otherwise, one was forced into a form of servitude that involved trading time for food and shelter. With the money saved, I could quit my job, move to a place like Thailand, and live on interest income. While I wisely chose not to exercise my freedom option, I still had to find something to do with the money.

I dismissed an investment in mutual funds quite quickly because I was familiar with findings that the vast majority of mutual funds underperformed the market indices on an after-fee basis.[2] I also became aware of the oft-neglected but crucial fact that investors tended to add capital to funds after a period of good performance and withdraw capital after a period of bad performance. This caused investors' *actual* results to lag significantly behind the funds' *reported* results. Fund prospectuses show time-weighted returns, but investors in those funds reap the typically lower capital-weighted returns. A classic example of this phenomenon is the Munder NetNet Fund, an Internet fund that lost investors billions of dollars from 1997 through 2002. Despite the losses, the fund reported a *positive* compounded annual return of 2.15 percent for the period. The reason? The fund managed little money when it was doing well in the late 1990s. Then, just as billions in new capital poured in, the fund embarked on a debilitating three-year losing streak.[3] Although I had felt immune to the temptation to buy after a strong run in the market and to sell after a sharp decline, I thought this temptation would be easier to resist if I knew exactly what I owned and why I owned it. Owning shares in a mutual fund meant trusting the fund manager to pick the right investments. Trust tends to erode after a period of losses.

Mutual funds and lower-cost index funds should not be entirely dismissed, however, as they offer an acceptable alternative for those wishing to delegate investment decision making to someone else. Value mutual funds such as Bruce Berkowitz's Fairholme Fund or Mason Hawkins's Longleaf Funds are legitimate choices for many individual investors. High-net-worth investors and institutions enjoy the additional option of investing in hedge funds, but few of those funds deserve their typically steep management and performance fees. Warren Buffett critiqued the hedge fund fee structure in his 2006 letter to shareholders: "It's a lopsided system whereby 2 percent of your principal is paid each year to the manager even if he accomplishes nothing—or, for that matter, loses you a bundle—and, additionally, 20 percent of your profit is paid to him if he succeeds, even if his success is due simply to a rising tide. For example, a manager who achieves a gross return of 10 percent in a year will keep 3.6 percentage points—two points off the top plus 20 percent of the residual eight points—leaving only 6.4 percentage points for his investors."[4]

A small minority of value-oriented hedge fund managers have chosen to side with Buffett on the fee issue, offering investors a structure similar to that of the limited partnerships Buffett managed in the 1960s. Buffett charged no management fee and a performance fee only on returns in excess of an annual hurdle rate. The pioneers in this small but growing movement include Guy Spier of Zurich, Switzerland-based Aquamarine Capital Management and Mohnish Pabrai of Irvine, California-based Pabrai Investment Funds. These types of funds bestow a decisive advantage, ceteris paribus, on long-term investors. Table 1.1 shows the advantages of an investor-friendly fee structure.

TABLE 1.1   Effect of Fees on the Future Wealth of a Hedge Fund Investor

	Typical Hedge Fund Fee Structure: "2 and 20"		Buffett Partnership-Style Fee Structure	
	Management fee: 2%		Management fee: 0%	
	Performance fee: 20%		Performance fee: 20%	
	Annual hurdle rate: 0%		Annual hurdle rate: 6%	
Assumed gross return	5.0%	10.0%	5.0%	10.0%
Resulting net return	2.4%	6.4%	5.0%	9.2%
Gross value of $1 million				
... after 10 years	$1,628,895	$2,593,742	$1,628,895	$2,593,742
... after 20 years	2,653,298	6,727,500	2,653,298	6,727,500
... after 30 years	4,321,942	17,449,402	4,321,942	17,449,402
Net value of $1 million				
... after 10 years	$1,267,651	$1,859,586	$1,628,895	$2,411,162
... after 20 years	1,606,938	3,458,060	2,653,298	5,813,702
... after 30 years	2,037,036	6,430,561	4,321,942	14,017,777
Value lost due to fees				
... after 10 years	$361,244	$734,156	$0	$182,580
... after 20 years	1,046,360	3,269,440	0	913,798
... after 30 years	2,284,906	11,018,842	0	3,431,625

I also considered investing my savings in one of a handful of public companies that operate as low-cost yet high-quality investment vehicles. Berkshire Hathaway pays Warren Buffett an annual salary of $100,000 for arguably the finest capital allocation skills in the world. Buffett receives no bonus, no stock options, and no restricted stock, let alone hedge-fund-style performance fees.[5] It certainly seems like investors considering an investment in a highly prized hedge fund should first convince themselves that their prospective fund manager can beat Buffett. Doing this on a pre-fee basis is hard enough; on an after-fee basis, the odds diminish considerably. Of course, buying a share of Berkshire is not quite associated with the same level of privilege and exclusivity as being accepted into a secretive hedge fund.

Berkshire is not the only public holding company with shareholder-friendly and astute management. Alternatives include Brookfield Asset Management, Fairfax Financial, Leucadia National, Loews Companies, Markel Corporation, and White Mountains Insurance. While these companies meet Buffett-style compensation criteria, some public investment vehicles have married hedge-fund-style compensation with a value investment approach. Examples include Greenlight Capital Re and Biglari Holdings. These hedge funds in disguise may ultimately deliver satisfactory performance to their common shareholders, but they are unlikely to exceed the long-term after-fee returns of a company like Markel, which marries superior investment management with low implied fees.

In light of the exceptional long-term investment results and low fees of companies like Berkshire and Markel, it may be irrational for any long-term investor to manage his or her own portfolio of stocks. Professional fund managers have a slight conflict of interest in this regard. Their livelihood depends rather directly on convincing their clients that the past performance of Berkshire or Markel is no indication of future results. Luckily for them, securities regulators play along with this notion, thereby doing their part in encouraging a constant flow of new entrants into the lucrative fund management business.

Rest assured, we won't judge too harshly those who choose to manage their own equity investments. After all, that is precisely what I did with my savings in 2003 and have done ever since. You could say that underlying my decision has been remarkable folly, but here are a few justifications for the do-it-yourself approach: First, investment holding companies like Berkshire and Markel are generally not available for purchase at net asset value, implying that some recognition of skill is already reflected in their market price. While over time the returns to shareholders will converge with internally generated returns on capital, the gap is accentuated in the case of shorter holding periods or large initial premiums paid over net asset value. Even for a company like Berkshire, there is a market price at which an investment becomes no longer attractive.

In addition, one of the trappings of investment success is growth of assets under management. Few fund managers limit their assets, and this is even rarer among public vehicles. Buffett started investing less than $1 million six decades ago. Today he oversees a company with more than $200 billion in market value. If Buffett wanted to invest $2 billion, a mere 1 percent of Berkshire's quoted value, into one company, he could not choose a company with a market value of $200 million. He would likely need to find a company quoted at $20 billion, unless he negotiated an acquisition of the entire business. Buffett is one of few large capital allocators who readily admit that size hurts performance. Many others evolve their view, perhaps not surprisingly, as their assets under management grow. Arguments include greater access to management, an ability to structure private deals, and the spreading of costs over a large asset base. Trust Buffett that these advantages pale in comparison with the disadvantage of a diminished set of available investments. If you manage $1 million or even $100 million, investing in companies that are too small for the superinvestors offers an opportunity for outperformance. Buffett agrees: "If I was running $1 million today, or $10 million for that matter, I'd be fully invested. Anyone who says that size does not hurt investment performance is selling. The highest rates of return I've ever achieved were in the 1950s. I killed the Dow. You ought to see the numbers. But I was investing peanuts then. It's a huge structural advantage not to have a lot of money. I think I could make you 50% a year on $1 million. No, I know I could. I guarantee that."[6] The corollary: When small investors commit capital to megacaps such as Exxon Mobil or Apple, they willingly surrender a key structural advantage: the ability to invest in small companies.

Echoing Buffett's sentiments on the unique advantages of a small investable asset base, Eric Khrom, managing partner of Khrom Capital Management, describes the business rationale he articulated to his partners early on: "The fact that we are starting off so small will allow me to fish in very small pond where the big fishermen can't go. So although I'm a one man shop, you don't have to picture me competing with shops that are much larger than me, because they can't look at the things I look at anyway. We will be looking at the much smaller micro caps, where there are a lot of inefficiencies. . . ."[7]

The last argument for choosing our own equity investments leads to the concept of capital allocation. Contrary to the increasingly popular view that the stock market is little more than a glorified casino, the market is supposed to foster the allocation of capital to productive uses in a capitalist economy. Businesses that add value to their customers while earning acceptable returns on invested capital should be able to raise capital for expansion, and businesses that earn insufficient returns on capital should fail to attract funding. A properly functioning market thereby assists the process of wealth creation, accelerating the growth in savings, investment, and GDP. If the role of the market is to allocate capital to productive uses, it becomes clear that a few dozen top investors cannot do the job by themselves. There are simply too many businesses to be evaluated. By doing the work the superinvestors must forgo due to limited bandwidth, we put ourselves in a position to earn the just reward of good investment performance. This idea of capital allocation ties in with the previous point regarding our ability to invest in companies that are too small for the superinvestors. We may safely assume that Buffett and the others will allocate capital to mega-caps such as Coca-Cola, if those companies deserve the money. On the other hand, companies such as Strayer Education and Harvest Natural Resources may be left without capital even if they can put it to productive use. Smaller investors can fill this void and make money, provided that they make the right capital allocation judgments.

Cast Yourself in the Role of Capital Allocator

It is little surprise that the world's richest investor is a capital allocator rather than a trend follower, thematic investor, or day trader. Buffett is famous for his buy-and-hold strategy, which has been the hallmark of Berkshire's portfolio investments and outright purchases of businesses. Buffett looks to the underlying businesses rather than stock certificates to deliver superior compounding of capital over the long term. Buying businesses cheaply has not generated his long-term returns—it has merely accentuated them.

Buffett raised eyebrows in the investment community many years ago when he bought Coca-Cola at a mid-teens multiple of earnings. Most value investors could not understand why Buffett considered it a bargain purchase. Buffett was allocating capital to a superior business at a fair price. He knew that Coca-Cola would compound the capital employed in the business at a high rate for a long time to come. Buffett did not need P/E multiple expansion to make the investment in Coca-Cola pay off.

Similarly, famed value investor Joel Greenblatt paid roughly 20 times earnings for Moody's when it went public in 2000. Greenblatt was allocating capital to a superior business, one that could grow earnings at a high rate without requiring additional capital, thereby freeing up large amounts of cash for share repurchases. Despite trading at a relatively high earnings multiple at the time of the initial public offering (IPO), Moody's shares more than quintupled in the subsequent six years. Of course, the company ran into major trouble when the U.S. housing bubble burst a few years ago. Despite the steep decline, Moody's traded at $48 per share in early 2013, up from a comparable price of $12.65 per share the day it was spun off from Dun & Bradstreet in October 2000.

Role versus Objective: A Subtle but Important Distinction

Our role in the stock market may at first glance seem like a trivial issue. It is hardly a secret that rational investors seek to maximize risk-adjusted after-tax returns on invested capital. What is our role, therefore, if not to make the most money by identifying investments that will increase in price? This question is misplaced because it confuses objective (making money) and role.

We typically view our role in the market as insignificant. While most investors do have a negligible impact on the overall market, the accompanying small fish mind-set does not lend itself to successful investing. Even when I invested a tiny amount of money, I found it helpful to adopt the mind-set of chief capital allocator. I imagined my role as distributing the world's financial capital to activities that would generate the highest returns on capital.

Consider the following subtle difference in how investors may perceive their portfolios in relation to the available investment opportunities. Many of us inappropriately consider the scale of our portfolio ahead of the scale of potential investments. To illustrate this, imagine we wanted to invest $100,000 in one of the stocks in Table 1.2 in late 2001.

When selecting a company from this list, we might analyze financial statements and consider various valuation measures. But even before embarking on a detailed analysis, some of us may think, "I have $100,000 to invest, which will buy me a tiny stake in one the above companies. It looks like I can buy a few thousand

TABLE 1.2 "Mind-Set A"—Selected Investment Opportunities,
November 2001[8]

Ticker	Company	Stock Price	Market Value	$100,000 Buys . . .
AET	Aetna	$30.52	$4.4 billion	3,277 shares
DAL	Delta Air Lines	29.31	3.6 billion	3,412 shares
F	Ford Motor	17.88	32.4 billion	5,593 shares
GM	General Motors	47.69	26.5 billion	2,097 shares
LMT	Lockheed Martin	45.01	19.8 billion	2,222 shares
NYT	New York Times	45.15	6.8 billion	2,215 shares
TIF	Tiffany & Co.	29.17	4.3 billion	3,428 shares
TM	Toyota Motor	53.71	99.0 billion	1,862 shares

shares of any of these stocks" ("mind-set a"). Without realizing it, we are committing the fallacy of considering the scale of our portfolio ahead of the scale of potential investments.

On the flip side, if we adopted an asset allocator's mind-set, we might ask, "If I could buy one of the above companies, which would I choose?" This question focuses attention on the relative scale of the potential investments rather than the size of our portfolio. By applying this mind-set even before embarking on in-depth analysis of the various companies, we might make the observation shown in Table 1.3.

Toyota alone was valued more highly than all the companies on the left combined (based on market value rather than enterprise value, which in this case would have been a more appropriate measure). The investor with mind-set b might wonder: "Would I rather own Toyota or Aetna, Delta, Ford, GM, Lockheed Martin, the *New York Times*, and Tiffany combined?" While after careful analysis the answer might indeed be Toyota, it is obvious that we would need well-founded reasons for that choice. Had we kept a small fish mentality, however, we might have completely missed this issue of relative scale and invested in Toyota, ignorant of the severity of the implied relative value bet.

In Table 1.4, we revisit the previous comparison as of late 2004.

As a comparison of the market values shows, Toyota outperformed a portfolio of the companies on the left over the three-year

TABLE 1.3 "Mind-Set B"—Selected Investment Opportunities, November 2001

Ticker	Company	Market Value	Ticker	Company	Market Value
AET	Aetna	$4.4 billion	TM	Toyota Motor	$99.0 billion
DAL	Delta Air Lines	3.6 billion			
F	Ford Motor	32.4 billion			
GM	General Motors	26.5 billion			
LMT	Lockheed Martin	19.8 billion			
NYT	New York Times	6.8 billion			
TIF	Tiffany & Co.	4.3 billion			
		$97.8 billion			$99.0 billion

TABLE 1.4 "Mind-Set B"—Selected Investment Opportunities, October 2004[9]

Ticker	Company	Market Value	Ticker	Company	Market Value
AET	Aetna	$12.8 billion	TM	Toyota Motor	$125.3 billion
DAL	Delta Air Lines	0.4 billion			
F	Ford Motor	23.7 billion			
GM	General Motors	21.4 billion			
LMT	Lockheed Martin	23.8 billion			
NYT	New York Times	5.7 billion			
TIF	Tiffany & Co.	4.1 billion			
		$91.9 billion			$125.3 billion

period ending in late 2004.[10] While this may come as a surprise, it simply means that mind-set b is not a sufficient condition for investment success: Good decision making requires thorough analysis of underlying fundamentals. (Giving the previous table another thought, it is interesting that, in theory, by selling short all of Toyota in late 2004, we could have bought not only the companies on the left but also 93 percent of McDonald's.)

The Buck Stops Here

Once I had put aside my small fish mentality and embraced a capital allocator's mind-set, I started making better investment decisions. I found it easier to conclude, for example, that auto companies might not make good investments despite their recognized brands, large sales, and low P/E ratios. The capital allocator mind-set helped me realize I did not have to pick a winner in the auto industry when many companies outside the auto industry had better business models and were available at reasonable prices.

The new mind-set also raised the hurdle for investments in unprofitable companies because I knew intuitively that I would be forgoing current profits and the reinvestment of those profits in expectation of a future windfall. This seemed a rather speculative proposition. Many market participants, especially growth investors, exhibit a high tolerance for money-losing companies. An even more common trait is a willingness to ignore nonrecurring charges, even though such expenses reduce book value in the same way as recurring expenses. While no one would buy shares in a money-losing company unless he or she believed in a profitable future or in a favorable sale or liquidation, it seems that many investors' tolerance for losses is exaggerated by the subconscious reassurance that their investment amount is limited and they cannot be forced to commit more capital to a company even if it continues to lose money. Though our exposure is indeed legally limited to the initial investment, any impression that someone else will take care of a company's losses is an illusion:

- If other investors end up funding the losses of a company we own, they will either (1) dilute our interest or (2), if they lend money to the company, increase its interest expense and leverage. Both scenarios are blows to our prospects for a decent return on investment.
- If the company is able to fund losses with the liquidity available on the balance sheet, our percentage stake will not get diluted, but book value per share will decline. As Figure 1.1 shows, the impact of losses, whether recurring or not, on book value is perverse because, for example, a 20 percent drop in book value requires a 25 percent subsequent increase just to offset the decline.

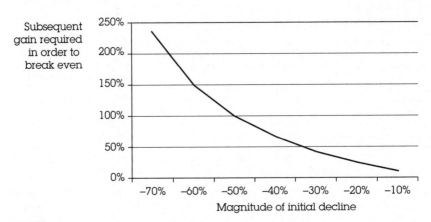

FIGURE 1.1   The Perverse Impact of Losses—Subsequent Gain Required to Break Even
Source: The Manual of Ideas.

Perhaps most important, the capital allocator mind-set enabled me to draw a sharp distinction between value and price, echoing Ben Graham's teaching, "Price is what you pay; value is what you get."[11] If I directed the allocation of the world's capital, I would not be able to rely on the market to bail me out of bad decisions. The greater fool theory of someone buying my shares at a higher price breaks down if the buck stops with me. Successful long-term investors believe their return will come from the investee company's return on equity rather than from sales of stock. This mind-set produces a very different process of estimating value than if we rely on the market to establish value and then try to gauge whether a company is likely to beat or miss quarterly earnings estimates.

Acting as a capital allocator rather than a speculator or trader required tremendous discipline at first, as I sometimes felt the temptation to outsmart other investors by betting that an earnings report would beat consensus estimates or an acquisition rumor would prove correct. Trading on such tenuous propositions required tacit agreement with the market's underlying valuation of a business, as I would have been betting on an incremental change in the stock price and not necessarily buying a fundamentally undervalued business. I learned that self-restraint was crucial, as buying an overvalued company in expectation of positive news could backfire. There is simply no way to know how an overvalued stock will react to an apparent earnings beat. Investors may be impressed by the strong earnings but disappointed by future guidance. The market may also have already priced in an earnings beat, with investors having bought the rumor, only to sell the news. Asset allocator Jeremy Grantham, chief investment strategist of GMO, agrees that investors have a hard time restraining themselves from playing the market: "Most professionals, including many of the best, prefer to engage in Keynes's 'beauty contest,' trying to guess what other investors will think in the future and 'beating them to the draw' rather than behaving like effective components of an efficient market; spending their time and talent seeking long-term values."[12] A money manager volunteered his outlook for energy investing in the *Wall Street Journal* in late 2005: "I think the sector is probably a little overvalued, but I wouldn't be surprised to see a run for energy stocks as we get to year-end. . . . People who are behind will go there to catch up."[13] The manager could not have been referring to investors who view themselves as capital allocators.

The Scale of Investments: How Much Is a Billion Dollars, Really?

In a world in which the valuations of many firms stretch into the billions or even hundreds of billions of dollars, developing intuition for the scale of such mind-boggling figures is critical. In late 2004, I came across Sirius Satellite Radio, which was valued at more than $8 billion, having reported revenue of $19 million and a net loss of $169 million in the previous quarter. Was $8 billion too much to pay for a company with little revenue and a net loss of more than eight times revenue? Since no traditional valuation measure could be used to arrive at an $8 billion valuation, why should the company not be worth $4 billion, or $16 billion? When a valuation appears to get out of hand, it helps to ask what else an equivalent sum of money would buy. At $50 per barrel of crude oil, $8 billion would have been enough to meet the oil demand of India for almost three months. Or assuming U.S. per capita GDP of $37,800, it would have taken the lifetime GDP of 4,200 Americans to equal $8 billion. It would have taken the lifetime savings of a *multiple* of 4,200 Americans to buy Sirius. Does it make sense that possibly tens of thousands of Americans would have had to spend their lives working and saving just so they could buy a money-losing company? While this question did not tell me how much Sirius was worth, it alerted me to a situation in which the company's per-share value might have deviated from the market price.

Mohnish Pabrai makes an eloquent case against investing in companies that become too large.[14] He compares companies to mammals, echoing Charlie Munger's latticework approach. According to Pabrai, nature seems to have imposed a size limit on mammals and companies alike. There have never been mammals much larger than an elephant, perhaps because mammals are warm-blooded and need energy to survive. It gets progressively more difficult for the heart to circulate blood to the extremities as a mammal grows bigger. Similarly, the top management of a large and growing corporation becomes progressively more removed from the multiplying touch points with customers, suppliers, and partners. This reduces management effectiveness, eventually causing scale to become a disadvantage and providing competitors with an opportunity to beat the incumbent. Pabrai observed nearly 10 years ago that no company on the Fortune 500 list of the most valuable corporations had net income much in excess of $15 billion (this changed in 2005 when Exxon Mobil posted record profits due to rising oil prices). It seems that any company successful enough to make much more than a billion dollars per month triggers a particularly fierce competitive response and sometimes piques the interest of trustbusters.

Owner Mentality

You have to give Wall Street credit. It was not easy to start with the simple concept of business ownership and end up in a world of quarterly earnings guidance, credit default swaps, and high-frequency trading. Wall Street was supposed to foster the allocation of capital to productive uses while minimizing frictional costs and enabling other industries to deliver the goods and services demanded by consumers. In the case of Wall Street and the broader economy, the tail really has come to wag the dog.

You have probably heard a wide range of reasons for buying a stock over the years: "This company has a great management team." "I love its products." "It will take over the world." Those three examples are among the more palatable justifications, even if they contain no mention of the price paid for the business. Other arguments include: "This company operates in an industry with huge growth potential." "This company is just one of many I'm buying because I think the market will go up." "This is a small-cap stock, and today is December 31st—I'm betting on the 'January effect.'" "This company is a great acquisition candidate." "A taxi driver gave me a hot tip from a man he drove to 11 Wall Street." "This company's name starts with 'China.'"

While it may be in the interest of bankers and brokers to complicate matters to boost demand for financial guidance and trading, those of us concerned primarily with investment performance might do best to follow the advice of Henry David Thoreau in *Walden:* "Simplify, simplify." But how do we simplify the complicated and treacherous game investing has become? The only way to do it reliably may be to focus on what a share of stock actually gives us, legally speaking. If the stock market shut down tomorrow, how would we estimate the value of the stock we own? We might try to figure out the financial profile of the business in which we are part owners. How much cash could this business pay out this year, and is this amount more likely to increase or decrease over time? Somewhat counter-intuitively, the recipe for evaluating a business purchase is the same whether the stock market is open or closed. A functioning market offers one unique source of value, however: It occasionally provides an opportunity to buy a business at well below fair value. Those who take advantage of this opportunity may want to write a few thank-you notes to those on Wall Street who put career risk ahead of investment risk and put duty to their own pocketbooks ahead of fiduciary duty. On second thought, "a few" notes may not be enough.

Adopting the Right Mind-Set

Thinking like a capital allocator goes hand in hand with thinking like an owner. Investors who view themselves as owners rather than traders look to the business rather than the market for their return on investment. They do not expect others to bail them out of bad decisions.

Investment professionalization has had unintended consequences, as the ultimate owners of capital (households and endowments) have become increasingly detached from security selection. Short-term-oriented security holders, such as mutual funds and hedge funds, have displaced long-term owners. The results have been a greater tendency to choose portfolios that reduce occupational risk rather than investment risk, increased trading mentality, and less participation in company affairs. As Vanguard founder John Bogle pointed out, "The old own-a-stock industry could hardly afford to take for granted effective corporate governance in the interest of shareholders; the new rent-a-stock industry has little reason to care."

The incentive structure of the asset management industry discourages fund managers from standing up to corporate executives, as funds prize access for business and social reasons. When Deutsche Asset Management, a large Hewlett-Packard shareholder in 2002, voted for the contentious HP-Compaq merger, it may have been due to pressure from HP executives. According to a report, "Merger opponent Walter Hewlett has sued HP, saying its management threatened to lock Deutsche Bank, Deutsche Asset Management's parent company, out of future HP investment-banking business if it had voted against [the deal]. Because of that pressure . . . Deutsche Bank, which previously had indicated it would vote against the deal, at the last minute switched its votes in favor of it. . . ." Disintermediation of ownership has placed massive amounts of stock in the hands of mutual funds, weakening corporate governance, sustaining excessive executive pay, and tolerating imperialistic mergers and acquisitions.

In hindsight, was there a way to profit from knowing that Deutsche's vote for the HP-Compaq deal might be influenced by factors other than its merits to HP shareholders? Perhaps we could have used a cynical view of Deutsche's incentives as a reason to invest in Compaq, which traded at a wider-than-typical merger arbitrage spread, reflecting investors' belief that the unsound merger might be called off. The bigger lesson may be to avoid giving money to entities that have less than their clients' or shareholders' best interests in mind.

It is hard to overstate how important owner mentality is when investing in stocks. Management works for the shareholders, not the other way around. There is no law that prevents owners from asserting their rights, regardless of whether they own one share of stock or a million. Of course, there are practical limits to influencing management as a small shareholder, but we need to think big to succeed. If our analysis shows a company would be a great investment if only we could get management to pay a special dividend, repurchase stock, spin off a division, or remove an underperforming CEO, chances are good that someone with the power to effect such a change (read: a large shareholder or hedge fund) agrees with us. I am surprised by how often I have invested in companies that ended up announcing seemingly unexpected actions to unlock shareholder value. The only way to find such companies consistently is to think about what changes we would make if we had the power and how much value such changes would create. If the latter is sufficiently high, we may get rewarded, even though someone else will do the hard work.

Stock Selection Framework

In this book, we examine equity idea generation in nine categories, each of which requires a slightly different approach to idea generation and evaluation. However, it also makes sense to think about an overarching approach to choosing equity investments. In this regard, we consider a stock selection framework that is (1) flexible enough to allow for analysis of any stock, regardless of company size or industry, yet (2) concrete enough to be useful in making informed investment decisions. To achieve both objectives, the framework needs to go far beyond the basic dividend-discount model of equity value, which fails miserably at the second objective. Perhaps it is precisely the lack of real-world applicability of that basic model that compels so many investors to select stocks based on such subjective criteria as first-mover advantage and technology leadership without understanding how those criteria fit into a more holistic view of stock valuation.

Notwithstanding the complexity inherent in a universal stock selection framework, developing a holistic approach to stock selection is an eminently achievable task. After all, the stock market itself is a holistic framework that ranks all companies along the same dimension—market value. Biotech companies are not valued in biotech dollars that are not convertible into construction dollars. On the contrary, because market value is a variable that is defined in the same way for every public company, investors know exactly what percentage of a biotech firm they could own in exchange for a piece of a construction company. Similarly, biotech investors do not commit capital because they like the sound of biotech companies' names or because they are fascinated with furthering DNA research. They invest for the same reason as all other investors: to make a buck. Consequently, we ought to have a model that boils all companies down to the same dimension—equity value. By comparing that value with market value, we can make informed investment decisions.

Figure 1.2 outlines an approach that may be able to handle, at least in principle, the vast array of equity investment opportunities available in the public markets. Although the following framework may not be practicable for most small investors, it does illustrate how we may think about security selection if we adopt the mindset of chief capital allocator.

The stock selection framework begins by asking whether the net assets are available for purchase for less than replacement cost. If this is not the case, we exclude the company from consideration because it might be cheaper to re-create the equity in the private market. If the equity is available for less than replacement cost, then we consider whether it is so cheap that liquidation would yield an incremental return. If this is the case, we may consider liquidating the equity. In the vast majority of cases, an equity will trade far above liquidation value, in which case we turn our attention to earning power.

Once we focus on the earning power of a going concern, the key consideration becomes whether the business will throw off sufficient income to allow us to earn a satisfactory return on investment. Many related considerations enter the picture here, including the relationship between net income and free cash flow, the ability of the business to reinvest capital at attractive rates of return, and the nature of management's capital allocation policies.

Key Takeaways

Here are our top 10 takeaways from this chapter:

1. In investing, it is hard enough to succeed as an original; as a copycat, it is virtually impossible. Each of us must carve out a *personal* way to investment success, even if you are a *professional* investor.
2. One of the masters' key teachings is as important as it is simple: A share of stock represents a share in the ownership of a business.
3. Investors tend to add capital to investment funds after a period of good performance and withdraw capital after a period of

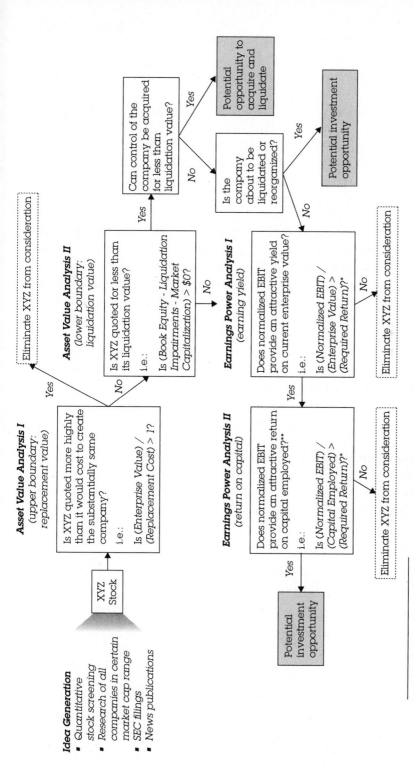

FIGURE 1.2 Illustrative Stock Selection Framework
Source: The Manual of Ideas.

*Required return depends on conviction regarding normalized EBIT and other factors.
**Additional considerations: Can capital be reinvested at the normalized return on capital? Are above-average returns on capital sustainable?

19

bad performance, causing their actual results to lag behind the funds' reported results.

4. Those considering an investment in a hedge fund may first wish to convince themselves that their prospective fund manager can beat Warren Buffett. Doing this on a prefee basis is hard enough; on an after-fee basis, the odds diminish considerably.

5. It is little surprise that the world's richest investor is a capital allocator rather than a trend follower, thematic investor, or day trader. Buffett looks to the underlying businesses rather than the stock certificates to deliver superior compounding of capital over the long term.

6. While most of us have a negligible impact on the stock market, the accompanying small fish mind-set does not lend itself to successful investing. Instead, we benefit from casting ourselves in the role of the world's chief capital allocator.

7. Although our exposure to the losses of the companies in which we invest is legally limited to our initial investment, any impression that someone else will take care of a company's losses is an illusion.

8. Losses have a perverse impact on long-term capital appreciation, as a greater percentage gain is required to get us back to even. For example, a 20 percent drop in book value requires a 25 percent subsequent increase to offset the decline.

9. Mohnish Pabrai makes an eloquent case against investing in companies that become too large, echoing Charlie Munger's latticework approach. According to Pabrai, nature seems to have imposed a size limit on mammals and companies alike.

10. Thinking like a capital allocator goes hand in hand with thinking like an owner. Investors who view themselves as owners rather than traders look to the business rather than the market for their return on investment.

Notes

1. See Hagstrom (2005).
2. Multiple studies have been published on mutual fund performance, including Brown and Goetzmann (1995), Malkiel (1995), Carhart (1997), and Khorana and Nelling (1997). Carhart concludes: "The results do not support the existence of skilled or informed mutual

fund portfolio managers." Malkiel finds: "In the aggregate, funds have underperformed benchmark portfolios both after management expenses and even gross of expenses."

3. See Ferri (2003).
4. See Buffett (2007).
5. See Berkshire Hathaway (2010).
6. See Stone (1999).
7. *The Manual of Ideas* interview with Eric Khrom, New York, 2012.
8. Source of price and market value information: Yahoo! Finance, http://finance.yahoo.com, accessed November 23, 2001.
9. Source of price and market value information: Yahoo! Finance, http://finance.yahoo.com, accessed October 22, 2004.
10. A more accurate gauge of Toyota's outperformance would be an analysis based on stock price (including paid dividends) rather than market value, which can be affected by events such as mergers and acquisitions that do not necessarily improve the per-share return to an investor.
11. See Buffett (2009).
12. See Grantham (2005).
13. See McDonald (2005).
14. See Pabrai (2002–2004).

CHAPTER 2

Deep Value: Ben Graham–Style Bargains

Inelegant but Profitable Strategy of Cigar Butt Investing

The problem is to distinguish between being contrary to a misguided consensus and merely being stubborn.
—Robert Arnott and Robert Lovell Jr.

"Welcome to the bargain bin of investing!" This alternative chapter title sums up Graham-style investing quite well. Ben Graham outlined his approach decades ago in *Security Analysis*, the investment classic he co-authored with fellow Columbia University professor David Dodd. Graham-style investing unabashedly starts with the price of a stock. Unless the price looks like a bargain based on some tangible metrics, Graham-style investors have no interest. The company in question could be the best business the world has ever seen, but the cheapskate segment of the investment community will give it no consideration. This discipline enables deep value investors to succeed where other investors dare not tread—in the underbelly of public equity markets.

Those of us who liked to dig through the bargain bins of CD stores—back when stores like the Virgin Megastore in Manhattan's Union Square still existed—may identify a few unique features of bargain bins. They tended to be somewhat hidden within the stores, certainly getting less attention than the latest top 10 selections. Instead of being arrayed on easy-to-browse shelves, the CDs were essentially tossed into a large bucket, putting the onus on the shopper to discern between the mediocre, the bad, and the worse—in the hope of finding the occasional good. The bargain CDs came with a no-return policy, putting all the risk squarely on the shopper. Finally, they came with considerably less opportunity to meet someone cool of the opposite sex while browsing, unless one was looking for a date who wouldn't mind being taken to a meal at McDonald's. You see, it took a certain type of person to enjoy bargain bin shopping—and it is no different with Graham-style equity investing.

Value investor Ethan Berg describes his bargain-hunting sensibility as follows: "I had observed in major items I purchased in my consumer life that with a little digging there regularly were anomalies on how things were priced, or more accurately, mispriced. My Red Sox season tickets were $20 a seat but with the same view as seats two rows away at $65 a seat and across an eight-foot aisle that were $45 a seat. I purchased my car used, at one-fourth of its original cost, even though it still had what I estimated to be approximately 85 percent of its useful life remaining."[1]

The Approach: Why It Works

Bargain hunting is something most us embrace in principle, but true bargain hunters are few and far between. On the line that represents the trade-off between quality and price, most investors find themselves creeping toward quality, accepting a higher price in return for greater certainty and peace of mind. There is nothing wrong with such a transformation. After all, Warren Buffett has famously undergone the same shift in his investment approach. That said, Buffett has hinted that the shift has been at least partly motivated by the mushrooming of his investable assets.

In his personal portfolio, Buffett has ventured into Graham-style bargains long after Berkshire started focusing on high-quality franchise businesses. Several years ago, Buffett was reported to have invested some of his personal portfolio into South Korean *net nets*—companies trading for less than their current assets minus total liabilities. The investment approach of Zeke Ashton, managing partner of Centaur Capital Partners, has evolved similarly. "We very much prefer our ideas to take the form of high quality businesses with excellent management that can grow value over the longer term, but we will buy mediocre assets if the price is right."[2]

Track Record Dating Back to the Father of Security Analysis

Economists Eugene Fama and Kenneth French have extensively studied the relationship between stock performance and book-to-market ratios. Their seminal paper covered the period from 1963 to 1990 and included nearly all stocks on the New York Stock Exchange, Amex, and Nasdaq stock markets. The stocks were divided into deciles based on book-to-market and were re-ranked annually. The highest book-to-market stocks outperformed the lowest book-to-market stocks by 21 to 8 percent, on average, with each descending decile performing worse than the previous. Fama and French also examined the beta of each decile and found that value stocks had lower risk, while growth stocks had the highest risk. The study had a profound impact in part because Fama was a long-time champion of the capital asset pricing model. Figure 2.1 shows the updated relative performance of value versus growth stocks.

Many value investors have achieved strong investment returns over their careers by following a strategy that involved buying stocks trading at a discount to their readily ascertainable asset values. Ben Graham, Walter Schloss, John Neff, and Marty Whitman are just a few names that come to mind. Of course, we note that many of the most successful investors, including Warren Buffett and Joel Greenblatt, have migrated away from balance sheet values toward good businesses, producing even more impressive returns.

A holy grail of value investing might be uncovering opportunities that both provide asset protection on the balance sheet and include businesses with high returns on capital. This combination is virtually impossible to find unless a company has experienced a steep near-term profit decline. In such an instance, a firm may appear to be a low-return business when in fact normalized profitability implies attractive returns on capital. Another potential holy grail is a company whose balance sheet assets are partly noncore, that is, not actually employed in the operating business.

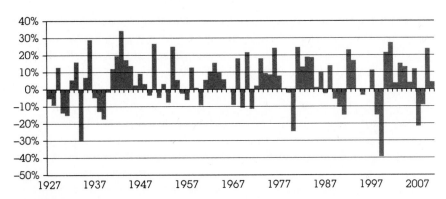

FIGURE 2.1   Annual Performance Difference between U.S. Value versus Growth Stocks, 1927–2012
Source: Kenneth French.[3]

The longevity of the Graham-style approach to investing in statistically cheap equities is remarkable, according to Toby Carlisle, managing member of Eyquem Investment Management:

> *It's a testament to Ben Graham's genius that his net current asset value strategy should be so robust, by which I mean that it should continue to work in different markets, both temporally and geographically, 76 years after it was first published. The strategy has been the subject of numerous papers. Two notable papers are Professor Henry Oppenheimer's* Ben Graham's Net Current Asset Values: A Performance Update, *and James Montier's* Graham's Net-Nets: Outdated or Outstanding? *Professor Oppenheimer studied net current asset value stocks in the United States between 1970 and 1983, finding a mean return of 29.4 percent per year against an index return of 11.5 percent. Montier looked at the performance of net current asset value stocks globally between 1985 and 2007, finding a mean return of 35 percent per year against an index return of 17 percent per year.*[4]

Some Companies Are Worth More Dead Than Alive

Investors often forget that corporations were not always meant to live forever. Many years ago, the idea of a company focused more on the limited liability such an entity could afford the individuals involved in a specific, time-bounded project. Over time, the idea of a corporation evolved into that of a legal person meant to perpetuate itself indefinitely. While the notion of perpetual equity creates economic value in the case of lasting business franchises, it may detract from value in situations in which orderly liquidation of assets might be preferable. Few managers will agree with such a notion, and even shareholders will typically disagree that liquidation represents the best course for maximizing value.

In many situations, the more appropriate objective may be to limit a business to its core competency while maximizing the return of cash to shareholders. Such a business may exist for a long time and may even retain an option to resume reinvestment of capital, should its competitive position or the market structure improve markedly. By prioritizing return of cash to shareholders, low-return businesses can assist investors in earning a strong investment return, assuming the equity purchase price was favorable. The truism that over the long term an investor in a business will earn a return closely matching the return on capital of the business is only partly true. If the business dividends out all free cash flow, a long-term shareholder will earn a return equal to the free cash flow yield implied in the original purchase price. The return on capital earned by the business is irrelevant when the payout ratio is 100 percent. As the payout ratio declines, the economics of the business becomes increasingly important.

Table 2.1 shows the impact of dividend policy on the returns of an equity investor. We assume a modest return on equity of 10 percent and show that the return to an equity investor can be quite a bit higher with optimal capital allocation. In this example, if the company retains all earnings, the investor earns a return equal to the return on equity. On the other hand, if the company pays out all earnings, the investor earns a return equal to the earnings yield implied in the stock purchase price, which in this case equals 20 percent.

The dynamics described highlight the importance of returning cash to shareholders when the cash would otherwise be redeployed in a mediocre business. Sometimes the logical consequence is a push toward liquidation, but the latter is neither required nor optimal if a company has a cash-generative business segment with low capital reinvestment requirements. On the other hand, if an outside purchaser of the business is willing to pay a price that implies a low

TABLE 2.1 Impact of Dividend Policy on the Return of an Equity Investor

	End of Year 0	Year 1	End of Year 2	Year 3	Year 4	Year 5	Year 6
Key assumptions							
Stock purchase	($100)						
Forward P/E	5.0x	5.0x	5.0x	5.0x	5.0x	5.0x	
ROE		10%	10%	10%	10%	10%	10%
No dividend							
Beginning equity		$1,000	$1,100	$1,210	$1,331	$1,464	
Net income		$100	$110	$121	$133	$146	$161
Dividends paid		$0	$0	$0	$0	$0	
Ending equity	$1,000	$1,100	$1,210	$1,331	$1,464	$1,610	
Market capitalization	$500	$550	$605	$666	$732	$805	
Dividends received		$0	$0	$0	$0	$0	
Sale of stock		$0	$0	$0	$0	$161	
Total cash inflow	($100)	$0	$0	$0	$0	$160	
Pretax return	10%						
50% payout							
Beginning equity		$1,000	$1,050	$1,103	$1,158	$1,216	
Net income		$100	$105	$110	$116	$122	$128

28

		($50)	($53)	($55)	($58)	($61)
Dividends paid						$100
Equity (ex-dividend)	$1,000	$1,050	$1,103	$1,158	$1,216	$1,276
Market capitalization	$500	$525	$551	$579	$608	$638
Dividends received		$10	$11	$11	$12	$12
Sale of stock		$0	$0	$0	$0	$128
Total cash inflow	($100)	$10	$11	$11	$12	$140
Pretax return	15%					
100% payout						
Beginning equity	$1,000	$1,000	$1,000	$1,000	$1,000	$1,000
Net income		$100	$100	$100	$100	$100
Dividends paid		($100)	($100)	($100)	($100)	($100)
Equity (ex-dividend)		$1,000	$1,000	$1,000	$1,000	$1,000
Market capitalization	$500	$500	$500	$500	$500	$500
Dividends received		$20	$20	$20	$20	$20
Sale of stock		$0	$0	$0	$0	$100
Total cash inflow	($100)	$20	$20	$20	$20	$120
Pre-tax return	20%					

Source: The Manual of Ideas analysis.

return based on the current distributable cash flow of the business, then shareholders may indeed benefit from a sale of the business.

Ben Graham's pioneering work provides a framework for thinking about the value of a business in liquidation. When estimated liquidation value exceeds the market price, a company may be viewed as worth more dead than alive. In *Security Analysis*, Ben Graham and David Dodd argued for certain adjustments to be made to the balance sheet to reflect the typically messy process of liquidation. As we discuss later in this chapter, the appropriate adjustments vary based on multiple factors.

Our experience suggests that investors tend to overestimate liquidation values, as the reality of a dying business tends to hide nasty surprises for investors. Nonetheless, when a public company is quoted materially below conservatively appraised liquidation value—and when liquidation is actually possible—investors can earn a handsome annualized return. The relatively short holding period in most such cases means that vulture investors need a constant stream of similar opportunities to keep their capital employed.

The option of liquidating an undervalued business to realize value derives directly from the legal rights of shareholders as owners of a real-life business. Writes Seth Klarman, chairman of The Baupost Group:

> *A liquidation is, in a sense, one of the few interfaces where the essence of the stock market is revealed. Are stocks pieces of paper to be endlessly traded back and forth, or are they proportional interests in underlying businesses? A liquidation settles this debate, distributing to owners of pieces of paper the actual cash proceeds resulting from the sale of corporate assets to the highest bidder. A liquidation thereby acts as a tether to reality for the stock market, forcing either undervalued or overvalued share prices to move into line with actual underlying value.*[5]

Investors' Obsession with Income

We find it quite fascinating that investors seem to appreciate assets in their personal lives but place greater emphasis on income when it comes to their portfolio holdings. By income, we refer to the income statement figures of a business rather than merely the dividend payout. Many of us are prone to taking on debt to buy the assets we desire today, regardless of whether those assets accrete value over time. We appreciate the present value of an asset we need or want. However, when it comes to public equity investments, many of us discount a company's balance sheet while placing a premium on periodic income. This is why faddish companies occasionally rise to incredible market valuations despite a relative absence of hard assets, and why asset-rich companies occasionally trade well below replacement value. Reflects Jeroen Bos, investment director of Church House Investments: "Virtually all the companies I buy are loss-making, haven't paid a dividend . . . [but] they are at a discount to their working capital. They have losses, but these losses are containable for the next two or three years, and management is working."[6]

There is no question that income and cash flow deserve a place in a valuation exercise. They may even deserve primacy in most equity analyses. Consider companies like Coca-Cola, Johnson & Johnson, and Procter & Gamble, which have relatively few hard assets but whose income streams possess great value. As long as such franchise businesses have conservatively financed balance sheets that pose no risk to the equity, those balance sheets may be mostly disregarded for valuation purposes. Unfortunately, investors may have loosened their definition of a franchise business to such an extent that they ignore the balance sheet more often than is appropriate. In the long run, the income of most businesses does relate to the net assets a business has at its disposal. This is especially true for businesses that exhibit high capital intensity. They may earn abnormal returns on capital employed for a while due to an imbalance of supply and demand or some other transient factor, but virtually all such businesses revert to the mean. Investors suffer mightily when they overestimate the duration of the abnormal earning period of a business.

Which businesses are prone to inefficient value appraisal due to investors' focus on income? We find a category of businesses particularly interesting—companies that seek to offer a current yield to investors yet depend heavily on the hard assets on their balance sheet. For example, the market typically assigns a cap rate to real estate operating companies, making net operating income a key driver of the market quotation. When income declines, investors may find it difficult to decide whether the erosion is temporary, especially if fear prevails in the market. In such cases, a real estate business can trade materially below replacement value. Add leverage to the balance sheet, and the depth of investor pessimism becomes unpredictable. Considerations such as the existence of nonrecourse debt may be ignored by most market participants in such times of perceived distress. Examples also include other types of publicly traded limited partnerships, many of which operate in the energy industry but have defensible businesses that differ materially from hard-to-predict oil and gas exploration businesses.

Massimo Fuggetta, portfolio manager of Bayes Fund, outlined his investment thesis on an undervalued real-estate-related company in early 2011: "One of my favorites today is Barratt Developments, a UK house builder priced below one pound and 25 percent of tangible book value, while until 2007 it was valued between one and two times book. They ran into trouble with a wrongly-timed and -priced acquisition and are still suffering under a weak construction environment. But as the market eventually normalizes, I think they should be valued at many times the current price." Two years later, Barratt's stock price had more than doubled as the fundamentals of the business began to revert toward the historical mean.[7]

Consider also companies that offer products whose price is determined by the market. If the price series is reliably mean-reverting but investors become fearful at the bottom, they may undervalue the assets of the companies involved. Professor Pavel Savor of the Wharton School drew our attention to this anomaly in 2010 as U.S. oil refiners, including Alon USA, Tesoro, and Western Refining, fell to multiyear lows. The stocks rebounded strongly as refining spreads reverted toward their historical mean. Regulatory impediments to adding capacity in the U.S. refining industry all but ensured that spreads would have to widen as demand inevitably picked up.

On a more mundane level, the combination of a narrow-moat business and a lack of current profitability tends to sour the investment community on a company's stock, relegating a wide range of companies to Graham-style bargain status. Many of those businesses hide little value on their balance sheet, but the diligent investor will occasionally uncover gems that are ignored despite their strong net asset values. Andrew Shapiro, president of Lawndale Capital Management, articulated a case for Reading International, an asset-rich company that remained stubbornly ignored by the wider investment community. Similarly, Eric Dumont, general partner of Eudaimonia Investments, laid out a lucid sum-of-the-parts thesis on Corridor Resources, a Canadian natural gas exploration and production firm. The balance-sheet-focused investment case was well within Mr. Market's ability to comprehend, but investors' apparent focus on income left Corridor languishing in obscurity. Timing remains a tricky issue in these types of situations, but if an investor's value appraisal is correct, rewards typically await.

The staffing industry represents another example of an equity segment that is prone to mispricing due to the market's focus on near-term income. Long-term-oriented investors may do quite well by embracing a time arbitrage strategy. States Nick Kirrage, fund manager of Specialist Value UK Equities at Schroders:

> *Staffing businesses . . . have big fixed overheads and quite volatile top lines, and profits can be quite volatile. Typically, the staffing industry understands this, and they therefore run with balance sheets that are either heavily net cash or very lowly geared. But the market becomes very focused [on] short-term profits, so once [per] cycle, the share prices collapse very, very strongly, and people just assume that profits either won't recover or it will take too long for them to recover—and they can't really be bothered to wait. For people who are willing to wait for three to five years, that's wonderful, because you're not taking balance sheet risk. Therefore, the chance of you permanently losing money is very low. The chance of you making quite a lot of money, because the operating leverage works both ways, is very high.[8]*

Scott Barbee, portfolio manager of Aegis Value Fund, articulates an approach that marries the downside protection features of asset value with the upside potential associated with earning power: "We generally like to buy companies trading at a significant discount to their asset values and at mid to low single-digit multiples of normalized earnings two to three years out. This way, the assets provide downside protection while the earnings potential gives us upside."[9] Barbee's approach seems particularly applicable to money-losing businesses whose market value has declined to tangible book value or below. A key consideration seems to be whether the current money-losing period reflects a permanently damaged business or a cyclical or otherwise temporary decline in profitability.

Uses and Misuses of Ben Graham–Style Investing

Deep value investing has outperformed the market averages over long periods of time, so why wouldn't everyone with a long time horizon embrace it? While all investors strive toward essentially the same goal—to make money in the market—their paths may differ considerably. The historical success of an approach means little if an investor cannot understand or embrace the underlying drivers of success. It turns out that Graham-style investing may be appropriate for a relatively small subset of the investment community, as it requires an unusual willingness to stand alone, persevere, and look foolish. "I have learned how to suffer," reflects Jake Rosser, managing partner of Coho Capital Management.[10]

The Rewards of Psychological Discomfort

On more than one occasion, we have heard investors respond as follows to a deep value investment thesis: "The stock does look deeply undervalued, but I just can't get comfortable with it." When pressed on the reasons for passing, many investors point to the uncertainty of the situation, the likelihood of negative news flow, or simply a bad gut feeling. Most investors also find it less rewarding to communicate to their clients that they own a company that has been in the news for the wrong reasons.

Comfort can be expensive in investing. Put differently, acceptance of discomfort can be rewarding, as equities that cause their owners discomfort frequently trade at exceptionally low valuations. If discomfort were entirely related to fundamental factors such as a company's business prospects and intrinsic value, then little reward might exist for accepting discomfort. However, the latter seems to be at least partly due to investors' psychological makeup. Most of us find it easier to accept a mistake if we can do so in good company. Investing in Enron and losing money may make us feel less bad because many smart people suffered the same fate. However, if we lose money in a company that has been widely panned by analysts and shorted by the smartest hedge fund managers, we may feel especially inadequate.

Consider an investment in a casualty of Apple's rise to dominance—Research in Motion, Nokia, or Sony. Many analysts predicted the demise of those companies as their share prices declined. If we invested in such a company and lost money, we might feel quite lonely. Similar reasoning may apply to an investment in the much-maligned and heavily shorted for-profit education industry. Misery loves company, so it makes sense that rewards may await those willing to be miserable in solitude. Observes Michael Mauboussin, chief investment strategist of Legg Mason Capital Management and chairman of the Santa Fe Institute: "Buffett's advice is so good but so hard. The point when there's a valuation extreme is precisely the point when the emotional pull—in the wrong direction—is strongest."[11] Adds James Montier, portfolio manager at GMO: "People love extrapolation and forget that cycles exist. The good news is that you get paid for doing uncomfortable things, when stocks are at trough earnings and low multiples their implied return is high, in contrast you don't get paid for doing things that are comfortable."[12] John Lambert, investment manager at GAM, seeks to generate ideas in "areas of currently depressed sentiment and hence probable low valuations."[13]

If we owned nothing but a portfolio of Ben Graham–style bargain equities, we may become quite uncomfortable at times, especially if the market value of the portfolio declined precipitously. We might look at the portfolio and conclude that every investment could be worth zero. After all, we may have a mediocre business run by mediocre management, with assets that could be squandered. Investing in deep value equities therefore requires faith in the law of large numbers—that historical experience of market-beating returns in deep value stocks and the fact that we own a diversified portfolio will combine to yield a satisfactory result over time. This conceptually sound view becomes seriously challenged in times of distress. By contrast, an investor in high-quality businesses that are conservatively financed and run by shareholder-friendly managements may fall back on the well-founded belief that no matter how low the stock prices of those companies fall, the businesses will survive the downturn and recover value over time.

Playing into the psychological discomfort of Graham-style equities is the tendency of such investments to exhibit strong asset value but inferior earnings or cash flows. In a stressed situation, investors may doubt their investment theses to such an extreme that they disregard the objectively appraised asset values. After all—the reasoning of a scared investor might go—what is an asset really worth if it produces no cash flow? Is store real estate really worth anything if the store makes no money and the entire retail industry is struggling? Bill Ackman's investment case for J.C. Penney made tremendous sense given the assumptions used in his analysis, but fearful investors may tweak the assumptions in such a way that little estimated value remains for the equity holders. This dynamic serves to make the stock prices of companies like J.C. Penney exceedingly volatile, providing an opportunity for investors willing to assume the discomfort of buying when everyone else seems to be selling.

Each of us knows best how much discomfort we are willing to assume in the service of superior investment returns. We should not fool ourselves, either. Investors typically do worst when they enter situations in which they lack staying power, whether due to financial or other reasons. Plenty of money can be made in businesses that make us perfectly comfortable. The drivers of success merely shift—for example, away from a willingness to look foolish by going against the crowd toward an ability to analyze the durability of competitive advantage. Many analogies serve to illustrate this point. In real estate, money can be made both in premium beachfront property and in fixer-upper homes in middle-income neighborhoods. The skills and sensibilities of the people profiting in these distinct areas differ markedly. The people who tend to succeed seem able to match their strengths to the requirements of the opportunities they pursue.

Not a Low-Turnover, Long-Term-Oriented Investment Approach

Graham-style deep value investing might be called the original value investing. Yet, it is somewhat incongruent with a key trait of many value investors—patience, exhibited by low portfolio turnover. When we invest in an asset-rich but low-returning business, time may be working against us. As long as management can hold on to the assets and keep reinvesting capital in the business at low returns, shareholders may earn unimpressive returns despite a bargain purchase price. Warren Buffett once described the Graham approach as walking down the street and picking up cigar butts. They are kind of soggy and repulsive, but we do get a free puff out of them. Cigar butt stocks are meant to be one-time hits, delivering a nonrecurring return—and hopefully doing so quite quickly. No one wants to be stuck with a soggy cigar butt.

Some confusion exists among investors because many regard deep value investors as the ultimate patient investors, willing to operate in obscurity and invest in companies that may go on for months with little or no news. Less patience seems to be required to invest in high-flying stock market darlings due to busy news feeds, ample Wall Street analyst coverage, and lively online discussion. Cigar butts may indeed require a greater willingness to stick around than do highly liquid market leaders. However, the nature of cigar butts implies that success in this area is likely to come with material portfolio turnover, perhaps on the order of 100 percent. If we assume that a deep value portfolio turns over once annually, the investor can still realize a long-term capital gain for tax purposes. However, the investor will not benefit from an ability to build up a large deferred tax liability over time.

By contrast, investors who also seek out value but do so in businesses with attractive reinvestment opportunities may remain invested in the same companies for many years, reaping the benefits of tax-deferred compounding. Rosser describes his evolution toward higher-quality businesses:

> *Net nets and sum-of-the-parts opportunities were previously part of our toolkit but have since been thrown out. We still endeavor to own companies with strong balance sheets but we are much more interested in companies that possess an earnings engine that does not need fixing. Ultimately, the reward on such companies is an order of magnitude greater than what can be earned on closing the valuation gap on a company trading for less than its liquidation value. In short, we have migrated from the Ben Graham cigar butt approach, focused on closing the gap to intrinsic value, to the Charlie Munger approach, focused on the purchase of compounding machines at a slight discount.*[14]

Ultimately, both Buffett-style and Graham-style investors can make money in the market. Key considerations include an investor's personal preference for the kind of security analysis needed for each style and the discipline needed to apply the chosen approach consistently. Perhaps this is why many investors either adopt an approach and stick with it or evolve from one approach to the other. Few investors apply both approaches successfully at the same time in the same investment vehicle.

Ben Graham–style investing shows that a buy-and-hold approach to investing is not always a virtue. When we attempt to extract value from poor businesses with valuable assets, impatience becomes a virtue. We are not referring to impatience with the stock price—quite to the contrary. If our analysis is correct, stock price declines would move us closer to buying more shares rather than selling the investment. Instead, we refer to impatience with regard to the course of the business itself. For most investors, this represents a theoretical exercise, except perhaps for the occasions when they withhold votes from management to express displeasure. This is why many of us look for situations in which an activist shareholder may have already entered the fray. We see promise that our impatience may actually be acted upon by a resourceful fellow shareholder. If the activist's method for catalyzing action is a proxy fight, the votes of more passive but equally concerned shareholders may become crucial.

If we assume that the passage of time usually diminishes the annualized return shareholders can expect from a cigar butt stock, then the question arises whether a mechanical turnover rule makes sense. If a company has done nothing to realize shareholder value over a year or two, should we sell the stock to avoid getting trapped? We would advise against such a rigid rule, as every removal of discretion also removes an option from us—an option to do the right thing under the circumstances. As a result, we may advocate for a thesis review session at regular intervals, but we would not automatically sell a security simply because of the passage of time.

In an annual or quarterly thesis review session, we may focus on how reality has played out in relation to our original investment thesis. If needed management actions have been slower than expected, we want to understand why. Most important, we need to incorporate whatever experience we have had with a particular situation into a judgment about the likely future course of value creation in the same situation. If we still expect satisfactory value creation from this point forward, then it makes sense to remain invested. The past is like a sunk cost—it should not figure into our assessment of the expected investment return, except to the extent that it helps us better anticipate the future course of events.

Beware of Portfolio Concentration in the Land of Cigar Butts

Creative destruction remains alive and well in the global economy. Some would even argue that the pace of change has accelerated, creating additional peril for many businesses. Newspapers and television networks were considered some of the most predictable businesses for many decades, but the advent of the Internet has put their future in serious jeopardy. In an insightful editorial in the *Wall Street Journal*, Internet pioneer turned venture capitalist Marc Andreessen argued that "software is eating the world."[15] We find it difficult to argue against Marc's conclusions, and denial is never a recipe for success, whether in investing or in life. If we accept that creative destruction will continue at least at the pace experienced throughout recent history, then it becomes obvious that businesses trading at deep value prices are likely to be among those that are creatively destroyed. How quickly and comprehensively the intrinsic value of a weak business franchise may be destroyed is a tough call. It seems unwise to allocate a large portion of investable capital to any one deep value opportunity, even if the latter promises a large expected return.

Another argument against portfolio concentration lies in the nature of value creation in deep value situations. Strategic actions rather than skilled operation of the core business typically unlock value for shareholders of cigar butt equities. It is usually more difficult to extrapolate future strategic events from recent actions than it is to extrapolate future operating performance from recent results. Even in situations in which management has credibly articulated a path of strategic value creation, the timing and value realization of future events remain highly variable. Sometimes companies have a window of opportunity to realize satisfactory value. If they miss this window, value destruction can be swift. Think of asset-rich but cash-poor companies that may need to sell assets before an approaching creditor deadline. As a result of the unpredictability inherent in strategic events, high concentration in any single deep value situation could produce a disappointing result at the portfolio level.

Finally, investors who like to hedge their exposure to specific companies or industries may find it difficult to do so with cigar butts. Value creation in a deep value investment will typically correlate rather modestly with value creation in the related industry. When Kmart was working its way through bankruptcy, comparable store sales trends at Walmart and Target bore little correlation to the value Kmart's creditors were likely to extract. When Circuit City was struggling to stay out of bankruptcy, Best Buy's sales trends should have been all but irrelevant to Circuit City shareholders. To the extent Best Buy was taking market share from Circuit City, value creation at the two companies may even have been negatively correlated. Sometimes, value in a Graham-style situation will reside at the periphery or outside the industry in which the core business operates. In the case of Kmart, most of the value derived from the store real estate rather than the retail business itself. These factors make it exceedingly difficult to hedge most deep value investments by short-selling equities in the same industry.

Another popular hedging technique—the purchase of put options—also faces serious hurdles in the land of cigar butts. Deep value equities tend to have smaller market values, both because they are cheap and, more important, because if they were larger, more investors would analyze them, perhaps rendering them less undervalued. Due to the below-average market capitalization of Ben Graham–style bargains, no functioning options market may exist in individual securities. In cases in which options are available at acceptable bid-ask spreads, the options premium may be prohibitively large because of high implied volatility. The stock prices of many Graham-style bargains have declined precipitously, heightening historical volatility. Greater investor awareness of the likelihood of future strategic actions may also increase the volatility option writers will assume in their pricing models. Finally, put options in fearful stocks tend to be quite expensive due to many investors' desire to hedge their losing positions. Occasionally, short sellers become quite aggressive in declining equities, making the outright short sale of stock expensive. When short sellers are forced to incur a negative rebate due to low availability of borrowed shares, they may resort to buying put options instead, making the latter too expensive for most value-oriented investors. As a result, hedging may become impractical, forcing investors to size their unhedged positions in a way that does not endanger the portfolio.

Screening for Graham-Style Bargains

The deep value approach tends to be highly congruent with quantitative screening for ideas. Graham-style investing involves relatively few subjective judgments in the early stages of the investment funnel. Aiding the process is the fact that most stock screeners include data on the balance sheet variables of relevance to deep value screens. Scott Barbee sums up his idea generation approach as follows: "Our primary methodology is a simple stock screen looking for companies trading at discounts to tangible book value."[16]

Ben Graham's Net Net Screen

Value investors will be intimately familiar with the basic Graham-style net net screen, which searches for equities trading at a discount to their net current asset values. This represents a more stringent requirement than a discount to tangible book value, as the Graham formula ignores long-term assets. Instead, the formula focuses on assets that are generally more liquid and more easily disposed of without major impairment in a liquidation scenario.

The ubiquity of mechanical screens has narrowed the investable universe for investors seeking net net bargains, but they still exist. Investors willing to go around the world in search of Graham-style equities are likely to find quite a few opportunities. In recent years, Japan has offered perhaps the widest array of net nets, including cash-generative businesses with positive going-concern values. Still, a risk exists that deep value becomes less rewarding as the number of net current asset value bargains dwindles.

According to Soo Chuen Tan, managing member of Discerene Value Advisors, if only a small number of equities meet the quantitative criteria, the group may not offer the hoped-for value. With smart investors eager to invest in Graham-style bargains, any remaining net nets are likely to possess disqualifying risks. As a result, investors may want to keep track of the historical proportion of net nets in various markets around the world. When the proportion exceeds the average, conditions may be ripe for successful deep value investing. Tan has gone to such places in search of attractive net nets, presenting investment case studies for specific companies in Greece, Japan, and Malaysia at past ValueConferences events.

Martin Whitman's Modified Net Net Screen

Marty Whitman, chairman of Third Avenue Management, has updated Ben Graham's approach to reflect the improvements in corporate disclosure since Graham's time. Whitman distinguishes between assets in a way that reflects economic reality more appropriately than does the simple accounting distinction between short- and long-term assets. According to Whitman, some long-term assets may be more readily marketable than certain short-term assets.

For example, a Class A office building in Manhattan may be easier to sell without impairment than the inventory of a failing retailer. As a result, it may make sense to redefine the net net formula: Instead of mechanically considering all short-term assets and excluding all long-term assets, enterprising investors may benefit from making commonsense adjustments to all assets. In some cases, companies failing to meet Ben Graham's net net criteria may trade at wider discounts to net asset value than do most net nets.[17]

Enhanced Screening: Repurchases, Insider Buying, Shrinking Working Capital Requirements

We find several ways to augment the likelihood that our Graham-style screen yields a list of market-beating investment candidates. Rather than require specific improvements in operating performance, we focus on criteria that may correlate with improvement in the effectiveness of a deep value screen.

VALUE CREATION VIA BUYBACKS Share repurchases tend to be particularly accretive in the case of companies generating cash from operations while trading below tangible book value. If such companies apply free cash flow toward buying back stock, they accrete tangible book value per share, widening the gap between the market price and accounting net worth. It becomes exceedingly difficult for the stock price to decrease when the discount to book value per share keeps getting wider if the stock price remains constant. At some point, market participants are likely to regard the magnitude of the discount as too large to ignore, leading to revaluation of the equity. When the stock price of Sears Holdings declined below book value a couple of years ago, Bruce Berkowitz argued that the game would be over for short sellers of Sears stock if Eddie Lampert simply kept buying back stock. Berkowitz appeared to refer to the per-share accretion dynamic described here.

One caveat does apply in this regard: Even if tangible book value per share is increasing in the repurchase scenario, intrinsic value per share may not necessarily be doing the same. If a business trades above fair value, repurchases will destroy value even as they create growth in per-share book value. In such a scenario, the downside would increase even as the ratio of price to tangible book value decreases. Ultimately, repurchases create value only if they occur at prices below intrinsic value. That said, if we correctly judge that a company trading below book value is undervalued, then the book-value-per-share accretion dynamic will force revaluation faster than might be the case in the absence of repurchases.

WHEN INSIDER TRADES MATTER MOST Insider buying is another factor that has signal value in the context of deep value equities. While purchases by insiders do not create fundamental value for the shareholders—a slightly improved incentive structure notwithstanding—insider buying sends a strong signal that is magnified by the fact that insiders face a higher emotional hurdle in buying a pessimistic stock. We know that the mood of insiders generally swings in close concert with that of other market participants—this is why we see more merger and acquisition activity when prices are high rather than low. When insiders act against the psychological tendency to simply hunker down and not throw good money after bad into a stock that has underperformed, they express a view that the market has overreacted on the downside.

Most insiders, by virtue of being businesspeople rather than investors, may weigh operating performance more heavily than the equity valuation in their stock purchase decisions. As a result, it may be rare for insiders to buy stock unless they believe the fundamentals of the business are at least okay. Only the savviest insiders, perhaps the likes of John Malone and Eddie Lampert, would buy stock in a scenario in which they see major fundamental trouble, with the latter more than outweighed by a cheap stock price. If we accept that insiders weigh operating performance more heavily than the implied equity valuation, it becomes apparent why insider buying has more signal value in the case of beaten-down rather than high-flying equities. Whereas in the case of a high flyer, management's optimistic view of the fundamentals may be exceeded by the market's optimism, even a modestly optimistic outlook may top the market's expectations in the case of a Graham-style bargain.

THE UPSIDE OF A DECLINING SALES TREND Most companies build up working capital as they grow sales, a cash-draining business model feature that explains why many fast-growing businesses raise equity capital even as their operations accrue income. When a business with high working capital requirements hits a speed bump or enters a permanent period of stagnation, working capital needs decline, freeing up cash. In addition, lower capital expenditure (capex) requirements typically mean that the depreciation recorded on existing plant and equipment exceeds maintenance capex. This dynamic causes many slow-growth businesses to report free cash flow well in excess of net income. If the market is overly focused on sales declines or the income statement, an opportunity may exist to acquire a business at a high free cash flow yield. If management returns much of the cash to shareholders rather than reinvests it in hopes of reigniting growth, significant value can accrue to the shareholders of a struggling business.

A caveat might be appropriate in this context, as revenue declines may become too steep to allow for value creation. If sales evaporate, a company's capital base may erode due to losses, destroying shareholder value. Jeroen Bos stresses the importance of a strong top line, as sales restoration might be more difficult to achieve than margin improvement: "I like to see a company that has huge volumes but is not making money . . . than a company where sales are just completely evaporated, and it has to earn those back."[18]

Beyond Screening: Working through a List of Deep Value Candidates

Unless we choose to invest in a diversified basket of deep value equities, mimicking the approach successfully executed by the late Walter Schloss, we need to carefully evaluate each security to maximize the probability of success. This is no small feat, and most investors fail because they do not calibrate their analysis to the nature of Graham-style ideas. We accomplish little if we approach companies trading around liquidation value with a checklist designed for detecting wide-moat investment opportunities.

In this context, it makes sense to start with the quotation the market is putting on a company, although we might normally prefer to appraise an equity security *before* learning of the market's appraisal. When we confront an equity that is undeniably cheap (though perhaps not undervalued), we gain insight by extracting the key question embedded in the market price—and answering that question correctly.

For example, if a company is valued at half of conservatively stated liquidation value, we need not check boxes on the competitive moat or the margin profile. Rather, we focus our analysis on one key question: Will this company be liquidated and, if so, when? If the answers are "yes" and "soon," we may have identified an excellent investment opportunity, even if the underlying business leaves much to be desired. Similarly, if a company is generating cash and buying back stock at 25 percent of tangible book value, the key question might be: Will the company keep generating cash, and will it keep buying back stock? If the answer to both questions is yes, then it becomes difficult to argue that the stock price will do anything other than increase over time. Finally, if a company trades at a negative implied enterprise value, the key question might be: Is net cash going up or down over time, and will management do something stupid with the cash?

Adjusting Balance Sheet Values in a Liquidation Scenario

Graham and Dodd laid out their balance sheet adjustment process in *Security Analysis*, and the book remains an indispensable resource for thinking about liquidation scenarios. As we have argued elsewhere, liquidations tend to be even messier in real life than might be reflected in the discounts typically applied to assets on the balance sheet. Whenever we build an investment case that assumes a liquidation scenario, we find it crucial to think long and hard about the fudge factor that might be appropriate in a given situation.

We use *fudge factor* as a catchall bucket for items that lie outside the typical balance sheet liquidation analysis. For example, we typically penalize small companies to a greater extent, as negative liquidation-related items tend to be larger relative to the estimated liquidation value. The smaller a company, the higher might be the percentage of residual value eliminated by items such as legal fees, cash incentives for insiders, and other business shutdown expenses. Occasionally, the smaller a company, the greater the liquidation discount needed for items such as accounts receivable, as those owing the company money may perceive a higher chance of getting away without satisfying their obligations.

On the flip side, a positive development might materialize on the liability side of the balance sheet, but this is decidedly the exception rather than the rule. Nonetheless, investors may occasionally gain a profitable insight by scrutinizing the major liability items. Andrew Williamson, fund manager of the Hawkwood Deep Value Fund, cites an example of "a quasi-liquidation situation in the U.S., where there is a tax liability on the balance sheet, which is highly unlikely to be realized. [Due to] various accounting rules and management being very conservative . . . you might even say too conservative, [they] have put the full value of the potential tax liability on the balance sheet, which . . . is a very material chunk of the balance sheet. But when you read the notes, and you talk to management, and you assess it, there is almost zero probability [of] having to pay that tax liability."[19]

Companies at Cyclical Lows versus Those in Secular Decline

Assuming a low enough entry price, money can be made in both cheap businesses condemned to permanent fundamental decline and businesses that may benefit from mean reversion as their industry moves through the cycle. We much prefer companies that find themselves at a cyclical low, as they may restore much, if not all, of their earning power, providing multi-bagger upside potential. Meanwhile, businesses likely to keep declining for a long time have to be extremely cheap and keep returning cash to shareholders to generate a positive investment outcome.

The question of whether a company has entered permanent decline is anything but easy to answer, as virtually all companies appear to be in permanent decline when they hit a rock-bottom market quotation. Even if a business has been cyclical in the past, analysts generally adopt a "this time is different" attitude. As a pessimistic stock price inevitably influences the appraisal objectivity of most investors, it becomes exceedingly difficult to form a view strongly opposed to the prevailing consensus.

Consider the following industries that have been pronounced permanently impaired in the past, only to rebound strongly in subsequent years: Following the financial crisis of 2008–2009, many analysts argued that the banking industry would be permanently negatively affected, as higher capital requirements and regulatory oversight would compress returns on equity. The credit rating agencies were seen as impaired because the regulators would surely alter the business model of the industry for the worse following the failings of the rating agencies during the subprime mortgage bubble. The homebuilding industry would fail to rebound as strongly as in the past, as overcapacity became chronic and home prices remained tethered to building costs. The refining industry would suffer permanently lower margins, as those businesses were capital-intensive and driven by volatile commodity prices.

If those examples of industries that did rebound seem obvious in hindsight, consider the following examples of industries that as of this writing remained perceived by many investors as permanently impaired: Natural gas exploration and production companies in the United States were permanently doomed to weak profits as the shale gas revolution would forever keep natural gas prices low. Ocean shipping companies would have a hard time returning to strong profits due to overcapacity, exacerbated by large outstanding new vessel orders. For-profit education companies were permanently condemned to low profits due primarily to U.S. regulatory hostility. In each of these three live examples, investors may be surprised by the degree to which the industries restore earning power in the future.

Oxymoron or Opportunity: Net Nets with Non-Capital-Intensive Businesses

Here is a trick question: How can a business with virtually no assets be valued as a Graham-style net net? Answer: The business must be hidden within a larger company that does have substantial tangible assets. In most cases, the latter will be employed in a low-quality, capital-intensive business, though the assets may also represent excess assets that could be monetized for the benefit of shareholders.

When the market value of a company falls to such an extent that current assets exceed the sum of market value and total liabilities, investors are likely to focus on the fact that the balance sheet is comprised of unattractive, low-yielding assets. This focus on hard assets occasionally blinds investors to the existence of a hidden business that is utilizing few, if any, tangible assets. For example, during a real estate depression, investors may value the assets of a real estate operating company at less than their carrying value, appraising the equity at a large discount to tangible book value. However, if the company also has a real estate asset management business that does not employ balance sheet assets but generates high-margin, recurring fee income, an opportunity may exist to acquire the equity at a price far below intrinsic value.

Some smart value investors focus their search for deep value opportunities on companies whose tangible book value provides downside protection, while a hidden capital-light business provides upside potential. When such a non-capital-intensive business can be identified, the value of the business relative to the market value of the entire company becomes a key consideration. If the hidden gem is worth only a small fraction of the overall market quotation, the related upside potential may be too limited to warrant investment. On the other hand, if the hidden gem is worth as much as the market value of the entire company, an asymmetric situation may exist, featuring low downside due to asset protection, along with large upside due to the value of the capital-light business.

In this context, we have seen investors make the mistake of overvaluing the apparently hidden good business. If investors rely on the past performance of that business as the definitive guide to the future, they might be disappointed. The good business may not actually be hidden; rather, other market participants may have rightly concluded that the business has ceased to be good. Such a negative development is not farfetched, as businesses with low capital intensity tend to be most susceptible to competitive threats. When something other than capital employed drives the profits of a business, that something can change quite easily unless the business has a sustainable moat. Businesses with low capital intensity may be more likely to exhibit winner-take-all dynamics, as capital is not a barrier to scale. Consider how quickly Apple crushed well-established companies Nokia, Research in Motion, and even Sony. This was only possible as Apple did not need to scale capital employed alongside market share. Investors who considered investing in the beaten-down equity of Nokia too early because the Finnish company seemed to have a capital-light business in addition to large net cash holdings might have been surprised by the degree to which the profitability of the capital-light business would be affected by competition.

Asking the Right Questions of Graham-Style Bargains

The nature of deep value investment ideas is such that an elaborate checklist might inevitably bias us against such opportunities. The following questions take into account the inherent deficiencies of businesses likely to qualify as Graham-style investments, while focusing on the key drivers of an informed investment decision in this context.

Is Value Growing, Staying Flat, or Shrinking over Time?

When we think about the intrinsic value of a business, we try to incorporate all the components of value into the analysis. Even if we take the position that we cannot predict the future, it is impossible to exclude it from the assessment. Instead of trying to predict a specific outcome, we may want to consider a few different scenarios. What would be a pessimistic outcome for this company? What would be an optimistic scenario? Can we conceptualize a base case while acknowledging the high likelihood that the future will play out differently? This exercise helps us arrive at an estimated range of equity values.

If we feel especially ambitious, we may assign subjective probabilities to the various scenarios. This second step is needed to arrive at a single intrinsic value estimate for a company. We multiply the estimated probabilities by the present value of the associated scenarios and add up the resulting values to estimate total equity value. As the probabilities used in such a calculation should add to 100 percent, we need to undertake a comprehensive assessment of the possible future outcomes.

This analysis is complicated in the case of Ben Graham–style bargains, as much of the value resides on the balance sheet. Considering the future scenarios for a struggling capital-intensive business may turn out to be quite a bit more difficult than thinking about the path ahead for a business like Coca-Cola or Procter & Gamble. As a result, many investors stay as close to the balance sheet as possible when appraising Graham-style equities. Unfortunately, this results in a snapshot analysis of value rather than an estimate of true discounted present value.

When we value a company based solely on readily ascertainable balance sheet values, we run the risk that those values erode over time, negatively impacting future value. If the future course of value lies on a downward slope, then the present estimate of value should reflect such a trajectory. We should be willing to pay substantially less for a declining business whose current readily ascertainable hard asset value is 100 than for a flat to improving business whose hard asset value is also 100. Were we to buy both companies for 50, the former would get less cheap over time, assuming a constant stock price.

We like to think about value in these types of situations as follows: If the primary valuation ratio remains constant, will the stock price increase or decrease over time? For example, if we buy a business for 0.5 times tangible book value and the market keeps valuing the business at 0.5 times tangible book value well into the future, what will happen to the stock price?

Mohnish Pabrai states in a similar context: "I value [consistency of earnings] more than the absolute cheapest business, because then we know there is some sustainability to the cheap business getting even cheaper, and eventually gravity takes over."[20] Robert Robotti, president of Robotti & Company, also looks for deep value situations in which intrinsic value grows over time. Consider how Robotti summed up the investment case for shipping company Stolt-Nielsen in mid-2012:

> We think the asset value today is over $50 [per ADR], and we think that asset value over the next three to five years grows reasonably well from that valuation. The stock trades at $18; book is in the high $20s. It trades at a discount to book and we think a very significant discount to intrinsic value. There is significant insider ownership—the Stolt-Nielsen family owns over half of the company. The company has bought back

stock in the past. The company pays a dividend. They've done
plenty of things to indicate that they really are concerned
with shareholder value. The headwinds over the last four
years have stopped the market from realizing that.[21]

Is Liquidation Value Really Much Higher Than Market Value?

We often read investment write-ups that assert a discount to liquidation value. We find many of these assertions suspect, as they tend to implicitly assume a benign environment for liquidation to take place. Imagine a case for an ocean shipping company that estimates liquidation value as the private market sale value of the company's ships minus the net debt on the company's books. Would an argument that the equity has strong downside protection because it trades below liquidation value be credible? In our experience, such an argument may hint at potential undervaluation of the equity, but it is rather weak when it comes to downside protection.

In reality, a liquidation scenario would most likely play out in conditions of industry distress, in which it might be exceedingly difficult to find buyers for a fleet of ships. Even if such buyers existed, they would hold tremendous negotiating leverage over a competitor seeking to liquidate assets. The value of other assets may also start looking shaky in such a scenario, as accounts receivable suddenly become more difficult to collect and prepaid assets lose value. Meanwhile, we can be quite sure that the company's liabilities will remain constant or even increase. In some countries, the obligations of a business toward employees increase in case of a mass layoff. Similarly, the operating expenses of a liquidating business may spike as lawyers enter the picture and management demands an incremental incentive to see through the liquidation process.

Graham adjusted balance sheet asset values downward in a liquidation scenario, but such adjustments may prove inadequate in modern practice. Many factors affect the likely course of a liquidation process, including the size of a company, the nature of the assets on the books, the incentives of management, the pace at which a liquidation is completed, the prevailing industry conditions, the number of parties who might be interested in the company's key assets, and the existence of contingent liabilities such as unresolved litigation or environmental liabilities. Some of these factors are rarely considered in a back-of-the-envelope liquidation analysis, rendering many such exercises too optimistic in their estimate of value.

The onerous process of liquidating a business rarely becomes the course chosen by the board of directors. According to Toby Carlisle, "The assets of a company are typically worth more as part of a going concern than in liquidation, so liquidation value is generally a worst-case outcome. In my experience, most 'net net' companies have been turned around, rather than liquidated."[22]

What Is the Catalyst to Unlocking Value?

Graham-style bargains are typically companies with few high-return reinvestment opportunities. In most cases, the return on existing assets is declining or has already turned negative. As a result, getting cash out of the company becomes a key priority for shareholders. The pace at which a company can flow cash through to investors often determines the rate of return. Left to themselves, many deep value companies stagnate seemingly indefinitely, reinvesting cash into a doomed business or attempting in vain to expand into a more attractive business by paying a high price for an acquisition. If a company is small, satisfying the financial demands of the management team alone can impede accretion of value to shareholders.

The existence of a potential catalyst, even if the precise value-unlocking event cannot be identified, becomes important in situations in which the existing assets earn low returns and cash cannot be reinvested at acceptable rates. This view is congruent with the opinion of some value investors that no catalyst is needed if a company is deeply undervalued. According to Guy Spier, "Value is its own catalyst. It's exactly the fact that people look at the situation and say, 'this is never going to rise,' which is probably the reason why it's cheap."[23]

The argument that value is its own catalyst does assume the possibility of a catalytic event. If such an event depends solely on management, perhaps because insiders have voting control, then value may not be its own catalyst. In the extreme scenario of a CEO-controlled company that pays no dividend and does not repurchase shares, and in which the company systematically diverts value toward management compensation, the equity may be worth little more than zero. The "little more" becomes the value of optionality, reflecting some chance that the CEO could change behavior or decide to sell the company. Reliance on either possibility seems to be a recipe for shareholder disappointment.

Value typically proves to be its own catalyst in situations in which the following conditions exist: First, the investor appraises intrinsic value correctly, taking into account not only the hard assets of a business but also the prospects of the going concern and the capital allocation posture of management. Second, a catalytic event can be imposed from the outside, either by another company or an activist investor. Whether such a scenario is possible depends not only on whether management has voting control but also on factors such as potential takeover impediments in a company's organizational documents, contingent liabilities that may deter outside suitors, and the ability of management to destroy key assets before a change of control can take place. After activist investors seized control of the ostensibly undervalued asset management firm BFC Capital, they realized that management had succeeded in destroying a key asset—the relationship with the firm's investing clients. This was apparently done in accordance with the law. The result was devastating nonetheless: The firm lost the vast majority of the assets it had managed, necessitating layoffs and eviscerating earning power. What may have been an undervalued equity before the fight between the CEO and the activists became an overvalued equity thereafter.

Key Takeaways

Here are our top 10 takeaways from this chapter:

1. Graham-style investing unabashedly starts with the price of a stock. Unless the price looks like a bargain based on tangible metrics, Graham-style investors have no interest.
2. Economists Eugene Fama and Kenneth French have studied the relationship between stock performance and book-to-market ratios. They have consistently found that equities with high book-to-market ratios outperform those with low ratios.
3. A holy grail might be uncovering equities that provide both asset protection on the balance sheet and own businesses with high returns on capital. This combination is virtually impossible

to find unless a company has experienced a steep near-term profit decline.

4. By prioritizing return of cash to shareholders, low-return businesses can assist investors in earning a strong investment return, assuming the equity purchase price was favorable.

5. Investors may overestimate liquidation values, as the reality of a dying business tends to hide some nasty surprises.

6. Acceptance of discomfort can be rewarding in investing, as fearful equities frequently trade at exceptionally low valuations.

7. When we invest in an asset-rich but low-return business, time may be working against us. As long as management can hold on to the assets and keep reinvesting at low returns, shareholders may earn unimpressive returns despite a bargain purchase price. As a result, catalysts become a relevant consideration.

8. Businesses trading at deep value prices are among those most likely to be creatively destroyed. It seems unwise to allocate a large portion of investable capital to any one deep value opportunity, even if it promises a large expected return.

9. Several considerations may augment the likelihood that a Graham-style screen yields a list of market-beating investment candidates. Share repurchases, insider buying, and cash generated through working capital shrinkage may be used as screening factors.

10. When we value a company based solely on readily ascertainable balance sheet values, we run the risk that those values erode over time, negatively impacting future equity value.

Notes

1. *The Manual of Ideas*, January 31, 2011, 111.
2. *The Manual of Ideas*, May 2009, 32.
3. See http://mba.tuck.dartmouth.edu/pages/faculty/ken.french/data_library .html.
4. *The Manual of Ideas*, April 2010, 15.
5. See Klarman (1991).
6. *The Manual of Ideas* interview with Jeroen Bos, London, 2012.
7. *The Manual of Ideas*, January 31, 2011, 135.

8. *The Manual of Ideas* interview with Kevin Murphy and Nick Kirrage, Schroders, London, 2012.
9. *The Manual of Ideas*, July 2010, 12.
10. *The Manual of Ideas*, January 2012, 12.
11. *The Manual of Ideas*, October 2011, 14.
12. *The Manual of Ideas*, October 2011, 19.
13. *The Manual of Ideas*, March 2012, 8.
14. *The Manual of Ideas*, January 2012, 12–13.
15. See Andreessen (2011), 11.
16. *The Manual of Ideas*, July 2010.
17. For more information, see www.youtube.com/watch?v=39qDeG5Foko.
18. *The Manual of Ideas* interview with Jeroen Bos, London, 2012.
19. *The Manual of Ideas* interview with Andrew Williamson, London, 2012.
20. See Pabrai (2012).
21. *The Manual of Ideas* interview with Robert Robotti, May 2012, www .youtube.com/watch?v=N1MVgz6dJd0, slightly edited for clarity.
22. *The Manual of Ideas*, April 2010, 16.
23. See Pabrai (2012).

CHAPTER 3

Sum-of-the-Parts Value

Investing in Companies with Excess or Hidden Assets

Vodafone does not consolidate Verizon Wireless and, as a result, sell-side analysts seem to ignore its significant value.

—David Einhorn

The investment thesis David Einhorn, president of Greenlight Capital, articulated on Vodafone in 2010 was as straightforward as it was surprising. Einhorn made the case that the market was ignoring the value of a 45 percent stake in Verizon Wireless because Vodafone did not consolidate the financial results of Verizon Wireless. While such an argument might be expected in the case of a small company that lacks an institutional following, Einhorn argued the existence of a major analytical oversight in the case of a company with a market value of more than $100 billion. Einhorn may not have argued that analysts were unaware of Vodafone's equity stake, but rather that it was not top of mind due to the reporting peculiarity. The fact that Einhorn felt comfortable putting forth such a seemingly unlikely argument reveals the degree to which he views sum-of-the-parts situations as fertile grounds for pricing inefficiency.

The Approach: Why It Works

Investors usually analyze a company as a monolithic whole, appraising value based on overall book value, earnings, or cash flow. However, many companies can be appraised most accurately by analyzing each of their distinct businesses or assets separately and then adding up those components of value to arrive at an estimate of overall enterprise or equity value.

Horsham, Pennsylvania-based Mace Security International operated three distinct businesses in 2007: a consumer-oriented pepper spray business, an enterprise security business, and a car wash business. If we had appraised the company by applying an earnings multiple to the overall reported net income, we might have committed a serious error. The company's three major businesses had vastly different profit margins, returns on capital, and growth prospects. Assume for a moment that one of the three businesses earned no profit and therefore did not contribute to overall income. If we had valued Mace based on a multiple of corporate earnings, we would have implicitly assigned no value to the breakeven segment. Meanwhile, that segment might have owned valuable assets, such as the land and buildings associated with car washes.[1] The example of Mace illustrates one of the reasons companies with two or more distinct assets may become undervalued. Investors sometimes focus unduly on a company's overall profitability even if a valuable segment is going through a period of depressed earnings.

Another reason for the market's occasional mispricing of companies with multiple sources of value may be investors' unwillingness to place value on assets that differ materially from a company's core assets. Consider an oil and gas exploration and production company whose shareholder base consists of energy-focused investors who value the company based on reserves, production, and other variables related to producing oil and gas. If the company also owns an innovative technology for getting oil out of the ground, investors may not give the technology much credit. Meanwhile, the technology may be marketable to other oil and gas companies, potentially creating a new, high-margin source of revenue without requiring material capital expenditure. A case in point is Calgary, Alberta-based Petrobank Energy and Resources, an oil and gas company whose quoted enterprise value and true sum-of-the-parts value seemed to diverge considerably in 2011.

From a practical standpoint, companies with distinct components of value often enjoy greater strategic flexibility, as they may divest a fairly valued asset to improve the balance sheet, repurchase undervalued shares, or reinvest capital in a high-return business. Management's ability to make such strategic choices sometimes attracts the interest of sophisticated investors who may push management toward a value-enhancing decision. When Bill Ackman, chief executive officer of Pershing Square Capital Management, pressured the board of Target to set up a structure that would highlight the value of Target's owned real estate, he was drawing attention to the sum-of-the-parts value of the company. Similarly, when John Paulson, president of Paulson & Co., argued that Hartford Financial Services should spin off its crown jewel property and casualty insurance business, he stated that the unit was "buried" within the holding company. The latter was covered by few property and casualty analysts and instead was treated primarily as a life insurance company, resulting in a lower market multiple of book value.[2]

John Lambert, investment manager at GAM, cites the example of telecom company Cable & Wireless to illustrate his focus in this context:

> *The company has been mismanaged for a decade, and with old management finally cleared out, we feel a new start is in the cards. The company's assets appear materially undervalued at the current highly depressed share price, in particular their UK network, their subsea network internationally, their high-growth hosting business and substantial tax assets, to name just a few. We believe a much sharper focus on cash flow, and operational performance, will reveal the value of these assets. . . . In the meantime, the depressed share price means the company could clearly be of interest to larger acquirers, with reported expressions of interest in both individual assets and the entire company in recent months.[3]*

Occasionally, market participants may misperceive the value of a company's core tangible assets, reflecting a failure to dig deeper than the balance sheet carrying values. Eric Khrom, managing partner of Khrom Capital Management, cites the example of the helicopter transportation company PHI, which was focused on off-shore oil and gas:

> *Oil prices were falling like a rock [during the crisis of 2008–2009]. . . . I took it as an approach that [the company] owns [over 300] helicopters. . . . There is actually a blue book on helicopter values. . . . What I discovered, unlike airplanes, is the fact that helicopters have a very stable asset value. They don't fluctuate as heavily as airplanes do . . . [helicopters] are interchangeable between many industries. You don't just have to use them for oil and gas; you can use them for police, tourism. If one country suffers, you can move them to another country. . . . I did the liquidation value analysis, and I noticed that [PHI] was trading for maybe thirty cents on the dollar. So, regardless of what happens with the oil and gas industry, and regardless if this company made another profit or not . . . the helicopter fleet itself was trading at a tremendous bargain. That wasn't something you could pick up in a screen. . . .*[4]

Uses and Misuses of Investing in Companies with Overlooked Assets

Good reasons exist for pursuing sum-of-the-parts opportunities, but not every such situation is attractive. More assets do not necessarily equal more value, especially if some of the assets are money-losing businesses with bleak turnaround prospects.

Is an Identifiable Asset Really a Separate Asset?

Sometimes investors, in their zeal to create a sum-of-the-parts opportunity, slice a company into too many parts, creating an attractive investment thesis in theory but not in reality. A retail chain may own lots of store real estate, but if the retailer is struggling, the real estate may not be worth nearly as much as if the retailer were doing well. One might object that the value of the real estate has nothing to do with how well the retail business is doing because those are two separate assets. Perhaps the retailer could enter into sale-leaseback transactions to monetize the value of the real estate. Although this may be possible, a buyer of the real estate in a sale-leaseback deal will care tremendously about the profitability of the retail business. If the tenant is shaky, the real estate value may be shaky, too. Instead of a sale-leaseback deal, a struggling retailer may opt to sell the real estate to a competitor. In this case, the fact that the retailer is being forced to close stores may correlate with an industry downturn, lowering demand for new store real estate. As a result, while store real estate undoubtedly has some value, the amount of value tends to correlate with the value of the related retail business. The two components of value may be analyzed separately, but they cannot be viewed as completely independent.

Think of large technology companies, such as Hewlett-Packard or Xerox, which sell hardware but also derive significant revenue from services. Investors sometimes ascribe value to the typically higher-margin services business without much regard for the fortunes of the hardware business. However, when the services business is built largely around hardware, the former could evaporate if the hardware business becomes obsolete. In such a scenario, a sum-of-the-parts valuation of interconnected hardware, software, and services units might trigger too optimistic an appraisal of value. Similar reasoning applies to vendor-financed capital goods or other large-ticket businesses. If the core business relies on captive financing for demand, it can be appraised separately only with some caveats.

What Is the Catalyst to Unlocking Noncore Value?

Even when different components of value can be viewed separately, caution may be warranted. Consider the example of Steinway Musical Instruments, the renowned piano maker that also owns a band instruments business and valuable real estate in New York. The company's office building in Midtown Manhattan and other real estate may be appraised independently, as strong demand exists for such real estate. The public equity of Steinway appears to have been quoted materially below intrinsic value for many years. Yet, investors who bought Steinway shares based on a sum-of-the-parts appraisal would have witnessed years of inaction on monetizing real estate. Management apparently saw no urgency to unlock shareholder value, while any shareholder efforts to compel action proved unsuccessful.

Steinway is hardly the only example of a company that owns hidden assets but fails to highlight them for the benefit of shareholders. In fact, managements rarely part with assets simply to reward shareholders. Asset sales may be followed by share repurchases or dividends. Either action shrinks the CEO's fiefdom—not exactly the favored outcome for most executives. As a result, when evaluating companies with multiple assets, the existence of a catalyst to unlocking value becomes quite important.

Catalysts are controversial among value investors, as some consider value a catalyst in its own right. When Ben Graham formulated the concept of margin of safety, it prompted the question of what might narrow the discount to intrinsic value. Mohnish Pabrai retells the story as follows:

> *Ben Graham was called into a [U.S.] Senate hearing by Senator Fulbright. He was trying to understand the nature of markets. . . . Senator Fulbright actually posed a question to Ben Graham—this is in the 1950s—and he said, Professor Graham, you buy a stock for $10 and you say that the intrinsic value is $20, what are the forces that would eventually make people realize it's worth $20 and it can actually get up to trading at $20? Graham's response to Senator Fulbright at the time was that, he just said, Senator Fulbright, this is one of those mysteries that we do not know the answer to. But he said that, if we are right on the intrinsic value, in some reasonable period of time, it will trade around its value.*[5]

The answer that the reasons behind the narrowing remain largely a mystery may not satisfy most investors, but it is acceptable to those who intuitively seek value. Tim McElvaine, president of McElvaine Investment Management, sees danger in "getting overly fixated" on a catalyst," as investors may find it "hard to get a catalyst for free."

We normally do not require a catalyst, but we find that situations with multiple sources of value are more prone to becoming value traps in the absence of anticipated strategic action. Few companies represent the most effective home for disparate businesses, relegating some of the assets to relative underperformance. Unfortunately, when intrinsic value stagnates over time, Mr. Market is in no hurry to revalue an asset, turning it into the feared value trap.

Stephen Roseman, portfolio manager of Thesis Fund Management, has made catalysts a key component of his investment approach. "One of the non-negotiable requirements I have with respect to committing capital—on the long side—is a tangible catalyst I can point to within the ensuing six to twelve months. Capital has a cost, and this discipline helps to improve returns in two distinct ways: it helps to avoid value traps, a common foible of value investing; and it helps to improve IRR as capital is deployed closer to events that might help realize value."[6]

Is the Offer "Buy One, Get One Free" or "Buy 10, Get One Free"?

One of our pet peeves of investment analysis is the assertion that an equity offers something for nothing. We see this quite a lot and may even have succumbed to the temptation ourselves—to state that because one piece of a company is worth as much as the quoted value of the entire enterprise, the other piece of the company is being offered free. An item is not really free if you need to purchase another item at the same time. The term *free* should be reserved for situations in which you walk up and take something without parting with anything of monetary value. In this sense, *free* exists only rarely in the world of physical goods, though it is more readily available online. Facebook, Google, and Twitter are all truly free—no credit card needed. Those companies rely on advertising-driven business models that allow them to monetize consumers' free use of their websites. Unfortunately, no publicly traded equity comes with an advertising-sponsored model. There is no advertising-driven stock exchange website on which investors can freely move shares of common stock into their brokerage accounts while being exposed to banner ads. When it comes to investing, the notion of free is more akin to the sales pitch "buy one, get one free."

Here is the rub, however: It matters tremendously whether the offer is "buy one, get one free" or "buy 10, get one free." As shoppers, we recognize the former as a more compelling offer. As investors, we often overlook this important distinction. How often have you read an investment write-up that trumpets an asset as free while failing to disclose the value of the free asset *in relation* to the amount we must pay for the other assets involved? In our experience, investment articles rarely disclose whether we are looking at a "buy one, get one free" or a "buy 10, get one free" offer. This is precisely why many sum-of-the-parts theses fail to deliver the desired investment performance.

An analyst may find a business selling for $1 billion. The true value of the business is also estimated at $1 billion, but the company owns $100 million in hidden real estate. The analyst can rejoice at having uncovered $100 million in free assets. The investment write-up might read something like this: "We value the operating business at $1 billion. With the company trading at a market value of $1 billion, we conclude that investors receive $100 million in excess real estate for free." The analyst can sound insightful while pitching an opportunity to pay $100 for $110. This would be quite all right if the investor could receive $110 quickly and easily. However, reality works differently. The investor's $10 freebie would evaporate if the intrinsic value of the business fell by just 10 percent.

Screening for Companies with Multiple Assets

Sum-of-the-parts investment opportunities come in a few different flavors, each of which demands a slightly different approach to screening. Excess assets typically consist of cash and cashlike assets, stakes in other businesses, real estate holdings, or a combination of these asset types. In a situation that involves excess assets, we typically focus on evaluating the core business in the context of a lower implied purchase price due to the assumed disposition or distribution of excess assets. The approach differs in the case of opportunities in which the pieces represent more than one operating business. In such situations, excess assets may be immaterial, with the analysis focused on appraising the value of each business unit. The resulting sum may be higher or lower than overall intrinsic value. In the case of a sum-of-the-parts situation like Berkshire Hathaway, the whole may be greater than the sum of the parts due to Warren Buffett's ability to create value through capital allocation. In the case of most other conglomerates, a discount to the sum of the parts may be appropriate.

Companies with Multiple Operating Businesses

No easy way exists to identify companies with multiple businesses via a low-cost stock-screening tool, as most screeners contain corporate-level data only. Absent access to tools such as Bloomberg or Capital IQ, investors may resort to the rather painstaking process of combing through the financial statement footnotes of annual reports. Companies listed in the United States typically include a footnote with segment information in their 10-K filings. Such segment data provide a basis for valuing the business units, especially when we analyze the information in conjunction with management's discussion and analysis contained elsewhere in the report. A review of the market multiples of relevant comparable companies may improve our understanding of the relative value of each segment.

Even if we have access to a segment-level screener like Bloomberg or Capital IQ, we may gain quite a bit from closer inspection of the segment data. In some cases, the business segments will be sufficiently similar to justify little distinction in the respective approaches to valuation. In such a case, a valuation estimate using corporate-level data may differ little from an estimate based on a sum of the constituent parts. A similar conclusion applies when the business segments are so intertwined that they cannot be reasonably separated for valuation purposes. Intersegment sales frequently indicate the degree to which the various segments depend on each other.

The value of a sum-of-the-parts valuation exercise grows when the various business segments demand distinct approaches to valuation. In such a scenario, the sum of the parts may differ markedly from the valuation estimate one might derive from corporate-level data. When the latter is significantly lower than the former, the equity may have been overlooked by market participants focused on high-level data. Promising ideas include companies with businesses in more than one industry, businesses with vastly different returns on capital, and companies with unexpectedly large businesses in fast-growing geographies.

We may also find examination of the various business units rewarding due to large differences in the operating trends of the various units. Envision a telecom services company with flat to modestly declining revenue. Investors may ascribe low valuation multiples to this apparently struggling company, unless they realize that a small but fast-growing mobile business is partly offsetting the revenue declines of a large fixed-line business. As the revenue share of the mobile business grows, the top-level decline in revenue may reverse. Segment-level analysis may help us anticipate a reversal in top-line growth before other market participants do so.

Companies with Large Holdings of Net Cash

By 2013, Apple had accumulated a net cash position of well over $100 billion, creating a low-yielding but highly liquid excess asset. Investors who made the case that Apple was undervalued treated the net cash on the company's balance sheet as an excess asset. Apple's earnings were roughly identical with or without the cash because of low prevailing interest rates, but the difference in actual versus adjusted market value was significant. As a result, Apple shares traded at a headline price-to-earnings multiple in the teens and a cash-adjusted P/E multiple in the single digits. Despite the ease with which one could detect and adjust for Apple's net cash position, many investors apparently failed to do so in their P/E ratio analysis.

Most stock screening tools include data on cash, short-term investments, and debt, enabling us to screen for companies with large cash holdings. We are particularly interested in companies that hold large amounts of net cash in relation to equity market value. Market participants occasionally overlook or deliberately ignore large net cash holdings, creating a potential opportunity for investors willing to distinguish between equity value and enterprise value. We are especially interested in situations in which net cash amounts to a third or more of market value, as undervaluation of the equity by 33 percent would imply 50 percent upside potential. If net cash is likely to keep growing absent share repurchases or strategic actions, the equity security becomes especially enticing. A growing net cash position widens the margin of safety, lowering the downside and increasing the upside in case of a constant stock price.

We find situations in which net cash exceeds market value as intriguing as they are rare. Mr. Market's judgment that an enterprise has negative implied value triggers a number of questions: How is the net cash position evolving over time? If net cash is growing, is the market justified in the implicit assumption that management will make a major capital allocation error? To be clear, we should not expect a clean story to go along with a company that trades at negative enterprise value. Instead, our focus should be on the likelihood of future destruction of shareholder value. If destruction is likely, a company with negative enterprise value may be no bargain after all. On the other hand, if intrinsic value is likely to keep growing, however slowly, the situation may offer low downside and material upside. In such a scenario, we may be most concerned with the time it may take for the perceived valuation discount to close, as time may drive our annualized return more than the magnitude of the eventual revaluation. We find insider buying to be a particularly strong confirmation of value, as companies trading at negative enterprise value tend to suffer from negative market sentiment. An insider's willingness to disagree with the market by purchasing shares typically represents a strong signal that enterprise value exceeds zero.

Companies that have a large percentage of their market value in net cash may be viewed as opportunities to go "long optionality," according to Mike Onghai, president of Snowy August Management. Onghai has leveraged his background as a technology entrepreneur to identify companies "managing their transition to another phase of online technology."[7] Such equities occasionally trade for less than cash, reflecting the market's pessimism regarding the potential success of their product transition. However, the companies retain significant optionality due to a possibility, however small, that their transition proves successful. Onghai became CEO of LookSmart in early 2013, a situation that met the criteria of negative enterprise value and ongoing product transition.

Companies with Investments in Other Companies

Most stock screeners include data on long-term investments, although case-by-case research is needed to understand the composition of those investments. When screening for companies with significant holdings in other businesses, we typically require long-term investments to amount to at least 10 percent of market value. We use market value instead of book value to avoid situations in which the value of long-term investments is de minimis because of a high price-to-book trading multiple. We set the minimum requirement at only 10 percent, as the carrying value of long-term investments may be lower than their market value in the most interesting situations.

For example, Company A may have long-term investments amounting to 20 percent of equity market value. Assume that this asset consists of an investment in another public entity, Company B. The carrying value will be the market value of the holding as of the balance sheet date. If the price of Company B stock has doubled since the balance sheet date, then long-term investments may amount to 40 percent of the market value of Company A.

This could be quite significant due to the possibility that the remaining 60 percent of market value may be lower than the intrinsic value of Company A excluding the investment in Company B.

In the case of Loews, the value of the company's holdings in other public companies has occasionally approached the enterprise value of the parent, implying essentially zero value for Loews' privately held assets and the capital allocation ability of management. When market conditions offer an opportunity to buy the Loews stub for virtually no capital, we may go long Loews shares, or we may choose to go long the stub only. The latter involves selling short proportional amounts of Loews' publicly listed investee companies. While the prospect of creating a zero-cost scenario is enticing, we prefer to appraise the value of the pieces to be shorted. If we judge those pieces to be undervalued in their own right, we may prefer to forgo short-selling them while going long Loews common stock.

Companies with Large Real Estate Holdings

The value of real estate may be well understood, but the market occasionally ignores the real estate holdings of public companies, especially if a company's core business is not related to real estate or the real estate assets are carried for materially less than fair value. Generally accepted accounting principles (GAAP) require most companies to carry real estate at historical cost, resulting in material understatement of value in cases in which the real estate was acquired or developed decades ago. For example, when Playboy Enterprises was taken private by Hugh Hefner in 2011, the Playboy Mansion was on the books for only $1 million but might have been worth $50 million or more. The disparity reflected the original purchase price roughly four decades earlier. Similarly, Maui Land & Pineapple acquired much of the land it owns in Hawaii in the early 20th century, resulting in a large disparity between carrying value and market value.

David Coyne, portfolio manager at Setanta Asset Management, describes an investment in MI Developments (MIM), which owned underappreciated real-estate-related assets in 2010. Coyne realized that MIM carried real estate at cost rather than market value.

While unable to get precise details from their filings, it was fairly clear that the majority of their real estate assets were

transferred over from Magna [MIM's former parent company]
in 1998 and 1999. Since 2003 the number of properties had
been stable (as far as I could tell, additional space was built
on existing land), so MIM did not get involved in the ensu-
ing global real estate madness. Underpinning the $1.4 billion
net book value of their real estate was $1.2 billion in future
minimum rental payments to be received from tenant Magna
(weighted-average time to lease expiry of just 6.7 years),
along with a whopping 14.5 percent rental yield on the net
value of the real estate assets. MIM's properties were mostly in
the Greater Toronto area, Austria and Southern Germany,
which were largely unaffected by the global financial crisis.
Based on some conservative back-of-the-envelope calculations
I estimated that the real estate could be undervalued by some
50 percent and that MIM could be trading on a true price-to-
tangible book of perhaps 0.25x.[8]

Screening for real estate assets presents some challenges, not
only because carrying value may differ materially from market
value but also because most stock screeners include the carrying value of land and buildings in property, plant, and equipment
(PP&E). We may need to examine the financial footnotes of each
candidate to determine the breakdown of PP&E. Making the latter a
key screening variable is likely to result in significant noise, making
such screens impractical.

As an alternative to mechanical screening, we may choose to
build a list of non-real-estate-related operating businesses with
large real estate holdings. It may make sense to do so by industry.
For instance, we may wish to analyze the store bases of retailers to
identify companies with large portfolios of owned store real estate,
which may consist of store improvements only or, more interest-
ingly, of owned land and buildings.

Beyond Screening: Proven Ways of Finding Hidden Assets

Assets that might be considered truly hidden evade discovery by
quantitative screening methods, necessitating a more qualitative
approach. While a brute force method might include reviewing

as many corporate disclosures as possible, we may improve our search efficiency in the following ways.

Scrutinizing the Holdings of Smart Investor-Detectives

The prospect of hidden assets attracts the attention of quite a few smart investors. Other things equal, the existence of such assets makes it more likely that a company is undervalued. In addition, the prospect of other market participants uncovering the noncore assets provides a potential catalyst for revaluation of the equity. Finally, in the case of an apparently undervalued equity, the perception that some assets are hidden from the view of most investors may explain why the company is undervalued. Seth Klarman has argued that we strengthen an investment case when we understand why the market may have missed, misjudged, or even created an investment opportunity. For example, if we uncover an apparently undervalued company whose stock price has plummeted, the investment thesis will be strengthened by knowledge that a large institutional shareholder was forced to sell shares due to a need to satisfy redemptions of capital by the shareholder's clients.

As we have sought to discover companies with hidden assets, we have also identified smart investors who appear focused on unusual situations, including equities with overlooked sources of value. We list 10 such investors, along with their CIK numbers for easy searching of the SEC filings database at www.sec.gov.

- **Bill Ackman**, Pershing Square Capital Management (CIK 0001336528). Ackman has made investing in companies with multiple assets a cornerstone of his investment strategy. In the past, his investments in McDonald's, Target, and Alexander & Baldwin appear to have been motivated at least in part by a potential for highlighting hidden value through corporate strategic action.
- **David Einhorn**, Greenlight Capital (CIK 0001079114). Einhorn lays out the thesis for Greenlight's largest holdings in quarterly letters to investors. He frequently describes situations in which the market appears to be ignoring a significant but not immediately obvious source of value. One example is Vodafone, the mobile telephony giant that also owns a large stake in Verizon Wireless.

- **Carl Icahn**, Icahn Associates (CIK 0000921669). Icahn was known as a corporate raider before the term *activist* came into vogue. He has a long history of pushing management teams to unlock value through corporate action, including strategic combinations, spin-offs, and recapitalizations.
- **Daniel Loeb**, Third Point (CIK 0001040273). Loeb became quite widely known several years ago for his scathing letters to several chief executives, but his long-term investment performance may deserve even more attention. He has embraced an opportunistic approach that includes seeking out companies with multiple sources of value. An example is Yahoo!, which had equity interests in Alibaba Group and Yahoo Japan at the time of Loeb's involvement.
- **Mick McGuire**, Marcato Capital Management (CIK 0001541996). McGuire, a former protégé of Bill Ackman, applies a value-oriented activist approach to investing in mid-cap equities with value that might be unlocked through management action. As of early 2013, Marcato was engaged in an activist campaign at auto parts maker Lear, which operated in two distinct segments: seating and electrical power management.
- **Lloyd I. Miller III**, private investor (CIK 0000949119). Miller has invested in many micro-cap equities with large holdings of net cash over the years. One of his strengths seems to be identifying companies whose cash holdings may be ignored by the market due to weak operating performance. Miller appears to have successfully found companies whose performance is likely to improve, prompting revaluation of the enterprise.
- **John Paulson**, Paulson & Co. (CIK 0001035674). Paulson was a successful special situations investor before he gained fame and fortune in the subprime mortgage collapse. Since the crisis, he has invested in several companies that might best be valued on a sum-of-the-parts basis, including Hartford Financial Services, which includes a property and casualty insurer that was buried within the parent entity, according to Paulson.[9]
- **Michael Price**, MFP Investors (CIK 0000918537). Price has had a storied investment career, joining Max Heine at Mutual Series in 1973. Price led Mutual Series to long-term outperformance by following a value investing approach that focused at least in part on identifying companies with excess or misperceived assets. Price continues to apply his time-tested approach at MFP Investors.[10]

- **Wilbur Ross**, WL Ross & Co., filing under Invesco Private Capital (CIK 0001128452). Ross is perhaps best known as an investor in distressed industries, such as the U.S. steel industry in the early 2000s. He has succeeded in finding value where other investors have seen mostly risk. By identifying assets the market was mispricing or ignoring, Ross has been able to construct compelling investment cases on companies in industries undergoing major change.
- **Marty Whitman and Amit Wadhwaney**, Third Avenue Management (CIK 0001099281). Whitman ranks among the most highly regarded investors who focus first on the hard assets on a company's balance sheet. While building a downside protection case based on readily ascertainable net asset value, Whitman has identified companies with assets that have remained below the radar of other investors. Wadhwaney has applied a similar approach globally, identifying opportunities in holding companies, among other ideas.

Combing through Areas of Specific Opportunity

We may systematically identify companies with hidden assets by first considering investment categories likely to include such companies. The categories need not meet traditional definitions; rather, any descriptive bucket of companies likely to own assets that may be out of sight qualifies as a category. An example might be companies with net operating loss (NOL) carryforwards that are not capitalized due to a valuation allowance. As in the case of NOL-rich companies, some categories may persist for a long time. Meanwhile, other categories, such as thrift conversions, may represent a temporally bounded opportunity.

THRIFT CONVERSIONS How would you like to find a company whose number of shares outstanding is materially lower than the number shown in equity databases and stated in the company's SEC filings? This fortunate error occurs in the case of some thrifts because a captive mutual holding company (MHC) sometimes owns a large percentage of common shares outstanding. The economics of those shares accrue to the remaining shareholders (or depositors if the thrift is not yet publicly traded). As a result of the value hidden in MHC-owned shares, thrift conversions represent one of the more conservative, time-tested ways of earning attractive risk-adjusted returns in the banking industry.

In a first-step thrift conversion, an institution that has been technically owned by its depositors may become a stock corporation and raise capital in an IPO. In these offerings, new investors are essentially buying their own capital and getting the existing institution's assets and business free. Seth Klarman illustrated the mechanics as follows:

> *A thrift institution with a net worth of $10 million might issue one million shares of stock at $10 per share. . . . Ignoring costs of the offering, the proceeds of $10 million are added to the institution's preexisting net worth, resulting in pro forma shareholders' equity of $20 million. Since the one million shares sold on the IPO are the only shares outstanding, pro forma net worth is $20 per share. The preexisting net worth of the institution joins the investors' own funds, resulting immediately in a net worth per share greater than the investors' own contribution.*[11]

In a second-step thrift conversion, an institution that is partly owned by an MHC typically completes a transition to full public ownership by offering MHC-owned shares to investors. Ideally, the vast majority of the stock of a publicly traded thrift is held by an MHC. While those shares are considered to be outstanding, the economics belong entirely to the non-MHC shareholders. The analogy would be treasury stock held by a corporation that had completed a share repurchase. The major difference is that treasury stock is not formally considered to be outstanding.

Thrift conversions had their zenith in the 1980s and 1990s. Some savvy investors such as Klarman, who had actively participated in conversions, have since moved on to bigger opportunities as their funds have grown in size. In addition, bank-focused investment funds as a category were decimated in the financial crisis of 2008, making it plausible that thrift conversions may not be as closely followed as they were in the past. Writes Klarman, "The arithmetic of a thrift conversion is surely compelling. Yet except for brief interludes when investing in thrifts was popular among individual investors, this area has been virtually ignored. Only a small number of professional investors persisted in identifying this source of value-investment opportunities and understanding the reasons for its existence over a number of years."[12]

Some opportunities for outsized risk-adjusted returns in thrift conversions probably remain available. In early 2013, Lamplighter Financial, MHC held 74 percent of the common stock of Waterstone Financial. Those MHC-held shares were not actually outstanding for economic purposes, as the economics associated with the shares belonged entirely to the holders of the remaining 26 percent of the common stock. As a result, the bank's apparent market value of $240 million compared to its true market value of only $62 million. Waterstone's adjusted market value amounted to only 4 percent of tangible assets of $1.7 billion, despite a doubling in the stock price over the previous six months.

RETAIL OR HOSPITALITY BUSINESSES WITH LARGE REAL ESTATE HOLDINGS Retailers, restaurateurs, and hotel operators rely heavily on the operation of various types of real estate. As a result, they tend to be capital-intensive businesses if we measure intensity based on the assets actually employed in customer-facing operations. Over the years, most retail or hospitality businesses have opted to forgo owner-ship of real estate in favor of leasing. In doing so, they turned a cap-ital-intensive endeavor into a business with modest capital intensity and improved returns on capital employed. Despite this trend toward separation of real estate ownership and business management, some companies retain large holdings of real estate.

The fact that a company owns the land and buildings associ-ated with its locations may not be immediately obvious from reviewing the balance sheet, as real estate is typically carried at historical cost. Companies that have been in operation for decades may have carrying values roughly in line with the real estate carry-ing values of firms that lease real estate but have made significant recent improvements to the operated properties. The store improve-ments retailers make preopening or while renovating a store are typically capitalized, with the nature of the asset typically disclosed in a footnote to the annual financial statements.

When we identify a retailer or hospitality company that owns much of the real estate it uses in operations, we may analyze the company assuming the hypothetical scenario that the company sells and leases back the real estate. Such an exercise will result in sepa-rate values for the real properties and for the operating business, the pro forma profitability of which may be reduced somewhat by the assumption that the company will incur incremental lease expense. If the intrinsic value assuming separation of the real estate assets is materially higher than the equity market value of the company, we may have identified a company with hidden assets.

Finding companies with truly hidden assets is becoming progressively more difficult as large numbers of smart and diligent fund managers comb through the equity markets. Many smart investors have a go-anywhere approach, as they manage lightly regulated limited partnerships with relatively small assets under management. For example, several smart investors made a case for Syms, a discount retailer with large real estate holdings, including in Manhattan. The fact that Syms had a market value of $100 million or less did not keep it hidden from value-seeking investors. Real estate assets may remain out of sight longer in the case of non-U.S. companies, especially stocks that trade on smaller, local stock exchanges. Data on such companies may be excluded from most low-cost databases, making it harder for investors to screen for those companies.

As motivated investors set out to uncover hidden assets around the globe, the focus may shift from simply identifying a hidden asset to determining how that asset will be monetized or capitalized by the market. A spin-off of the real estate, advocated by Bill Ackman in a few cases, may accomplish such revaluation. Strategic action may either return cash to shareholders (in the case of asset sales) or highlight the hitherto hidden value (in the case of a spin-off). Absent such action, the smart investors who find the hidden assets may be unable or unwilling to drive up the stock price toward fair value, as the latter might imply a market-average prospective return. The most enterprising investors typically demand larger anticipated investment returns, requiring incremental investment by less ambitious investors.

COMPANIES WITH LARGE NOL CARRYFORWARDS Generally accepted accounting principles require companies to take a valuation allowance against their operating loss carryforwards if sufficient future profitability cannot be expected based on recent performance. The hurdle is high enough that many companies that appear likely to reestablish profitability are required to maintain the valuation allowance until they have demonstrated an operational turnaround. As a result, research-oriented investors may uncover opportunities in which a real NOL asset is missing from the balance sheet, making shareholders' equity appear lower than it actually is. Alternatively, we may prefer not to regard NOLs as a hidden asset to be recapitalized to increase book value, but rather as a positive factor in estimating future free cash flows.

In some instances, NOLs are so material that a company may be able to shield income from taxes not just for a year or two, but for a decade or longer. Many rules apply to the use of NOLs, and the rules can be quite confusing, making it difficult to estimate utilization of NOLs with certainty. For example, even if a company's NOL covers our estimate of next year's pretax income, the company may still have to pay some taxes as the NOL may not be applicable to certain income items, perhaps based on the geographic origin of the profit. In addition, the future use of NOLs may be restricted due to high turnover in the shareholder base, which could result from a takeover or churn in a company's 5+ percent shareholders. The latter have a Schedule 13G filing requirement, giving the IRS a mechanism for calculating owner turnover. Despite the regulatory limitations, some companies become attractive acquisition targets due to their large NOL carryforwards.

FINANCE COMPANIES MASQUERADING AS PRODUCT BUSINESSES Before finance companies became shunned by the market, they often represented a large yet not immediately obvious driver of value at low-margin product companies. Much of the value of General Motors seemed to reside not in the auto business, but rather in GMAC, the firm's giant finance arm. Similarly, personal computer makers earned low margins on the sale of hardware, relying on warranty sales to boost their margins.

Even in a postcrisis world in which the risks of finance companies are well understood, companies selling commoditized products may earn a large percentage of profit from ancillary financial and insurance services. Certain types of warranties not only achieve high margins but also provide investable float. Before we discard a low-margin product maker as unworthy of further inquiry, we may want to check whether the company has a material financial services business. Ancillary and unusual financial products typically carry the highest margins and could tip the scales in favor of an otherwise average investment.

CONGLOMERATES By definition, conglomerates employ a hetero-geneous set of assets in generating overall results for shareholders. As such, the value of the operating and nonoperating assets owned by holding companies such as Berkshire Hathaway may be subject to debate, but the existence of the various assets is typically no secret. Matthias Riechert, portfolio manager at Polleit & Riechert Investment Management, cites a key driver of undervaluation by pointing to the example of a German construction-related conglomerate: "Hochtief has traded at a conglomerate discount for several years because man-agement has not been capable of closing this gap by implementing strategic changes."[13]

Investors' apparent acceptance of the argument that conglomer-ates deserve a discount to their sum-of-the-parts value may create opportunity in select situations. In the case of Berkshire Hathaway, Leucadia National, and Markel, a conglomerate premium may be more appropriate than a discount. Due to the skill and share-holder orientation of their management teams, each of the three companies possesses a soft asset that may be underappreciated by the market: superior capital allocation ability. The latter results in above-average expected returns on capital, justifying a premium equity valuation.

The conglomerate structure has been rather popular with large family-owned businesses in Asia. Such companies frequently own a variety of consumer-facing businesses in addition to material real estate and other holdings. Management tends to be heavily incen-tivized to create shareholder value, although abuse of the insiders' control position is also not uncommon. Nonetheless, to the extent that family-run conglomerates may be overlooked by the market due to their often complicated structures, an opportunity may exist for investors willing to appraise the major components of value.

Building a Watchlist of Companies with Hidden Value

Most concretely, we translate a search for hidden value into invest-ment in specific undervalued equities. To invest when the margin of safety is largest, we track a list of companies with noncore or hidden assets. As the implied sum-of-the-parts value of those com-panies varies based on the market prices of their investee compa-nies, we are able to dynamically track the estimated discount to fair value. An example is well-managed conglomerate Loews, which in early 2013 owned 90 percent of publicly listed CNA Financial, 50.4 percent of publicly listed Diamond Offshore Drilling, and 53 percent limited partnership and 2 percent general partnership interests in publicly listed Boardwalk Pipeline Partners. Loews held those publicly traded assets in addition to outright ownership of Highmount Exploration & Production and Loews Hotels & Resorts. The company also had significant cash and investments at the corporate level.[14]

When we build a watchlist of Loews-like companies, we put ourselves in a position to act quickly should the market panic and sell off their common stocks without regard for the sum-of-the-parts value. Occasionally, an opportunity may exist even if investors do not sell off the holding company shares but simply fail to recognize an increase in the value of the underlying assets. Ideally, we not only compile and grow the watchlist over time but also track the estimated discount between intrinsic value and the market price. When the discount reaches a historically wide level, we may do the analytical work required to make an investment decision.

Asking the Right Questions of Companies with Hidden Assets

Whenever we uncover an unexpected asset within a public company, we may feel tempted to build an equity thesis around this apparent source of edge. Unfortunately, not all hidden assets warrant investment in the affiliated corporate entity. We focus on the following points of inquiry when assessing potential sum-of-the-parts opportunities.

To What Extent Are the Hidden Assets Really Overlooked?

Situations with significant noncore assets often resonate with smart investors, as the investment story can be quite compelling. First, the existence of various assets may increase the likelihood that an equity is undervalued. Second, the hidden nature of the assets may explain why a stock is neglected by the market. This combination of a bargain price and an apparent nonfundamental reason for the bargain valuation appeals to sophisticated market participants.

Some hidden asset stories are so compelling that they attract quite a few smart investors, potentially eliminating both the valuation discount and the hidden nature of the assets. Investors may indeed become patsies by failing to realize how many other smart investors have bought into the same story of hidden value. If the perceived discount to fair value does not exist or is later eliminated due to new developments, the outcome might be made more painful because many like-minded investors head for the exits at the same time.

Examples of hidden value theses gone bad abound in the value investment community, whether the investment case was long only or long-short. We are reminded of the Porsche-Volkswagen pair trade, the post-spin-off equity of EchoStar, apparently overcapitalized mortgage lenders in early 2008, regional airlines Pinnacle Airlines and Republic Airways, the prebankruptcy equity of General Motors, and many other situations in which groups of smart investors mistakenly embraced a notion of hidden value.

We apply the following rule of thumb: If two or more superinvestors own an equity security, whatever value may reside in it cannot be regarded as hidden. Value is also not hidden if two or more superinvestors disagree on the merits of an investment case. For example, the hidden assets Bruce Berkowitz may have identified at Florida real estate company St. Joe could no longer be regarded as hidden once David Einhorn articulated a bearish investment thesis. Each of us will regard a different set of investors as superinvestors, and there is no rule on who should qualify. Over time, we strive to get to know an increasing number of fund managers who have successfully looked for hidden value opportunities in the past. Such investors may not be well known to the average market participant, but we may still regard them as superinvestors. For example, while most investors have not heard of Lloyd Miller, he appears to have consistently identified small- and micro-cap companies with material noncore assets.

What Is the Investment Case without the Noncore Assets?

Investors often focus unduly on assets perceived as hidden, falsely assuming that the market values the core business appropriately. If we ignore the core business, we may misperceive the upside opportunity as equal to the ratio of hidden asset value to equity market value. Unfortunately, Mr. Market may be aware of the assets we perceive as hidden. In such a scenario, the equity may trade at a low multiple of earnings or book value, not because other market participants have overlooked certain assets, but rather because they view the core business as impaired. By falsely concluding that the market is ignoring the noncore assets, we may overpay for the core business and end up with a value trap.

Whenever we identify a situation with apparently hidden assets, we first analyze the core assets. The latter should be well understood by other market participants, unless the company qualifies as a micro-cap or there is another reason for outright neglect. Ideally, after appraising the core business, we will conclude that the enterprise valuation the market is putting on the entire company is more than justified by the core business alone. In such a case, the assets we perceive as hidden may indeed be overlooked by other investors. It rarely pays to invest in perceived hidden value unless we like the core business as well.

What Is the Path to Value Capture?

Whenever hidden assets motivate us to consider an equity security, the question of how those assets will cease to be hidden becomes important. In this context, we may be less interested in the somewhat speculative question of what will prompt other investors to see what we are already seeing. Rather, we focus on the economically important issue of how the value inherent in the hidden assets will accrue to us as shareholders—and when. If companies with hidden assets do nothing to actually monetize the value of those assets, simply telling other investors about the hidden value may not suffice. Even if the market becomes fully aware of the noncore asset value, the equity may not be revalued due to skepticism that shareholders will capture the excess value.

In a scenario in which the value of a hidden asset remains constant over time and the asset is not monetized or distributed to shareholders, the discounted present value of the asset may be exceedingly low. As a result, prompt value realization becomes crucial to any investment case that rests primarily on the existence of hidden assets. Preferable courses of action from a shareholder's perspective include a spin-off of the noncore assets or monetization followed by a special dividend, share repurchase, or balance sheet deleveraging.

Key Takeaways

Here are our top 10 takeaways from this chapter:

1. Many companies can be appraised most accurately by analyzing each of their distinct businesses or assets separately and then adding up those components of value to arrive at an estimate of overall enterprise or equity value.
2. A reason for the market's occasional mispricing of companies with multiple sources of value may be investors' unwillingness to value assets that differ materially from a company's core assets.
3. Companies with distinct components of value often enjoy greater strategic flexibility, as they may divest a fairly valued asset to improve the balance sheet, repurchase undervalued shares, or reinvest capital in a high-return business.
4. Sometimes investors, in their zeal to create a sum-of-the-parts opportunity, slice a company into too many parts, creating an attractive investment thesis in theory but not in reality.
5. We normally do not require a catalyst, but we find that situations with multiple sources of value are more prone to becoming value traps in the absence of strategic action.
6. It matters tremendously whether the offer is "buy one, get one free," or "buy 10, get one free." As shoppers, we recognize the former as a more compelling offer. As investors, we often overlook this important distinction.
7. Sum-of-the-parts opportunities come in a few different flavors, each of which demands a slightly different approach to screening. Excess assets typically consist of cash and cashlike assets, stakes in other businesses, real estate holdings, or a combination of these asset types.
8. The value of a sum-of-the-parts analysis grows when the various business segments demand distinct approaches to valuation. In such a scenario, the sum of the parts may differ widely from the valuation estimate one might derive from corporate-level data.
9. Some hidden asset stories are so compelling that they attract quite a few smart investors, potentially eliminating both the valuation discount and the hidden nature of the assets. Investors may become patsies by failing to realize how many

other smart investors have bought into the same story of hidden value.

10. Whenever hidden assets motivate us to consider an equity security, the question of how those assets will cease to be hidden becomes important. In this context, we are less interested in the speculative question of what will prompt other investors to see what we are seeing. Rather, we focus on the economically important issue of how the value inherent in the hidden assets will accrue to us as shareholders—and when.

Notes

1. For more information on the example of Mace Security, see a Value Investors Club write-up dated July 8, 2007, available at www .valueinvestorsclub.com/value2/Idea/ViewIdea/2784. See also Mace's historical SEC filings, available at http://sec.gov/edgar/searchedgar/ companysearch.html (type "Mace Security" in the "Company name" field).
2. www.marketfolly.com/2012/03/john-paulsons-presentation-on-why .html.
3. *The Manual of Ideas*, March 2012, 8–9.
4. *The Manual of Ideas* interview with Eric Khrom, New York, 2012.
5. See Pabrai (2012).
6. *The Manual of Ideas*, January 31, 2011, 151.
7. *The Manual of Ideas* interview with Mike Onghai, 2012.
8. *The Manual of Ideas*, January 31, 2011, 117–118.
9. Paulson & Co. presentation on Hartford Financial Services Group, March 9, 2012, www.marketfolly.com/2012/03/john-paulsons-presentation-on -why.html.
10. Wikipedia, http://en.wikipedia.org/wiki/Michael_F._Price.
11. Klarman (1991), 183–184.
12. Ibid., 127.
13. *The Manual of Ideas*, January 31, 2011, 150.
14. Loews Corporation fact sheet, accessed on February 24, 2013, http:// ir.loews.com/media_files/irol/10/102789/LoewsCompanyOverview.pdf.

CHAPTER 4

Greenblatt's Magic Search for Good and Cheap Stocks

The key to investing is not assessing how much an indus-try is going to affect society, or how much it will grow, but rather determining the competitive advantage of any given company and, above all, the durability of that advantage. The products or services that have wide, sustainable moats around them are the ones that deliver rewards to investors.

—Warren Buffett

When Joel Greenblatt's *The Little Book That Beats the Market* was published in 2005, it quickly became a best seller, not necessarily because investors were clamoring for the book's content, but because Greenblatt was already somewhat of a legend in the investment business. His track record of 50 percent annualized returns during the 10 years he ran a hedge fund, Gotham Partners, was virtually unmatched in the industry. The rewards to Greenblatt and his partners had been so high that after a decade of managing other people's money, he had the luxury of returning all outside capital and focusing exclusively on managing his own wealth. While reliable data on Greenblatt's investment performance since the dissolution of his hedge fund are hard to come by, his track record of outperformance probably continued in the two decades since 1994.

Whereas mystique surrounding Joel Greenblatt may have cata-pulted *The Little Book* onto best-seller lists after it was initially pub-lished, the simple yet powerful message of the book has kept it relevant. The advice to buy good companies only when they're cheap seems almost glib at first glance. However, Greenblatt's definitions of *good* and *cheap* and the actionable framework pre-sented in *The Little Book* make his advice invaluable to anyone seeking market-beating returns. According to Legg Mason's Michael Mauboussin, "The value of Greenblatt's formula is that it identifies high-quality companies at cheap prices. If you can do that over time, you should be fine."[1]

Ethan Berg's description of his investment approach hints at the essence of Greenblatt-style investing:

> *When I was a newspaper boy, there was a weekly circular from a Boston retailer that advertised "Good stuff, cheap." I've essentially adopted that slogan for much of my own invest-ing. When I feel like sounding more academic, I refer to the approach as "mispriced, advantaged companies." To evalu-ate investments, I'd create a simple 2 × 2 matrix. The vertical axis would be a measure of value and the horizontal axis a measure of advantage. Over time, I've not so much changed the approach as refined it. I've supplanted earnings measures with cash flow measures. When assessing presence of advan-tage, I used to rely mostly on pattern recognition. Now, I'll uti-lize some more quantitative data such as return on equity, when appropriate.[2]*

The Approach: Why It Works

The definition of a good business is no trivial issue. If we asked 10 different investors to define *good*, we might get as many dif-ferent answers: high margins, high returns on equity, good capital allocation practices, a wide moat, revenue growth, a large market opportunity—the list goes on. Each of these definitions may indeed describe a generally desirable characteristic of a business, but they all fail to provide an easily applicable, comprehensive definition of *goodness*. Take high margins: While generally desirable, they're not required. Walmart is a perfect example of a good yet low-margin business. Take high returns on equity: While desirable, they are not a panacea for heavily indebted companies. Similarly, good capital allocation practices are a high priority for shareholders, yet if the best capital allocation choice available to management is to return capital via buybacks or dividends, investors will not reap the rewards of a business able to compound capital at a high rate of return. Meanwhile, companies with wide competitive moats may keep beating their competitors, but they are not guaranteed to translate that advantage into superior operating performance. Finally, some of the biggest mistakes in investment decision making have involved fast-growing companies with large market opportunities.

Table 4.1 shows the returns to an investor buying into a business with high returns on capital employed. The example assumes a 50 percent return on initial capital employed and a modest 10 percent return on capital reinvested in the business. As the table shows, an investor will generally earn a respectable annualized return on an investment in such a business, even if the exit multiple of capital is lower than the multiple paid at purchase. If the exit multiple is at least as high as the purchase multiple, the annualized return to the equity investor can be quite handsome. We assume a five-year holding period. The longer the holding period, the smaller the role of the exit multiple in determining the investor's annualized return.

The Magic of Making Money

Greenblatt's way of identifying good businesses has been critical to the success of his magic formula. Rather than simply spell out the definition, it might be helpful to reason our way to it. Reconsider the example of Walmart: Of course, shareholders would be better off if Walmart expanded its profit margins, other things being equal. However, Walmart shares have performed well as a long-term investment despite relatively low margins, as the company has efficiently used the capital it employs in running the business. If it took Walmart $1 trillion of capital—physical structures, inventories, and the like—to generate $25+ billion in operating income each year, it would be all but impossible for shareholders to achieve acceptable returns. However, if Walmart can generate $25+ billion in profits while tying up less than $150 billion of

TABLE 4.1 Illustrative Investment Return to a Good Company Investor

		Year 1	Year 2	Year 3	Year 4	Year 5	IRR
Company Perspective							
Capital employed at start of period		100	140	183	230	280	
Return on beginning Year 1 capital		50%	50%	50%	50%	50%	
Return on incremental capital			10%	10%	10%	10%	
Net profit		50	54	58	63	68	
Reinvestment percentage		80%	80%	80%	80%	80%	
Amount reinvested		40	43	47	50	54	
Capital employed at end of period		140	183	230	280	335	
Amount returned to investors		10	11	12	13	14	
Blended return on average capital			45%	36%	30%	27%	
Equity Investor Perspective							
Investor buys . . .							
. . . and sells for 1x capital	−100	10	11	12	13	348	35%
. . . and sells for 2x capital	−200	10	11	12	13	683	31%
. . . for 2x and sells for 1x capital	−200	10	11	12	13	348	16%
. . . for 3x and sells for 1x capital	−300	10	11	12	13	348	6%
. . . for 10x Yr 1 and sells for 10x Yr 10 profit	−500	10	11	12	13	694	8%
. . . for 20x Yr 1 and sells for 10x Yr 10 profit	−1000	10	11	12	13	694	−6%

Source: *The Manual of Ideas.*

capital, shareholders can do well despite a net income margin of only about 3 percent.

The Walmart example brings us to a key requirement of successful investing. As investors, we want a public company to give us back more money than we put into it, preferably much more. Looking through from the publicly traded stock to the level of the operating business, this requires the business to take the capital available to it and turn it into as much additional capital as possible. Success is measured in percentage rather than absolute terms, so that $100 of additional capital created by a business employing $200 of capital is more impressive than a business employing $1,000. Determining the capital actually employed in the business requires some judgment. For example, if a company like Apple has $100+ billion of cash and investments sitting on the balance sheet, it would be inappropriate to consider those liquid assets to be employed in the business. Apple's profits, excluding interest income, would be no different if the company had $50 billion or $100 billion of cash in the bank. As a result, when determining how good Apple is as a business, we should not penalize the company by including the large cash hoard in the denominator of our percentage return calculation. Instead, we should include only as much cash in the formula as is required to be on hand for running the business.

The magic formula definition of a good business is no different: The higher the return on capital employed, the better the business. To normalize for different tax rates, we use operating income as the numerator of the equation. To normalize for the effects of financial leverage, we use capital employed as the denominator. Greenblatt defines capital employed as current assets excluding cash, minus current liabilities excluding debt, plus net fixed assets, typically consisting of the property, plant, and equipment line item on the balance sheet. The first two items represent the net working capital of a business, that is, the amount of cash tied up in operating the business on a day-to-day basis. Net fixed assets represent the capital tied up in the business for the long term, perhaps for buildings and improvements, vehicle fleets, or other long-term tangible assets. Not included are intangibles and goodwill. It makes sense to exclude these items, as the amount of money paid for past acquisitions does not affect the intrinsic quality of a business. Goodwill is not actually used in running a business—it is simply an accounting entry reflective of the price paid to acquire a business.

The Magic of a Low Price

We'll look at some of the shortcomings of that definition of a good business later in this chapter. For now, the main objection might be that high returns on capital at the business level may not translate into high returns on our capital, which is invested in the shares of the business at an enterprise valuation that typically differs from the amount of capital employed in the business. More often than not, high-return businesses trade at premium market valuations, ostensibly putting their expected stock market return on the same footing as the shares of lower-quality businesses. After all, no investor would commit capital to a low-quality business, unless the price paid was less than that paid for a higher-quality business.

The magic formula overcomes this objection easily, as the price paid for a business, expressed as a ratio of operating income to enterprise value, is the second and last quantitative factor considered by Greenblatt's stock ranking methodology. Just as the latter ranks stocks by return on capital employed, it also ranks them by operating earnings yield. The two factors are then weighted equally to arrive at a combined ranking for each company. Greenblatt's use of operating income to enterprise value as the way of determining cheapness is congruent with his use of operating income to capital employed as the way of determining quality, as the effects of leverage and taxes are stripped from both calculations. Says Nick Kirrage, fund manager of Specialist Value UK Equities at Schroders, "The [valuation metric] we predominantly look at is a Graham and Dodd-type P/E—cyclically-adjusted P/E—or actually cyclically-adjusted EV/EBIT, to take account of the capital structure."[3] Pavel Begun, managing partner of 3G Capital Management, also uses an adjusted valuation metric, seeking out companies trading at 8 to 11 times free cash flow. "The specific price we're willing to pay depends on the quality of the business and also on the growth prospects of the business. . . . [When] I say eight to 11 times free cash flow, that means normalized sustainable free cash flow as opposed to current-period free cash flow. What we attempt to do when we look at a business is ask, what is the free cash flow the company can generate in a mid-cycle type environment?"[4]

It is not hard to conceptualize why stocks ranked highly by the magic formula should outperform. If businesses with high returns on capital employed ought to trade at premium valuations, yet the businesses selected by Greenblatt's methodology trade at low valuations, we are able to have our cake and eat it, too, at least in theory.

Future Outperformance: Not Guaranteed, but Likely

In theory, the historical outperformance of Greenblatt's methodology should prompt investors to flock to it in droves, thereby eliminating its prospective attractiveness. In practice, several considerations suggest that the magic formula may be likely to outperform over time.

First, the institutional imperative makes adherence to the methodology difficult. Institutional managers care not only about investment risk but also, perhaps more acutely, about career risk. Many managers cannot afford to follow a winning strategy if it involves enduring long stretches of relative underperformance. It is much safer from a career standpoint to be wrong when everyone else is losing money than to be wrong when everyone is making money. During the period studied by Greenblatt, the magic formula handily outperformed the S&P 500 Index, yet the strategy also experienced nonoverlapping three-year periods of underperformance. While most fund managers may be able to endure a quarter or a year of underperformance, they may be left with few investors after a two- or three-year period of subpar results. Laments Alon Bochman, managing partner of Stepwise Capital, "It's really difficult to make an institutional product out of it, not because it's a poor formula, but because we institutional investors are poor at sticking to something good . . . it's extremely hard to stick with a strategy that has underperformed for years, as the magic formula can [do]."[5]

Second, investors have a hard time turning off their emotional biases. Even a quick peek at the list of candidates generated by the magic formula screen—available at magicformulainvesting.com—is likely to make an investor's stomach churn. Many companies on the list are either in out-of-favor industries or have major company-specific issues, such as regulatory scrutiny, accounting problems, executive turnover, or deteriorating operating momentum. While many investors may agree conceptually that buying good companies when they are out of favor is a path to long-term outperformance, a much smaller number are actually willing to follow such a strategy. Observes Bochman, "It's really hard for a human being who understands something about analysis to buy these stocks. [The magic formula] will buy stocks of drug companies when their main product is coming off patent, or it might buy a company that is being threatened by a lawsuit, where the suit amount is a very large part of the enterprise value. . . . You just don't want to go there."[6] Dan Sheehan, general partner of Sheehan Associates, recalls a missed opportunity in McDonald's, a good business that became cheap following the release of the documentary film *Super Size Me* in 2004.[7] With fears swirling that fast food might become the next tobacco, investors avoided the stocks of quick-service restaurant companies, creating some compelling investment opportunities for those able to look through the fear.

As a quantitative method, the magic formula screen is perfectly sanguine about picking a headhunting firm during a recession or a laser eye surgery provider when the media is calling into question the safety of laser eye surgery. Professional investors legitimately want to use Greenblatt's list as a starting point from which to do further research and ultimately make a subjective judgment regarding an investment opportunity. Unfortunately, their subjective judgment is frequently tainted by emotional bias. As a result, the investor may dismiss the headhunting firm by thinking, "Of course it's cheap, we're in a recession!" Similarly, the investor may dismiss the laser eye surgery company by thinking, "Of course it's cheap, they might go out of business!" Amir Avitzur, president of Avitzur Asset Management, alludes to a broader issue, as a company's stock price "is the one piece of information that [investors] see all day long . . . slowly but surely, they start to believe that the price is really the value of the company. . . . Unfortunately, when you focus on the price, you usually don't know when to buy, and even worse, you usually don't know when to sell."[8]

The magic formula methodology never runs out of investment candidates. Several value investment strategies have become de facto obsolete over time. For example, whereas Ben Graham successfully searched for so-called net nets more than a half century ago, such companies have become virtually extinct in the United States today. The few companies whose current assets exceed the sum of their equity market value and total liabilities are typically depleting those current assets at a rapid pace, or other reasons exist why theoretical liquidation values might not be realized. As a result, few professional investors can build their businesses around net nets. By contrast, Greenblatt's method simply ranks public companies relative to each other. There is no absolute cheapness requirement, whether net net or a book value that exceeds market value. As a result, the approach will keep providing investors with an investable list of relatively attractive public companies.

Finally, investors tend to remain skeptical of winning strategies even after long periods of outperformance. Investors have been taught—you might say brainwashed—that markets are efficient and there is no free lunch. As a result, they struggle with the notion that a simple quantitative strategy can systematically outperform the best efforts of large numbers of securities analysts and portfolio managers. For example, stocks that trade at a low multiple of price to book value have outperformed the broader market in a statistically significant way for a long time. Economists Eugene Fama and Kenneth French have studied this phenomenon extensively (latest data are available at kennethfrench.com). Ironically, even after having observed this contradiction of the efficient markets hypothesis for many years, Fama, in true professorial fashion, tried to explain it away by invoking the efficient-markets hypothesis (EMH) adherents' favorite axiom: If a strategy outperforms, it must be riskier! Unfortunately for Fama, the strategy of buying stocks with low price-to-book multiples also exhibited relatively low volatility. Volatility, of course, is the EMH adherents' favorite definition of risk. Undeterred, Fama concluded that low price-to-book stocks must be riskier in other ways. The continuing lack of disappearance of the low price-to-book anomaly suggests that investors may not flock to Greenblatt's method even after many years of demonstrated outperformance.

Uses and Misuses of Investing in Good and Cheap Companies

When a commonsense, easy-to-follow investment strategy outperforms as soundly as Greenblatt's method has done over the long term, it is tempting to argue that equity investors who do not adopt it are irrational or even foolish. It's not that simple, however, as investors cannot and should not turn themselves into computer algorithms made of flesh and blood. As human beings, we cannot deny our shortcomings, whether they are cognitive or emotional, just as we should not deny our unique capacity for qualitative insight and judgment.

A few years ago, Joel Greenblatt and Blake Darcy launched Formula Investing, an investment service operated by Gotham Asset Management, to enable investors to implement the magic formula without the biases inherent in qualitative security selection processes. Formula Investing takes a quantitative approach to building client portfolios in an effort to replicate the impressive back-tested results of Greenblatt's methodology. For those looking to outperform the market without the need for active portfolio management or security analysis, Formula Investing may offer an appropriate alternative.

Know Thyself (and Know Thy Clients)

Somewhat paradoxically, long stretches of *under*performance are one of the reasons the magic formula should continue to *out*perform over time. Unfortunately, this likely outperformance is of little relevance if we—or perhaps more likely, our clients—are part of the reason the approach will keep working. If our investment operation is likely to be among the ones that will abandon the strategy after one, two, or three years of underperformance, whether due to capital withdrawals or a "this doesn't work" epiphany, it makes little sense to embark on the strategy in the first place. In this case, the most plausible scenario might be to incorporate certain aspects of Greenblatt's methodology into our own approach, though only to the extent that we still view the resulting strategy as decidedly ours. The latter will give us the confidence to stick with it during times of underperformance.

If we decide the magic formula is not for us, what insights from the approach could we adopt to elevate our own strategy to greater success? The answer might differ from one investor to the next, but here are a few general observations:

Not every troubled industry or company is going away. Investors perceive most stocks that rank highly on the magic formula to have major issues: for-profit education companies due to hostile regulation, oil services companies in the wake of the Gulf of Mexico oil spill, defense contractors toward the tail end of the wars in Iraq and Afghanistan, staffing companies in a recession, pharma companies facing near-term patent expiries—the list goes on. While these are all legitimate issues that negatively affect future business performance, the success of the magic formula suggests that investors, on average, tend to overestimate the magnitude and speed with which negative factors will erode profitability.

Consider all the articles about the imminent demise of specific companies, industries, or even countries. If the truth looked anything like the media reporting or analyst commentary, there might be few companies left to consider for investment today. Even Apple, the world's most highly valued company in 2012, was once written off as a soon-to-be-dead business. The lesson seems to be that if we feel tempted to embrace the market's rampant bearishness on certain businesses, we may want to recalibrate our expectations a bit and ask whether other investors might be overreacting. To gauge the latter, it helps to consider a beaten-down company's market quotation and to decide what would have to be true about the future for such a low valuation to be justified. Similarly, we may want to consider the market quotation that would be appropriate if the future turned out less bleak than feared by Mr. Market.

Another lesson of the magic formula might be a greater appreciation of businesses capable of generating high returns on capital. This appreciation may be lacking somewhat among so-called deep value investors who focus on companies trading at a discount to readily ascertainable asset values. Not only do some companies consistently achieve high returns on capital but also they are in fact capital-light businesses for which the returns metric is quite irrelevant. As a result, an exclusive focus on balance sheet values eliminates a whole range of businesses that might be attractive investments.

For example, the intrinsic value of a software company has virtually nothing to do with the value of its hard assets—the desks, chairs, and computers used to write, update, market, and sell the software. Instead, the intrinsic value resides in the company's technology, human capital, contracts, and other intangibles. If this type of non-capital-intensive business has a stated return on capital of 20 percent or even 50 percent, the equity might be of little value. If a software company can achieve only a 50 percent return on the carrying value of its desks, chairs, and computers, the investment case is likely nonexistent. Similarly, whether such a company trades at a price to tangible book ratio of 1x or 10x may not matter much. More important are metrics such as the free cash flow yield or the ratio of price to normalized earning power.

This does not mean that as deep value investors we should relax our investment discipline or venture outside our comfort zone.

After all, few investors are equally skilled at valuing capital-light and capital-intensive businesses. Deep value investors tend to traffic in the latter, and that is not only fine but also exceedingly profitable if done well. However, if we face a choice between two businesses, each trading at a price to tangible book ratio of 0.9×, we may find it more valuable to spend our time assessing other aspects of each company than appraising the value of every little asset on the balance sheet. The fact that Company A may trade at an adjusted tangible book value of 0.82× while Company B may trade at 0.88× should not tip us in favor of Company A. Rather, we may want to analyze each company's business segments with an eye toward capital-light businesses hiding within the structure of a capital-intensive company. For example, a choice between two real estate companies trading at similar discounts to the appraised value of their real estate assets may come down to whether one company also has a non-capital-intensive, fee-generative investment management business.

Finally, the historical outperformance of the magic formula confirms that price matters. No matter how high the returns on capital of a business, it will not rank highly overall if the earnings yield, as measured by operating income to enterprise value, is low. This insight seems trivial but is easily forgotten when investors fall in love with a company. How many times have we seen an investment thesis that extols the virtues of a company but lacks any reference to the market quotation? Simon Caufield, managing director of SIM Limited, puts it well: "Almost any asset is a buy at the right price, and almost any asset is a sell at the wrong price."[9] As investors who run the risk of falling in love with a business and overpaying for it, imagine if we set a minimum on the free cash flow yield or earnings yield we needed to see before even considering an investment. We would be freed from the constant temptation to overpay, just a little and just this once, for a great business. Instead, we could focus on assessing only those businesses meeting our explicit valuation criteria. We wouldn't have the pick of all the businesses in the world, but if we chose wisely from the list of available companies, we might end up with a good business at a good price.

Diversification versus Concentration

A fascinating finding of Greenblatt's initial study of the historical performance of the magic formula was the performance observed for each decile of stocks. Equities scoring in the top 10 percent out-performed those scoring in the next 10 percent, which in turn outperformed those in the subsequent 10 percent, and so forth. This cascading of historical performance based on a combination of just two simple factors seemed almost too neat to be true, but the two-factor system did not result from an exercise in data mining.

The finding that the magic formula worked not only at the extreme of companies ranking highly based on the twin criteria used but also that it had a predictive quality in terms of the relative performance of equities across the entire spectrum of public com-panies led some investment managers to suggest that the method might also be used for constructing low-risk long-short portfolios of equities. In such a strategy, a fund manager would go long stocks in the top decile and short stocks in the bottom decile. Unfortunately, Greenblatt's analysis of the historical data showed that such portfo-lios would not outperform the long-only strategy of buying compa-nies in the top decile. The gross leverage of a long-short portfolio would come back to bite the investor at some point, setting back the portfolio in drastic fashion. If a long-short portfolio employed no gross leverage, performance would fall far short of the long-only approach. A key reason is that stocks in the bottom decile, while severe underperformers, still showed a slightly positive return over time, reflecting the market's upward trajectory over the long term. While a long-short strategy might become feasible in a stagnating or declining market, the magic formula is probably not the optimal ranking methodology to serve as the foundation of such a strategy.

Just as long-short portfolios face unattractive risk-adjusted returns if they are built entirely upon a magic formula ranking, long-only portfolios could suffer debilitating volatility if they consist of a very small number of highly ranked equities. The magic for-mula approach has outperformed handily over time, but there have also been big outliers. Some highly ranked equities subsequently lost virtually all of their value, while some others delivered mul-tibagger returns. Professional investors will likely keep attempting to identify such outliers ex ante, but we are yet to learn of some-one who has consistently succeeded in doing so. As a result, even if we add qualitative selection criteria to the magic formula invest-ment strategy, a concentrated approach may remain inappropriate. Greenblatt has argued that a portfolio of 30 highly ranked equi-ties may provide an optimal level of diversification. If we wish to devise a strategy that picks the top 5 or 10 candidates based on our refined methodology, it might be a good idea to reduce the magic formula portion of the overall portfolio from 100 percent to a ratio of the number of stocks we choose divided by 30. For example, a 10-stock magic formula portfolio could comprise a third of our overall portfolio.

Leave It or Tweak It?

When we asked Joel Greenblatt about tweaks that could improve the already impressive performance of the magic formula, he stated: "In our experience, eliminating the stocks you would obviously not want to own eliminates many big winners." Greenblatt did go on to describe a few basic tweaks his team makes to the off-the-shelf calculation:

> *First, we created our own database, we do not use a commercially available database. Instead, we have a team of analysts who analyze the balance sheet, income statement and cash flow statements of each of the companies in our investment universe. Second, we have developed a model for financials and those are included in our diversified value weighted funds. Third, we have made some tweaks to the metrics we use to take advantage of the added information that we get from doing the fundamental work ourselves.*[10]

Greenblatt's first point highlights the importance of good data, as inputs into the magic formula should be stripped of unusual, one-time items. Otherwise, the most highly ranked companies will tend to be those with the highest nonrecurring gains. The latter are irrelevant to likely future performance, rendering many selections of little use. Most commercially available databases do a decent job of stripping out large unusual items, although some items are also missed because the accounting definition of extraordinary items tends to be narrower than the definition appropriate in this context. As a result, some nonrecurring items may not be evident from a glance at the income statement. Reading an earnings press release or the financial footnotes in a regulatory filing is therefore a helpful exercise if we wish to verify that the data used in the magic formula calculation does indeed represent recurring items.

Greenblatt's second point brings up a limitation of the standard magic formula methodology, whose data inputs are not meaningful for banks and most other financial firms. For example, the standard definition of enterprise value—equity value plus debt minus cash—does not apply to banks. Similarly, income before interest and taxes is not a useful measure for banks, as interest income and interest expense represent core operating items.

Greenblatt's last point might be most significant for us, as he hints at the possibility of improving the performance of the magic formula by using adjusted metrics—instead of *trailing* operating income to enterprise value and *trailing* operating income to capital employed. As *future* performance determines the going-concern value of a business, using credible estimates of this year's or next year's profitability might be preferable to relying on trailing figures. Even more valuable might be thoughtful estimates of *normalized* operating income. As a result, while elimination of obviously unattractive candidates may not be a good idea, tweaks that improve the quality and relevance of the data used in the magic formula seem promising.

The last point contains a subtle warning: If we wish to use the magic formula as an idea generation tool, we may want to restrain ourselves from subjecting the list of investment candidates to our standard idea evaluation process, as we may end up excluding ideas with the highest prospective returns (they usually make our stomachs churn the most). To improve the performance of Greenblatt's quantitative method, we need to employ tweaks that help the magic formula work better, not tweaks that add entirely new hurdles. Examples of potentially detrimental factors include considerations like insider buying and selling, insider ownership, recent news, analyst upgrades and downgrades, stock price momentum, profit margin trends, and other factors that are exogenous to the magic formula. If a checklist approach could improve the Greenblatt method, then multifactor models would likely outperform the magic formula. They do not, according to data compiled by Greenblatt. The only way to systematically boost the expected return of Greenblatt's method is to make adjustments that are *endogenous* to the strategy itself.

To devise an optimal evaluation and selection process for magic formula ideas, it helps to refocus on the basic rationale underlying the approach. While the market is pretty good at valuing high-return businesses that have reached a steady-state phase of limited reinvestment opportunities, Mr. Market makes two mistakes with some consistency: It overvalues high-return businesses whose returns on capital derive from explosive but ultimately transitory trends or fads. Examples include Boston Chicken, Green Mountain Coffee Roasters, Herbalife, Heely's, Taser, and Travelzoo. On the flip side, the market may undervalue unhyped quality businesses with sustainable high-return reinvestment opportunities. The magic formula succeeds largely by finding some of these companies when they trade at high earnings yields. If we work through a list of Greenblatt-style investment candidates with an eye toward sustainable capital reinvestment opportunities, we might get closer to embracing likely winners and avoiding likely losers. States investment manager Marko Vucemilovic, "When I began my investment career I was obsessed with EVA [economic value added] and the book called *The Quest for Value*. Greenblatt's magic formula screen took EVA concepts and simplified them, similar to what Graham did with his statistical approach to stock selection based on asset values. I have read Greenblatt's books and greatly admire his work and track record . . . we do similar screens, but with a bit more focus on sustainably high ROICs. Otherwise we would have a portfolio full of cyclical or dying businesses."[11]

Screening for Good and Cheap Companies

When *The Little Book That Beats the Market* was published, Greenblatt also made available a practical tool to his readers. The free Magic Formula Investing website (www.magicformulainvesting .com) shows up-to-date screen results and allows users to set a minimum market capitalization for the screened companies. Users can select whether they wish to see 30 or 50 highly ranked stocks. Within that top group, the website lists companies in alphabetical order rather than based on their magic formula score. The latter is hidden, as Greenblatt sought to avoid a situation in which most investors bought the same top handful of companies.

The paucity of data shown on each highly ranked company is a key drawback of the website, as neither the return on capital employed nor the operating income yield are available to users. In fairness, the site may not represent a focus for Greenblatt following the launch of Formula Investing (www.formulainvesting.com), an investment service. Ultimately, the free Magic Formula Investing website is an interesting tool for eyeballing companies that meet Greenblatt's criteria, but investors who actively employ the strategy may prefer to build a screening tool that provides access to considerably more data on each screen result.

The following discussion shows how to build your own magic formula screening tool—and extend it to make it even more powerful.

Replicating Greenblatt's Winning Screen

As a prerequisite for creating our own magic formula screen, we need to secure a reliable source of fundamental and pricing data that can be pulled into an Excel spreadsheet. Two low-cost tools are StockScreen123 (www.stockscreen123.com) and Stock Investor Pro of the American Association of Individual Investors (www.aaii.com). The latter relies primarily on Thomson Reuters' data and offers great functionality at a reasonable price.

Whenever we use a limited number of screening criteria, as is the case with Greenblatt's two-factor system, we like to do as much of the work as possible in Excel rather than in the third-party tool. This gives us more flexibility, as we can manipulate the data in an Excel spreadsheet in virtually any way we desire. As a result, instead of attempting to construct an elaborate screen in the third-party application and then import the passing companies into Excel, we immediately import all companies meeting certain minimum criteria. These minimum criteria have little to do with the magic formula. Instead, we may require that a stock have a market capitalization of at least $50 million, trade on a national exchange, or be domiciled in a certain country. One of the minimum criteria we need to make our Greenblatt-style screens usable is a requirement that the companies we consider be outside the financial sector. While a modified Greenblatt methodology can include financial firms, this requires a separate screening setup.

Using the AAII Stock Investor Pro screener, which includes roughly 10,000 public companies listed on U.S. stock exchanges, we narrow the list of stocks to be imported into Excel as follows: First, a requirement that the companies have a market value of at least $25 million shortens the list by more than 40 percent to ~5,900 companies. Second, an exclusion of financial sector companies reduces the number to ~4,200. Finally, a requirement that the ending date of each company's most recently reported period be no older than six months narrows the list to ~3,900 companies. We could cut this number down further, but in the interest of having our magic formula screen consider a broad range of public companies, we choose to import the entire remaining list into Excel. When doing so, we import all relevant data for each company, especially items such as trailing operating income, enterprise value, and capital employed. If certain data items are not readily available in the third-party data service, we bring all the data needed to calculate such items into Excel. For example, for capital employed, we import current assets, cash and short-term investments, current liabilities, short-term debt, and net property, plant, and equipment.

Once in Excel, we add two special columns to the spreadsheet—a ranking based on operating income to capital employed and another based on operating income to enterprise value. We accomplish this quite easily with the standard RANK function. We then add a third column that will contain the sum of the twin rankings. Finally, we sort this third column in ascending order and—*voilà!*—we have the most highly ranked magic formula stocks in front of us.

From here, we can add any other informational columns to the spreadsheet. This may help us flag any companies that look particularly intriguing. In general, we like to see the actual percentage values for the two magic formula criteria. We also include tax rates, as those are not considered in the ranking but may affect an investment decision. If we find a company with a low tax rate and a high operating income to enterprise value yield, we may decide to research it further, as the after-tax earnings yield is likely to be highly attractive (unless the company has a large net cash position that is skewing the EBIT-to-EV calculation). In addition to adding any informational columns we desire, the flexibility of Excel lets us tweak the magic formula without much effort. For example, the more valuation-minded among us may decide to weight the EBIT-to-EV ranking more heavily than the EBIT-to-capital ranking. We accomplish this simply by adjusting the formula in the column containing the sum of the two rankings.

Replacing the Rearview Mirror with Consensus Estimates

One of the key adjustments we like to make to the original magic formula is to use forward-looking earnings data in the calculation. The future is what counts in investing, and while historical data have the advantage of certainty, forward-looking estimates have the advantage of relevance. Even if those estimates turn out to have been inaccurate, future earnings are likely to be more closely aligned with current estimates of future earnings than with actual past earnings.

Even better than using consensus estimates would be to develop a view about the future that is correct but not yet reflected in the consensus. Value investor James Bradford's understanding of the improving fundamentals of railroad Union Pacific likely put him ahead of the consensus view in early 2011:

> *ROA is going up and there are real reasons for this: traffic congestion and increased gas prices. The interstate highway system is like a competing train line that did not have to pay for the tracks. Now those "tracks" are getting costly. Gas prices and congestion are going to move Union Pacific's return on invested capital from 9 percent to 16 percent over the next few years, up from 6 percent a few years back—so you have a business going from bad to good. Increased pricing and volumes is a good combination. No one is ever going to build an east-west rail line again so you have something really special with those tracks.*[12]

We are also mindful of a few shortcomings of using forward-looking data in lieu of historical figures, which is why we like to use both approaches in our idea generation process. First, only relatively large public companies tend to have reasonably credible consensus earnings estimates. Unfortunately, by eliminating many small companies from consideration, we exclude members of a group that has historically outperformed the overall magic formula return.

Second, consensus estimates sometimes exhibit autocorrelation, especially in times of rapid changes in earnings. Studies have shown that Wall Street analysts like to cluster their earnings estimates around the latest mean estimate, so as not to be seen as going out on a limb. This career-preserving tendency can cause a slower-than-warranted downward adjustment in the mean consensus estimate. Since many magic formula candidates face near-term earnings pressures, they may be more likely than other stocks to suffer from the phenomenon of a slowly adjusting mean. Put bluntly, the estimate on which our ranking relies may be about to drop materially.

Finally, consensus estimates generally reflect forward EPS rather than operating income. As a result, the effects of financial leverage and taxes, normally stripped from the magic formula, are included when we use forward-looking data. While we could often deduce operating income from EPS, we prefer to mitigate the leverage issue by putting in place a leverage constraint. A simple but effective way of doing so may be to require an enterprise value to equity value ratio of less than ~1.5.

Going International

While comprehensive data on the performance of Greenblatt's method in non-U.S. markets is hard to come by, it seems reasonable to assume that the approach can be extended globally. If we can run the magic formula screen on an equities database that includes both U.S. and non-U.S.-listed companies, the increased number of companies to choose from should enhance prospective performance. Unfortunately, reliable data on global stocks are generally only available from expensive databases, such as Bloomberg or Capital IQ, making it difficult for noninstitutional investors to embrace a global magic formula strategy. For those willing to live with a somewhat limited set of data, we recommend the free *Financial Times* global stock screener (http://markets.ft.com/screener/customScreen.asp).

Beyond Screening: Hope for Improvement Springs Eternal

Before we delve into the right questions to ask of magic formula investment candidates, it might be helpful to consider a few more ways of improving the performance of the methodology. Ultimately, each of us gets to decide to what extent it makes sense to experiment with the formula in hopes of improving it. However, if we use historical data to identify potential performance-enhancing changes to Greenblatt's approach, we need to be wary of the data mining trap, namely, that we do not settle on an approach that happens to have performed well historically but makes little sense. For example, if the magic formula worked best when positions were initiated on Tuesdays and exited on Thursdays, this would not mean we should embrace such a nonsensical approach.

Throwing Out Capital-Intensive Businesses

A review of companies ranked highly by the magic formula reveals that hiding among the types of capital-light businesses typically associated with Greenblatt's approach are also some capital-intensive cyclical businesses. The latter would normally stay off the list due to their modest average returns on capital. However, when those businesses approach a cyclical peak—or have just passed a cyclical peak—their trailing returns on capital employed can be attractive enough to catapult the stocks onto the magic formula list. Examples of such companies include oil and gas exploration and production firms, mining companies, and certain manufacturing businesses. When commodity prices jump far beyond their long-term trend line, many commodity-based businesses enjoy a period of exceptionally strong profitability.

It is not obvious that we should try to exclude cyclical businesses from consideration in the context of the magic formula, as qualifying companies are typically cheaper than their peers. This may be especially true for cyclical businesses, whose cheapness ranking is likely to be higher than their goodness ranking, even near a cyclical peak. The low valuation already reflects the market's expectation that profitability may suffer, so why go a step further and exclude these companies altogether? We draw an analogy to businesses benefiting from one-time gains—we exclude those companies because their clean numbers would not warrant inclusion. Similarly, capital-intensive businesses near the top of the cycle have unsustainably high returns on capital employed.

Any attempt to eliminate capital-intensive cyclical businesses from consideration opens the door to mistakes of judgment, as we might be tempted to brand companies we dislike as cyclical or capital-intensive businesses. Think of for-profit education companies in the wake of government regulation. It would be easy to argue that their best days are over, at least in terms of their margin profiles, and that, therefore, they may be lumped in with cyclical businesses. One way to prevent such mistakes is to think about cycle-average or normalized earnings for the companies we might be tempted to exclude. If a stock would still rank highly, it deserves to stay. Unfortunately, even here we run the risk of underestimating normalized earnings for companies toward which we are negatively predisposed. As a result, rather than engage in estimating the future, we could opt to use average earnings over the previous cycle (seven years of data should normally suffice). Finally, we could set up an easily interpreted rule that all companies in specific industries be excluded from consideration: Commodity mining companies would be prime candidates for such a list.

What's the Right Way to Account for Brand Value?

The magic formula approach overlaps to some degree with another popular approach—investing in companies with significant brand value. Advertising agency Oskoui+Oskoui defines *brand value* as the "monetary premium that results from having customers who are committed to a particular brand and who are willing to pay extra for it."[13] The intangible nature of brands keeps them out of the calculation of capital employed, boosting returns on the latter for any companies that do in fact have valuable brands.

To some extent, if we attempt to account explicitly for the value of a brand in an analysis of magic formula candidates, we run the risk of double counting, as the economic benefit of a brand is already reflected in operating income. Any brand value that fails to contribute to the profits of a company is hardly meaningful from an investment standpoint. Similar reasoning applies to the costs a company must incur to nurture a brand and keep it desirable in the minds of customers. Such expenses are also already reflected in operating income, so there is no need to reconsider them in the analysis. States Daniel Gladiš, chief executive officer of Vltava Fund: "If the brand is good and variable, it should show up in regular equity. That's why I use valuation, not brand itself. There are companies that have high branding, but they're not making much money. For example, car producers—lots of good brands, but free cash flow is not very high. I like free cash flow a lot; that's the key."[14]

Durable brands play an important role in supporting the sustainability of high returns on capital employed in a business. The Coca-Cola brand is almost certainly more responsible for the high returns of the Coca-Cola Company than any other single factor—management quality, global distribution, or even taste. Some other sodas may taste just as good as Coke, yet none comes close in terms of consumer preference. Sustainability of high returns on capital matters tremendously when we assess Greenblatt-style ideas, as sustainability of existing returns is almost a prerequisite for the ability to reinvest incremental capital at high returns. Analyzing the strength of a brand in this context can be helpful as part of a magic formula evaluation process. Of course, many non-brand-related factors can also support sustainability, including barriers to entry, high customer switching costs, scale advantages, network effects, and other sources of durable competitive advantage.

Nonlinear Ways of Combining Good and Cheap

When we reconstructed Greenblatt's magic formula screen for our research purposes, we noticed a curiosity: The series of operating income to enterprise value data was quite well behaved, with results increasing from less than zero for unprofitable companies to 20, 25, or even 30 percent for cheap companies meeting certain minimum enterprise value criteria. If some stocks had higher ratios of operating income to enterprise value, they either held net cash equal to the vast majority of their equity market values, or their income had benefited from one-time items.

On the flip side, we noticed that the series of operating income to capital employed data was not well behaved, with many highly ranked stocks exhibiting percentage returns in the hundreds, thousands, or even quasi-infinite returns. The latter stemmed from some capital-light businesses employing negative capital, perhaps because they had few fixed assets and payables exceeded receivables. We wondered whether it was meaningful to rank a company with a 5,100 percent return on capital employed ahead of a company with a 5,000 percent or, for that matter, 1,000 percent return on capital. It struck us that in such cases the relative investment attractiveness of those candidates depended less on the calculated return on capital and more on the relative amount of capital each company would be able to reinvest in the business at anywhere close to the stated returns.

We concluded that instead of simply adding up the twin magic formula rankings in linear fashion, it might make more sense to introduce an arbitrary hurdle, above which we would consider all companies tied from the perspective of returns on capital. For those companies, the cheapness factor would suddenly carry more weight, a result that made intuitive sense to us. In addition, when analyzing capital-light businesses tied for first place in terms of return on capital, we could look beyond each company's calculated return and focus exclusively on the predictability and sustainability of the company's competitive advantage. Finally, we could prioritize our research into each company's capital reinvestment ability, a key consideration for businesses meeting the criterion of impressive returns on existing capital employed.

Asking the Right Questions of Greenblatt-Style Bargains

Despite the popularity of checklists, not every investment should be approached with the same set of questions. We tailor our analysis of a security to the type of opportunity under examination. For example, if we analyze a company that trades at a large discount to net current asset value, we might inquire whether the firm can be liquidated without major asset impairments, not whether the long-term competitive position is favorable. Similarly, if we analyze a company that has received a takeover bid, we may focus on the terms of the deal and the likelihood of the transaction being consummated, not on the long-term outlook for the business. On the other hand, if we analyze a high-quality business that trades well above book value and at a high multiple of earnings, we should examine the company's prospects for sustained rapid earnings growth.

We may be able to improve the performance of the magic formula screen if we ask questions that take into account the nature of Greenblatt-style selections. Of particular relevance is that the methodology favors firms exhibiting high returns on capital employed. Such companies are generally not cheap based on the liquidation value of their assets. Instead, they might be cheap based on current and prospective earning power. As a result, a crucial determination when evaluating magic formula selections is whether they exhibit above-average returns on capital for transitory reasons or for reasons that have some permanence. Warren Buffett calls this moat; others may know it as sustainable competitive advantage.

It is also crucial whether a business operates in a growing industry that allows the company to reinvest a portion of cash flow at high rates of return. We seek out companies whose earnings yield is likely to increase over time if the stock price remains unchanged. Such companies not only sustain high returns on capital but also grow earnings by reinvesting in the business. As those companies generate high returns, they need to reinvest only a portion of cash flow to achieve respectable growth. As a result, they generally have cash available for dividends and stock repurchases. Buybacks executed at good prices accelerate EPS growth and value creation.

To narrow down the list of magic formula candidates to the most promising investments, we consider a number of subjective criteria. In addition to positive criteria, such as sustainability of competitive advantage, management quality, and industry growth, our selection methodology also takes into account a number of negative criteria, which we use to eliminate candidates from further consideration. As Charlie Munger might say, invert!

How Durable Is the Firm's Competitive Advantage?

Durability is critically important, because whenever rational investors value a firm at a large premium to tangible equity, competitors may attempt market entry. Warns David Coyne: "'Good' companies bring their own set of risks. While I recognize the benefits of brands and moats and compounding and other Buffettesque terms, I am wary of my ability to spot the genuine moats from Maginot lines. For misdiagnosed 'good' companies, sales, margins, returns and valuation multiples can all come under severe pressure, culminating in a sharply lower share price."[15]

If we can invest $1,000 in physical assets, follow a value-enhancement recipe, and then have those assets valued at $10,000 in stock market, we will be inclined to seek more of this good thing. Such a value-creating machine would become visible to potential competitors, though they may not have access to the exact recipe. The latter could include proprietary business processes, copyrights and patents, carefully nurtured consumer brand preferences, deliberately heightened customer switching costs, and other factors that allow a business to generate abnormal returns on the physical capital it employs. Given the propensity of opportunistic enterprises for entering into industries or industry niches in which the skilled application of a recipe can turn a $1,000 investment into $10,000 of market value, we strongly prefer magic formula companies likely to sustain their competitive advantage.

Yusuf Samad, former chairman of the UK Society of Investment
Professionals, embraces this approach:

*I focus on buying good companies at cheap prices. I believe
in taking a thorough fundamental approach to understanding a business and buying it at a cheap price. Over time, I
have refined my approach to focus on companies with an
understandable business and financials. The starting point is
that the business lines and sources of revenue should be clear,
and it should be possible to relate these easily to the financials. Good companies should have strong cash flow, well pro-
tected by high barriers to entry. To identify these companies, I
look for business models that incorporate one or more of the
following characteristics: repeat use of the product; a product that is well plugged into a customer's value chain; high
switching costs for customers; annuity income streams vs.
lumpy revenues; and provider of the backbone or infrastruc-
ture to an industry.*[16]

Adds Josh Tarasoff, general partner of Greenlea Lane Capital
Partners: "One of the most powerful ideas I have ever encountered is the one-decision stock: a company you can simply hold
for a decade or two and receive an outstanding outcome. My ideal
investment would be to purchase a company like this at a significant
discount to intrinsic value, and then hold it for a very long time.
This approach is a combination of letting the economics of a great
business play out, while also opportunistically taking advantage
of market inefficiencies." Contrast Tarasoff's idea of a one-decision
stock with that of investors who are willing to pay up in order to
invest in a great business. By looking for compounding machines
that trade at a discount to intrinsic value, Tarasoff eliminates
stocks that may be in vogue but offer scant long-term value.

Durability of competitive advantage relates quite closely to
a firm's "ability to raise prices in excess of inflation," according
to Michael McKee, president of MAC Investment Management.[17] It
is difficult to imagine a company whose competitive advantage is
eroding but whose pricing power remains intact. Josh Tarasoff distinguishes between nominal pricing power and real pricing power.
He points out that investors mistakenly interpret nominal pricing

power as reflective of a good business. According to Tarasoff, only real pricing power, that is, the ability to raise prices in excess of inflation, should be regarded as special. Tarasoff relates pricing power to the value a customer derives from a product or service. The wider the gap between value and price, the greater the power of a firm. When and to what degree a company chooses to exercise its pricing power depends on a number of factors, but the key consideration for investors is whether a firm could raise prices without materially impacting unit sales.

Several additional factors may assist us in judging the sustainability of competitive advantage. Pavel Begun highlights a few considerations by invoking the example of U.K. property surveyor LSL Property Services:

> *If you look at the main determinants of the contract renewal, you're going to find out the price is hardly ever the main consideration. Most of the time, it's the quality that the service provider delivers, and LSL is considered to be a top of the line service provider. To see a confirmation of that, you can go back to 2008, which was probably the worst for the surveying business in the U.K. in many years, because you had the Northern Rock situation. . . . [LSL] managed to get a tremendous amount of market share in that period.*

Begun also points out that "surveying costs represents only 0.1% of the average mortgage size," suggesting a likelihood of low price elasticity.[18]

Professor Michael Porter of Harvard Business School asserts: "Once a company achieves competitive advantage through an innovation, it can sustain it only through relentless improvement. Almost any advantage can be imitated." He adds, "Ultimately, the only way to sustain competitive advantage is to upgrade it—to move to more sophisticated types. This is precisely what Japanese auto-makers have done. They initially penetrated foreign markets with small, inexpensive compact cars of adequate quality and competed on the basis of lower labor costs. Even while their labor-cost advantage persisted, however, the Japanese companies were upgrading. . . ."[19] While we may agree with Porter on the importance of continuous innovation, we wonder how strongly correlated past innovation is to success in future innovation. Just because Japanese automakers have outinnovated the rest of the world to date, can we call their competitive advantage sustainable? It seems sustainability, as Porter defines it, depends heavily on management execution, a condition that makes sustainability extremely difficult to predict.

Opportunity to Reinvest Capital at High Rates of Return?

We have highlighted the ability to reinvest capital as a key consideration for Greenblatt-style candidates, but why is reinvestment so important? High returns on existing capital—the capital already employed in a business—are almost meaningless without an ability to invest new capital at above-average returns. Returns on existing capital, whether high or low, are already reflected in a company's operating income. In a static scenario, the driver of return to equity investors is the earnings yield—or free cash flow yield, to be more precise. If we pay less for a given level of earnings, we will earn a higher return. Whether the earnings number was achieved by employing X amount of capital or half of X is irrelevant. In a scenario without reinvestment, the only other driver of return will be whether management returns cash to shareholders or whether it insists on putting cash back into the business despite an absence of high-return projects.

In a scenario in which attractive reinvestment opportunities exist, the rate of return on existing capital becomes relevant because it tends to correlate with the rate of return on reinvested capital. For the types of businesses selected by Greenblatt's methodology, the percentage of free cash flow that can be reinvested is almost more important than the anticipated return. The latter is typically so high for magic formula stocks that the reinvestment percentage tends to be exceedingly low. When this percentage becomes meaningful, capital-light businesses can see explosive growth in revenue, income, and free cash flow.

Estimating the extent of the reinvestment opportunity available to a business is no small feat. Josh Tarasoff sheds light on this issue: "For a significant reinvestment opportunity to exist, there must be the potential for long-term unit growth. So, a large addressable market relative to the current business is desirable. Sustaining a high return on capital necessitates pricing power, a strong competitive position, and attractive underlying economics in terms of margins and capital turnover."[20] Adds Professor Max Otte, head of the IFVE Institut für Vermögensentwicklung: "If you look for franchises, you really have to think about the growth dynamics: will the business be able to grow without a lot of capital? Will growth in its niche be sustainable or defensible? That often has a lot to do with regional market share or market share in a narrow product space with lasting preferences."[21]

How Good Are Management's Capital Allocation Practices?

Since capital-light businesses typically enjoy attractive reinvestment opportunities for only a modest portion of free cash flow, the deployment of the remaining cash plays a vital role in the total return shareholders can expect on their investment. In the case of magic formula stocks, which are by design cheaper than other companies of similar quality, management usually adds to per-share value by repurchasing shares on the open market. Dividends are another viable option, though tax treatment can play a role in the ultimate attractiveness of a payout to taxable investors.

Acquisitions are typically a less favorable way of allocating excess capital, as target companies will seek at least a fair price. As a result, as a general preference, we like to see Greenblatt-style candidates use excess cash for buybacks rather than mergers and acquisitions (M&A). Finally, most management teams will be tempted to reinvest in the business even beyond the amount of capital justified by attractive returns. While it is difficult for outside shareholders to judge in real time whether a company's reinvestment levels are appropriate, management's attempts to expand into new businesses or launch new product categories may be warning signs that the company is venturing into potentially high-risk, low-return projects.

Are There Any Disqualifying Factors?

Just like it is usually easier to dismiss a flawed concept than to prove a valid one, it is generally easier to dismiss unattractive investment candidates than it is to embrace the right opportunity. As a result, we find value in putting any list of Greenblatt-style candidates through a multistep elimination process before devoting considerable time and judgment to finding the most compelling opportunities among the remaining candidates.

We may want to add the following elimination steps to our magic formula idea evaluation process:

- *Pro forma adjustments:* We eliminate companies that would not be on the list if their financial statements were adjusted to reflect true operating performance. This will apply to some companies that have recently reported one-time items or have engaged in a strategic transaction. In the latter case, reported results may fail to account for the pro forma performance of the combined entity.
- *Capital reinvestment:* We avoid companies with virtually no opportunity for high-return reinvestment of capital. Typically, these are companies in industries in long-term decline, such as paper check producers or newspaper publishers.
- *Threats to key revenue source:* We avoid companies dependent on a specific customer or contract, if loss of it has become a real possibility. Circumstances may include the acquisition of a major customer, an ongoing rebid process for a large contract, or the loss of critical patent protection.
- *Cyclicality:* We avoid capital-intensive businesses that generate high returns on capital only during cyclical upswings in their respective industries.
- *Faddishness:* We avoid companies providing a product or service that has a reasonably high likelihood of being a fad. This may be hard to judge while a fad is unfolding, but if we seem surprised by how quickly a concept or fashion has spread, or if we feel like a product will either take over the world or eventually peter out, we take notice.
- *Insider selling:* We avoid companies with heavy recent insider selling, particularly if such selling occurred at prices roughly equal to or below the current market price. While this criterion is exogenous to the rationale of the magic formula and should therefore be left out in a purist approach to Greenblatt-style opportunities, we simply cannot embrace an equity that is being abandoned by those who know it best.
- *Alignment of interests:* We avoid companies with major CEO conflicts of interest or corporate governance abuses. Once

again, this criterion is not directly relevant to the magic formula, but our investment philosophy prevents us from committing capital to situations in which we cannot trust the insiders.

- *Value proposition:* We avoid companies that offer a questionable value proposition to their end customers. We believe that in for a competitive advantage to be truly sustainable, the product or service should add value to a customer. Tobacco products, payday loans, mutual funds with large loads, and most investment newsletters fit into this category. When considering companies for elimination in this context, watch for products or services that make sensationalist marketing claims ("how I made 1,000 percent in 10 days") or that could not exist without heavy marketing to uninformed audiences.
- *M&A rollups:* We avoid companies that have meaningful integration risks due to major reliance on acquisition-driven growth. We also recognize that a magic formula company should typically consider its own shares to be a better bargain than a potential acquisition candidate.

Key Takeaways

Here are our top 10 takeaways from this chapter:

1. The advice to buy good companies only when they're cheap seems almost glib at first glance. However, Joel Greenblatt's definition of *good* and *cheap* and the actionable framework presented in *The Little Book That Beats the Market* make his advice invaluable to anyone seeking market-beating returns.
2. According to the magic formula, the higher the return on capital employed, the better the business. We typically calculate capital employed as net working capital plus net fixed assets.
3. Greenblatt's use of operating income to enterprise value as the way of determining cheapness is congruent with his use of operating income to capital employed as the way of determining quality, as the effects of leverage and taxes are stripped from both calculations.
4. In theory, the historical outperformance of Greenblatt's methodology should prompt investors to flock to it in droves, thereby eliminating its prospective attractiveness. In practice,

several considerations suggest that the magic formula is likely
to keep outperforming over time.

5. Just as long-short portfolios face unattractive risk-adjusted
   returns if they are built entirely upon a magic formula ranking,
   long-only portfolios could suffer debilitating volatility if they
   consist of a very small number of highly ranked equities.

6. Mr. Market makes two mistakes with some consistency: It overvalues high-return businesses whose returns on capital derive
   from explosive but ultimately transitory trends or fads. On the
   flip side, the market may undervalue unhyped quality businesses with sustainable high-return reinvestment opportunities.

7. One of the key adjustments we like to make to the original
   magic formula is to use forward-looking earnings data in the
   calculation. The future is what counts in investing, and while
   historical data have the advantage of certainty, forward-looking
   estimates have the advantage of relevance.

8. If we can run our magic formula screen on an equities database that includes both U.S. and non-U.S.-listed companies,
   the increased number of companies to choose from should
   enhance prospective performance.

9. Instead of simply adding up the twin magic formula rankings
   in linear fashion, it might make more sense to introduce an
   arbitrary hurdle, above which we consider all companies tied
   from the perspective of returns on capital. For those companies, the cheapness factor suddenly carries more weight.

10. High returns on existing capital—the capital already employed
    in a business—are almost meaningless without an ability to
    invest new capital at above-average returns. Returns on existing
    capital, whether high or low, are already reflected in a com-
    pany's operating income.

Notes

1. *The Manual of Ideas*, October 2011, 13.
2. *The Manual of Ideas*, January 31, 2011, 112.
3. *The Manual of Ideas* interview with Kevin Murphy and Nick Kirrage,
   Schroders, London, 2012.

4. *The Manual of Ideas* interview with Pavel Begun and Cory Bailey, 2012.
5. *The Manual of Ideas* interview with Alon Bochman, April–May 2012.
6. Ibid.
7. *The Manual of Ideas* interview with Dan Sheehan, 2012, www.youtube .com/watch?v=UgwBZ26R274.
8. *The Manual of Ideas* interview with Amir Avitzur, 2012.
9. http://greatinvestors.tv/video/the-importance-of-business-cycles-and-why-valuation-is-every.html.
10. *The Manual of Ideas*, July 2011, 10–11.
11. *The Manual of Ideas*, February 2010, 43.
12. *The Manual of Ideas*, January 31, 2011, 115.
13. *The Manual of Ideas*, March 2010, 43.
14. *The Manual of Ideas* interview with Daniel Gladiš, Zurich, Switzerland, February 2012.
15. *The Manual of Ideas*, January 31, 2011, 117.
16. *The Manual of Ideas*, January 2011, 154.
17. *The Manual of Ideas*, July 2012, 13.
18. *The Manual of Ideas* interview with Pavel Begun and Cory Bailey, 2012.
19. See Porter (1998).
20. *The Manual of Ideas*, July 2011, 99.
21. *The Manual of Ideas*, October 2009, 101.

CHAPTER 5

Jockey Stocks

Making Money alongside Great Managers

*Commoditization is correlated with management impact.
If you're the manager of a retailer, an insurance company,
a commodity company, a miner, or a bank, you can have
a huge impact on whether your business is great or good. If
you're managing a business that already has a wide moat,
you're more of a caretaker. Your job is to not screw up. Your
job is not to roll out New Coke.*[1]

—Pat Dorsey

When we talk about jockey stocks, it seems impossible to
ignore the words and experience of Warren Buffett. He
took control of Berkshire Hathaway in the mid-1960s at a time
when Berkshire could only be regarded as a highly deficient horse.
Through shrewd capital allocation, Buffett turned Berkshire into
a winner. Along the way, he invested successfully in many other
horses and jockeys. He refined his strategy throughout the process,
arriving at a somewhat surprising conclusion, given his strikingly
positive personal experience at Berkshire.

Buffett is widely known for seeking out good management
teams, but investors sometimes fail to appreciate the nuances of his
attitude toward corporate managers. For Buffett, the goal first and
foremost is not to invest in great managements but in great businesses. Were this not so, he might never have uttered these famous
words: "When a management with a reputation for brilliance tackles

a business with a reputation for bad economics, it is the reputation of the business that remains intact." Pat Dorsey, president of Sanibel Captiva Investment Advisers, reminds us of another Buffett quote: "Good jockeys will do well on good horses, but not on broken-down nags."[2] Jake Rosser subscribes to this view while sharing an insight congruent with Buffett's track record as chairman of Berkshire: "Even in unattractive industries, a superb management team with superior capital allocation abilities can trump poor industry economics. Wilbur Ross in steel or coal mining would be one example. Another example would be the management teams of Markel and Aspen Insurance. . . ."[3]

In this chapter, we examine the many nuances of making management quality a key investment consideration. We forgo the question of whether better management is desirable—of course, it is. Instead, we focus on the trade-offs investors face in the real, messy world of equity investing. These trade-offs may involve the ability of management to run the business versus allocate excess capital, the incentives of management, the quality of the business, and, inevitably, the judgment of the market as implied by the equity quotation. How do we as investors decide which trade-offs are acceptable and which are not?

The Approach: Why It Works

Chief executives can distinguish themselves in two major ways: business value creation and smart capital allocation. When the average investor thinks of good management, reference is usually made to business value creation. Steve Jobs may be the ultimate example of a CEO who created tremendous business value. His record on capital allocation is difficult to judge because it remained incomplete: Apple accumulated tens of billions of dollars in cash during Jobs's most recent tenure, but we do not know how Jobs might have allocated that excess cash. Would he have deployed it into a shrewd or misguided acquisition? Would he have repurchased stock, and, if so, would the repurchases have occurred at bargain prices or at a premium to fair value?

We also need to distinguish between business performance and the stock price. It may be a foregone conclusion that better management results in better business outcomes. However, whether it also results in market-beating stock performance depends not only on the actions of management but also on the valuation ascribed to the business by the market at the time of investment. Salesforce .com had excellent management in 2012, suggesting that the business was likely to outperform. Unfortunately, an investment in the equity seemed far from certain to outperform the stocks of other software companies, as Salesforce traded at a large premium to the peer group average.

Investors may not reap the expected rewards from finding excellent managers if other market participants also discover the same managers. Mr. Market has a tendency to deify certain executives, sending their companies' stock prices into the stratosphere and condemning new purchases of stock to likely underperformance. As investors, our goal should be to identify chief executives who are themselves underappreciated.

Experienced value investors will know that such executives not only are typically skilled at running their businesses and allocating capital but also tend to be soft-spoken and nonpromotional. "When considering management, we find humility and conservatism to be important qualities," states John Lambert.[4] The right breed of CEO generally feels the results should speak for themselves, and those results should be as conservatively stated as possible. In the eyes of such CEOs, accounting is a slow-moving profession that, if anything, should help the company paint a cautious picture of accrual income, possibly reducing the current-period tax burden. Concludes Lambert, "There are no hard and fast rules, but we would be wary of [managers] appearing overly confident or those for whom the share price appears to be more important than the business."[5]

Despite the possibility that some businesses with excellent management may be overvalued because of Mr. Market's love affair with those executives, investors typically find rewards in deploying capital toward well-managed companies. If we consider that long-run equity returns gravitate toward the mid-single digits, it is easy to conceptualize those returns diminishing toward zero—or worse—in the case of bad management. The epithet *bad* refers not only to less-than-capable managements and boards but also to those who dilute shareholder value through excessive compensation or periodically destroy value through empire-building acquisitions.

If we accept that real equity returns are likely to run in the mid-single digits, we may be more inclined to appreciate the few percentage points of value that may come from low executive compensation and value-maximizing allocation of capital. Sometimes the returns to shareholder-friendly capital allocation can be much higher than just a few percentage points, especially in times of high market volatility. When stock prices oscillate wildly around the fair values of the related businesses, management teams have a unique opportunity to create value through well-timed stock repurchases. In such situations, getting the timing right is easier than it may appear, as shrewd managers do not ask when a stock price will stop declining but rather whether their company is materially undervalued by an overly pessimistic Mr. Market.

Consider the example of the late Henry Singleton of Teledyne, which he built into an industrial conglomerate. Teledyne would probably have been a satisfactory investment even with average capital allocation. However, Singleton's aggressiveness in repurchasing stock whenever the market turned despondent rewarded shareholders with returns that exceeded the market average by a wide margin.[6] Doing what Singleton did is hard, even for executives who know their businesses intimately and therefore should have a better grasp of intrinsic value than do outside investors. Executives are only human, and they grow fearful in the same way investors do— and typically at the same time. It is little wonder that the number of mergers and acquisitions tends to be lowest when the prices of target companies are also the lowest. On the other hand, when exuberant investors push equity valuations through the roof, executives often find plausible-sounding reasons for paying premium prices for takeovers.

Skeptics of the jockey approach may wish to study the examples of Berkshire Hathaway, Fairfax Financial, and Leucadia National. Berkshire started out as a textile business with terrible economics and a terrible outlook for value creation, yet shareholders reaped big rewards. Berkshire, Fairfax, and Leucadia each succeeded in compounding equity at impressive rates, owing to the capital allocation skill and shareholder orientation of their leaders. Contrary to the claims of some statisticians, managers like Warren Buffett at Berkshire, Prem Watsa at Fairfax, and Ian Cumming and Joe Steinberg at Leucadia represent more than the long tail of a normal distribution. In this context, the existence of outliers reveals nothing about the causes behind those outliers.

Buffett almost certainly became an outlier not by chance but by design. Quite a few other managers may be able to approach Buffett-like value creation by adopting similarly shareholder-friendly capital allocation policies. The statisticians appear to ignore the possibility of the distribution mean shifting to the right as more managers emulate Buffett. This is analogous to many investors' correct but incomplete view that public market investing is a zero-sum game. While not all investors can earn above-average returns, the average return is far from predetermined. If investors consistently made terrible decisions, for instance by investing only in money-losing Internet companies, there might be just as many relative underperformers and outperformers as there are today, but the market return would be considerably lower. Just as every economically sound investment decision nudges the market return infinitesimally higher, so does a chief executive's creation rather than destruction of shareholder value nudge the CEO performance average slightly higher.

Uses and Misuses of Investing in Jockeys

It may be because investing is at least as much art as science that few investment managers find themselves on a Forbes list because they figured out a better way of discounting cash flows. Meanwhile, some investors have become quite wealthy by judging the long-term potential of a business or a CEO correctly. This simple truth leaves many of us unsatisfied, as it reveals little about the underlying recipe for success. When it comes to judging a great business, many soft factors enter the equation. This may be even more the case with people rather than businesses. Business analysts give us many tools for judging businesses, but how do we judge the people running those businesses?

Appearances May Be Deceiving

"Not in our time, in our fathers' time nor in our grandfathers' time has there been such a social debacle. . . . He had no need to overreach himself for power, for money, or for social position. He had them all!" Those were the words of the *New York Daily News*, commenting in 1938 on the scandalous downfall of Richard Whitney, former head of the New York Stock Exchange, who was forced to resign for fraud shortly after the SEC came into existence.[7] Nearly 70 years later, another head of the New York Stock Exchange was forced to leave under the cloud of scandal. Times change; human nature apparently doesn't.

No single factor is sufficient for evaluating management quality. Enron's Jeff Skilling went to Harvard. AIG's Maurice Greenberg built one of the world's most valuable corporations. WorldCom's Bernie Ebbers successfully competed against giants like AT&T. Countrywide's Angelo Mozilo pioneered financial products that became the envy of the money center banks. Lehman's Richard Fuld rose to the top of the Wall Street establishment. Before their companies failed due to fraud or mismanagement, many journalists, analysts, and investors regarded these executives as leaders to be celebrated. Yet, an impeccable resume or apparent success provides no guarantee of either business permanence or personal integrity.

The existence of a historical performance record in the current role makes management evaluation easier, but few CEOs have served in their current role long enough. Writes John Lambert: "A strong track record of achievement in directly comparable areas is obviously also nice to have. More often than not, we are seeing new management teams in companies where the previous incumbents have failed operationally or strategically, and hence assessing the abilities and direction of the new team becomes a critical task."[8]

Investors sometimes gloss over hints that a management team may be overly promotional or aggressive in applying generally accepted accounting principles. This leniency usually stems from the belief that the team in question will deliver near-term outperformance. Successful investors tend to warn against such a trade-off, pointing to the integrity of management as a key consideration. Tom Gayner, chief investment officer of Markel Corporation, dismisses the possibility of ignoring management transgressions if a high investment return might be expected: "The one area where I will not compromise is in the area of integrity. I may not make every judgment correctly when I'm trying to make sure I'm dealing with people of integrity but I will never knowingly entrust money to people when I am concerned about their integrity. Even if you get everything else right, the integrity factor can kill you. My father used to tell me that, 'you can't do a good deal with a bad person.'

And he was right."[9] Adds Mark O'Friel, managing partner of MOF Capital: "If the management of an investment target is trustworthy and shares common values with the investor, then the opportunity is worth closer inspection. Otherwise, it is best to stay away, short or, if given the capacity, replace management."[10]

The Compensation Factor

Charlie Munger's advice to "invert" serves us well when analyzing managers—not in identifying the greatest jockeys but rather in eliminating the bad actors, even if those individuals are esteemed by the business establishment. An acid test is compensation: Is management reaching for cash regardless of business performance, or is pay tied closely to results? If the latter is the case, do the criteria focus on shareholder value, or could they be satisfied in an empire-building, value-destroying scenario? Per-share growth in book value typically aligns better with the long-term interests of shareholders than does growth in EBITDA, which may be accomplished by saddling the balance sheet with debt. "We like companies that set strong goals in bonus plans and then stick to not paying out those bonuses if they don't hit the targets," states Lisa Rapuano, portfolio manager of Lane Five Capital Management.[11] In cases when the compensation criteria align with the interests of shareholders— think of bonuses tied to multiyear stock price performance—a gulf exists between packages that reward top executives when the stock goes up versus packages that consider the share price in reference to a benchmark. In the 1980s and 1990s, many CEOs became rich simply because they found themselves in the right place at the right time—a quality business in a bull market.

While the structure of compensation ranks among the key considerations for evaluating the alignment of interests between management and shareholders, stock ownership should not be ignored. A chief executive should own stock (not options) with a market value equal to at least several years of annual cash compensation. Anything less may make the CEO more interested in maximizing the pay package than per-share value. Rather than require "a specific number with respect to company ownership," Pavel Begun, managing partner of 3G Capital Management, looks for the ownership stake to "comprise a large percentage of the CEO's net worth."[12]

Mind the Attitude

Management's attitude toward shareholders is a key consideration. Attitude sounds like such a soft criterion that it may seem impossible to judge. However, several factors reflect directly on a CEO's attitude toward the owners of the business. Are the CEO's communications with shareholders open and honest, or do they appear to have been drafted by public relations people and vetted by lawyers? Annual letters by Warren Buffett and J.P. Morgan's Jamie Dimon serve as exemplary written communications, as they discuss forthrightly the prior-year performance of their businesses.

For public companies that host periodic earnings calls, we find it instructive to evaluate management's conduct during the Q&A portion of those calls. Do the executives answer questions comprehensively or focus on the positives while glossing over the negatives? Do they respond promptly or search for acceptable answers while prefacing their responses with fillers like "I would say that . . ." or "I'm not sure we can comment"? According to Jake Rosser, "Much can be gained through the analysis of managerial communications. How management communicates with its key stakeholders offers insight into their character. We like to see managers who do what they say they are going to do and are open and honest with respect to their challenges and mistakes. Management teams that are candid and don't blame others for company shortcomings tend to be better value creators over time than promotional types."[13]

The attitude of management also manifests itself when a trade-off exists between short-term results and long-term performance. Pavel Begun cites the example of Simpson Manufacturing, which makes connectors for buildings:

The main competitive advantage of the business is the reputation you have for the quality of the product, because that product is responsible for the integrity of a building. What happened when the Great Recession hit, you had a choice. . . . You basically could have said, "We want to preserve a certain margin . . . we're going to start making lower-quality connectors using a different type of steel, and we're going to pull back on R&D. . . . [This] will help us produce the short-term financial performance that is going to be more pleasing to the Street." But that's not what they did. What they did is say, it doesn't matter what happens in the short term because the reality is the only reason our business is going to be valuable in the long term is if we have great quality of our product, and we have the R&D effort behind it to make it even better. That shows you the mindset of the management. . . . We want guys who are going to be focused on the long-term business value as opposed to the short-term financial performance.[14]

Of course, inferior management teams quite frequently attempt to justify bad performance by arguing that they are investing for the long term. As a result, context is crucial when determining whether management is optimizing for the long term or simply failing to deliver anticipated results.

What Happens in the Boardroom . . .

Another consideration is the composition of the board of directors, whose role it is to set compensation and to hire and fire the CEO. We might ask, how independent and shareholder-minded is the board, really? Forget the independence criteria of the major proxy advisory firms, some of which have given Berkshire Hathaway poor marks and even recommended against Buffett's election to the board of the Coca-Cola Company. Sensible analysis of board composition focuses squarely on two questions: Do the directors have more at stake financially in the form of stock ownership or in director's fees and related-party transactions? If it became necessary, would the board have the wherewithal to oppose or even fire the CEO?

Economists Eugene Fama and Michael Jensen point out that "without separation of decision management from decision control, residual claimants have little protection against opportunistic actions of decision agents, and this lowers the value of unrestricted residual claims." They see the board as the solution to the problem of management opportunism, at least in theory:

The common apex of the decision control systems of organizations, large and small, in which decision agents do not bear a major share of the wealth effects of their decisions is some form of board of directors. Such boards always have the power to hire, fire, and compensate the top-level decision managers and to ratify and monitor important decisions.

*Exercise of these top-level decision control rights by a group
(the board) helps to ensure separation of decision management and control (that is, the absence of an entrepreneurial
decision maker) even at the top of the organization.*[15]

Warren Buffett expressed skepticism regarding board independence in a speech at a conference on takeovers in 1985. Buffett's
remarks in favor of shareholder choice in M&A situations went
so far as to place the board into the management rather than
the shareholder category. Buffett opposed giving management the
power to accept or reject an unsolicited takeover bid:

*Someone has to have the ability to make the decision on sell-
ing a business, and it's going to be the shareholders, it's going
to be the management, or it's going to be the government
or some combination thereof. You notice I don't include the
board of directors, because my experience overwhelmingly
has been that the boards of directors (there are exceptions)
tend to go along with what management wants. So I put them
in the management classification. And managements are
usually going to resist sale, no matter how attractive the price
offered. They will advance all sorts of high-sounding reasons,
backed up by legal and investment banking opinions, for
rejection. But if you could administer sodium pentothal, you
find that they, like you or me, simply don't want to be dis-
possessed—no matter how attractive the offer might be for the
owner of the property. Their personal equation is simply far
different from that of the owners. If they can keep the keys to
the store, they usually will.*[16]

Shares Lisa Rapuano: "We analyze the boards pretty aggressively,
to see if they are cronies or are qualified or have been part of not-
so-great companies in the past."[17] Whatever method we choose for
assessing boards should pass the following acid test to avoid disqual-
ification: Would our method have given low marks to the board of
Enron and high marks to the board of Berkshire Hathaway?
Some insiders brazenly put in place their own job protection
plan in the form of a poison pill. Deceptively referred to by companies as shareholder rights plans, most poison pills serve to entrench
management at the expense of shareholders. The plans make it

prohibitively expensive for investors or strategic suitors to acquire more than a specified percentage of stock without the prior consent of management. When boards consider whether to provide such consent, their own payoff may weigh at least as heavily as that of the shareholders. As a result, poison pills give incumbent managers a stronger bargaining position in terms of deal-related bonuses and continuing roles. The result is either a corresponding diminution of value to shareholders or the scuttling of a deal that might have benefited the shareholders.

Out-of-the-ordinary situations such as proxy fights sometimes reveal much about the attitude of top management. When Michael Eisner went to great lengths to oppose Roy Disney on the board of the Walt Disney Company, shareholders should have taken notice. Similarly, when Carly Fiorina spared little shareholder expense in crushing Walter Hewlett's opposition to Hewlett-Packard's merger with Compaq, shareholders might have opened their eyes to the kind of executive Fiorina was—and was likely to remain in the future. Those CEOs who go to great lengths to crush constructive criticism by major shareholders reveal an attitude that rarely belongs in the corner office.

In 2004, Gretchen Morgenson of the *New York Times* wrote about a little-noticed director-sanctioned looting of shareholder capital. John Shalam, CEO of Audiovox, got the company's board of directors to agree that the sale of an Audiovox unit would qualify as a "change of control" at Audiovox, triggering a $1.9 million payment to the CEO and another executive, Philip Christopher, EVP of the sold unit. The executives' creativity—and the board's acquiescence—did not stop there. Christopher argued successfully that Audiovox should pay him another $16 million for "personally held intangibles," things such as "personal contacts and personal and professional relationships with suppliers, customers, contractors, financiers, employees and ex-employees." Morgenson noted that "it took an asset sale for Audiovox shareholders to learn that for all those years when Mr. Christopher was being paid handsomely for managing the wireless unit—a job that includes building professional relationships . . .—the value of those relationships was accruing to him, not to the company and its owners."[18]

Tom Gayner points to an often overlooked check—leverage. "One of the great investors I've tried to learn from is Shelby Davis [founder of Davis Selected Advisers]. Shelby said that you almost

never come across frauds at companies with little or no debt. . . .
If a bad person is going to try and steal some money, they will
logically want to steal as much as possible. Typically, that means
they will have as much debt on the books as possible in addition
to equity in order to increase the size of the haul. Staying away
from excessive leverage cures a lot of ills." On the flip side, we
note the experience of many Chinese companies that went public
in the United States via reverse merger. Some of them appeared to
have large cash holdings with little or no debt. However, the cash
was often overstated, and the operating businesses were flawed or
nonexistent. The latter might explain why those companies failed to
put on leverage: A diligent banker might have uncovered the frauds
during the underwriting process. Chinese frauds routinely reported
different financials to the SEC and the Chinese tax authorities. As
both types of filings were publicly available, it would not have
taken Sherlock Holmes–style detective work to raise suspicion.

Leaving aside outright frauds, we find that management-related
risks often stem from inadequate alignment of interests between
shareholders and corporate executives. As each group seeks to
maximize its financial benefit, an issue arises because their goals
are only partially congruent. Both shareholders and managers feel
better off if the stock price increases, ceteris paribus. However,
if managers may trade off between maximizing equity value and
their own welfare, few will choose the former. "Buffett talks about
the 'institutional imperative' and the behaviors that stem from that
notion. One of the central management challenges for any large
institution or organization is how to keep the principal/agency conflict in balance. The familiar saying of, 'The inmates are running the
asylum' is really just another way of describing how agents tend
to push aside the interests of the principals over time," writes Tom
Gayner and adds that, "in general, the agents have the upper hand
and they've abused it."

Author Fred Schwed Jr. sums up the agency issues that plague
corporate executives this way:

> *Most businessmen imagine that they are in business to make
> money, and that this is their chief reason for being in busi-
> ness, but more often than not they are gently kidding them-
> selves. There are so many other things which are actually
> more attractive. Some of them are: to make a fine product or*

to render a remarkable service, to give employment, to revo-
lutionize an industry, to make oneself famous, or at least to
supply oneself with material for conversation in the evening.
I have observed businessmen whose chief preoccupation
was to try to prove conclusively to their competitors that they
themselves were smart and that their competitors were damn
fools—an effort which gives a certain amount of mental sat-
isfaction but no money at all. I have even seen some whose
chief interest lay in proving this point to their partners.[19]

Not All Situations Are Created Equal

Capital allocation choices that may be optimal for one business at one time may be inappropriate under different circumstances. Investors sometimes act in knee-jerk fashion, advocating dogmatically for share repurchases as the top capital allocation priority. This seems to make sense from a shareholder's vantage point, as the act of becoming and remaining a shareholder typically reflects an investor's judgment that the shares of a company are selling for less than fair value. Buying back stock seems like a sensible priority. Unfortunately, investors are fallible when it comes to portfolio decisions. By extension, they may misjudge the wisdom of share repurchases.

Shrewd CEOs have an opportunity to protect shareholders from an overly optimistic assessment of equity value. Repurchases destroy value if management overpays for stock or leverages the balance sheet to the point at which the equity becomes vulnerable to a cyclical downturn. Repurchases may also add less value than would reinvestment of capital in a growing business with attractive returns on capital. Lisa Rapuano sums up her preferences as follows: "We like companies that buy back stock when it is low and don't when it is high, or that pay out special dividends when the cash is not deployable for a good return. We like companies that eschew acquisitions or store openings or other capital deployments when they think the price is too high."[20]

We may differentiate between two types of situations when judging management's capital allocation discipline, according to Simon Denison-Smith, investment manager at Metropolis Capital.

[Discipline] can manifest itself in a number of ways. . . . The
purest (and lowest risk) flavor is to find a business model that

has clear organic growth potential, with a high return on the capital needed to be deployed to secure this growth and where the management has no need to look anywhere else for growth. Finding a business like this at a sensible price is rare. . . . Along slightly different lines are businesses in flat or slightly declining markets. These businesses will usually serve their shareholders best by focusing on retaining (and maybe growing) their dominant position within their niche, generating as much cash as possible and returning any excess that their strategy does not require to owners through dividends and buybacks.[21]

Denison-Smith's differentiation between growing businesses and flat or declining businesses hints at why jockeys may matter more under certain circumstances than under others. A shareholder-friendly capital allocator may have a greater positive impact in the second scenario. CEOs tend to regard a policy of reinvesting capital as the default choice, which aligns pretty well with the optimal course of action in the first scenario. On the other hand, a flat or declining business carries with it the risk that management will misallocate capital due to a desire to grow the business. Leaders of no-growth businesses should harbor no illusions about what is likely optimal from a shareholder perspective. They should act in accordance with that realization. It is hard enough to find a CEO willing to admit that redeployment of capital in the business looks futile. Finding a CEO who actually acts in a way that keeps the business on a steadily declining trajectory in favor of maximizing the flow of cash to shareholders is rare. As a result, when faced with a no-growth business, we pay particularly close attention to the statements, incentives, and actions of management.

Management tends to be of similarly high importance in times of financial distress or economic crisis. Few businesses are of such high quality that they retain much excess capital during sharp downturns in demand or credit availability. Whether out of financial necessity or a desire to build a financial cushion, many management teams become receptive to lowball offers of equity capital at the most inopportune time for shareholders. CEOs who own a large equity stake should be more likely to consider every alternative before accepting dilutive equity capital than may be executives whose primary concern a public relations firm might describe as "adding a liquidity cushion so we may continue to best serve the interests of our customers, suppliers, and other constituencies." If an equity raise becomes unavoidable, shareholder-friendly CEOs may prioritize raising equity via a rights offerings rather than a third-party injection of capital.

Screening for Jockey Stocks

In an ideal world, investors could screen the public company universe for management skill and for the closeness of incentive alignment between executives and shareholders. Imagine asking your stock-screening software to return a list of the 1 percent of public companies with the closest alignment of incentives or to show you the 1 percent of companies with the most shareholder-friendly management teams.

Unfortunately, such screening software does not exist, as determinations like shareholder friendliness, alignment of interests, or even the ability to run a business involve not only many variables but also an element of judgment. While we cannot exactly screen for jockey stocks, we can use screens to move a step closer toward identifying companies with good management, in terms of both ability and alignment of interests.

Management Ability

We find the following proxies for management ability to be particularly instructive: return on capital employed, growth of capital employed (per share), the margin profile, asset turnover, and capital expenditure trends.

PROXY ONE: RETURN ON CAPITAL EMPLOYED One of the key goals of corporate executives should be to widen the gap between the cost of capital and the return on capital. The concept of economic value added reflects the twin realities that investors have alternatives for the deployment of their capital and that higher-risk businesses should promise higher expected returns on capital. The latter makes intuitive sense yet is exceedingly difficult to incorporate into a sensible investment approach. Differentiating between the cost of capital of various businesses rarely drives the success of an investor. Some of the most successful investors assume the same cost of capital for virtually all companies, preferring to focus on other drivers of value. Warren Buffett uses a flat discount rate of 10 percent when thinking about the present value of the future cash flows of various businesses. If two companies yield a similar estimate of present value, the objective becomes to determine which business will have more resilient cash flows over the long term.

If we accept 10 percent as the default cost of capital, returns on capital become a focus. The latter can be calculated in many different ways, each serving a slightly different purpose. For example, return on (tangible) equity reflects most closely the income a company generates for the shareholders. It includes the benefits of financial leverage. On the flip side, return on equity tells us nothing about the degree of leverage used in generating the return, making cross-company comparisons and risk assessment difficult.

The return-on-assets measure eliminates some of the weaknesses of return on equity, but it introduces new shortcomings, revealing little about the value of businesses that utilize a large base of assets in generating returns for shareholders. For example, distributors that carry large amounts of inventory relative to their equity capital may concurrently show low return on assets and high return on equity. Similar reasoning applies to banks with large outstanding loan portfolios.

We prefer to focus on return on capital employed, which we calculate as operating income divided by the capital actually employed in running the business. The latter may be approximated as property, plant, and equipment plus current nonfinancial assets minus current nonfinancial liabilities. Commonsense adjustments should be made to this formula to arrive at the true amount of capital employed in the business. For example, if a business requires a certain amount of cash to be on hand, then the estimated amount should be considered capital employed. On the other hand, if a business owns real estate not used in running the core business, the estimated value of such real estate should be excluded from capital employed. This is analogous to the concept of enterprise value, which many investors rigidly calculate as equity market value plus net debt. However, enterprise value requires commonsense adjustments, for instance, when a large amount of cash on hand is de facto restricted because it represents seasonally high customer deposits or prepayments.

When we attempt to relate return on capital to the skill level of management, the analysis improves if we not only account for the absolute return but also consider the following: How does the return on capital employed compare to the average return of similar companies? How does the return compare to the historical return of the company, with particular attention to the period prior to the tenure of current management? How has the gap between the returns of the company and those of comparables trended over time?

PROXY TWO: GROWTH OF CAPITAL EMPLOYED (PER SHARE) At first glance, it may make little sense to use increases in the capital base as a way of gauging management ability. Major caveats indeed apply, as it is too easy for managers to grow capital without creating shareholder value. A company might engage in value-destructive acquisitions, or it might retain capital that should more appropriately be paid out or used for share repurchases.

We consider growth of capital only in conjunction with return on capital employed. Assuming satisfactorily high return on capital, management creates more value if it organically grows capital than if the latter remains constant. Consider newspaper publishers: They may earn high returns due to their low capital intensity, but the lack of reinvestment opportunities renders them quite unattractive. This logic applies to management teams that fail to reinvest capital at attractive rates of return. Good management will identify attractive reinvestment opportunities, producing what investors commonly refer to as organic expansion and market share gains.

To understand why return on capital employed is not sufficient to judge management, consider a company that increases returns while shrinking capital employed. This may result in an acceptable outcome if the company returns large amounts of capital to shareholders, but the value of the enterprise will most likely have decreased during the capital-shrinking process. A key reason for Berkshire Hathaway's acquisition of Burlington Northern may have been an ability by the railroad to employ large amounts of capital and grow capital employed over time. This combination of capital intensity and a moderate return on capital appears to have been more important to Buffett than a higher return on a smaller pool of capital employed.

PROXY THREE: MARGIN PROFILE   Gross and operating margins vary widely by industry, and while there is a correlation between margins and returns on capital, no causation is mandated. Walmart achieves high returns on capital despite a net margin in the low single digits. This is possible because the numerator of return on capital is an income figure rather than a margin figure. Walmart reports high income relative to capital employed, as it processes a large number of low-margin transactions. This results in high turnover of the asset base, which is primarily store inventory. Put simplistically, the faster a grocer turns over inventory, the more income it generates, and the higher the return on capital.

When we search for skilled managements, it makes little sense to screen for gross, operating, pretax, or net margin as an absolute number. Sure, high margins may be preferable ceteris paribus, but they tell us nothing about management quality. The latter may be assessed only if we compare a firm's margin profile to both that of a carefully chosen comparable company average and the historical experience of the firm under consideration.

When comparing margins across different companies, some caution is warranted: Some companies in the same industry may classify similar items differently, with some items included alternately in cost of sales or operating expense. A comparison of operating margins usually produces more meaningful insight than a comparison of gross margins. Another complication involves so-called special items, with some companies reporting high gross or operating margins for most periods, only to take large charges in other periods. A semiconductor company may seem better managed than its competitors because it reports higher gross margins. However, if the company subsequently takes an inventory charge, we may conclude that true gross margin was lower all along, rendering moot any determination of above-average management ability.

PROXY FOUR: ASSET TURNOVER   Turnover statistics inform on the capital efficiency of a business. One of the questions turnover data may answer is, How quickly are the goods flying off the shelves? Consider the following statistics in Table 5.1 from an earnings presentation by Dell.[22] The cash conversion cycle shows the numbers of days it takes Dell to turn sales into cash. Whereas for most companies this number is positive, indicating a certain period of

TABLE 5.1   Cash Conversion Cycle of Dell Inc.

	3Q12	4Q12	1Q13	2Q13	3Q13
DSO = days sales outstanding	42	42	43	46	45
DSI = days sales of inventory	11	11	12	13	11
DPO = days payables outstanding	84	89	87	89	88
CCC = cash conversion cycle	−31	−36	−32	−30	−32

CCC = DSO + DSI − DPO

Source: Dell Inc., *The Manual of Ideas.*

time until cash is collected, in Dell's case the number is negative because Dell pays suppliers more slowly than it keeps goods in inventory and collects cash for sales transactions.

Dell's negative working capital supports the view that the company is well managed. However, when a company has enjoyed a negative working capital position for a long time, we may wonder how much of the outperformance versus competitors is due to management and how much is due to the company's unique business model. As Dell pioneered the built-to-order model many years ago, an incoming CEO would likely enjoy a cash conversion cycle similar to the one shown here. Concluding that this CEO was better than the CEO of a competitor with a less favorable cash conversion cycle would be premature. A new CEO of Dell should instead be judged on how the company's cash conversion cycle trends during the new CEO's tenure. Even so, reasons other than the ability of the CEO could cause the statistics to trend up or down. For instance, the cash conversion cycle might become less favorable as a result of a management plan to increase shareholder value in other ways.

PROXY FIVE: CAPITAL EXPENDITURE TRENDS Many managers see a top priority in perpetuating the corporation. They regard capital expenditures or acquisitions—as opposed to dividends or stock repurchases—as default use of cash flow. While capital expenditures represent a capital allocation decision, they may also provide insight into management's ability to run the business. In particular, this may be the case if we can disaggregate maintenance and growth capex.

Some industries have high reinvestment requirements, with capex needed to maintain competitiveness. Consider the telecom services industry, in which many of the top players are highly profitable on the basis of GAAP, but their postcapex cash generation leaves much to be desired. In such an industry, a more capable management team may find ways to curtail capex while maintaining the competitiveness of the enterprise.

To incorporate capex data into an analysis of management ability, we screen for capex growth in relation to sales growth—the lower the ratio, the better. We also screen for capex in relation to depreciation and amortization (D&A). If a company manages to keep capex below D&A, it may generate free cash flow in excess of net income, perhaps justifying an above-average multiple of reported income.

Management Incentives

The power of incentives is widely appreciated, thanks in part to academic studies and the teachings of Robert Cialdini and Charlie Munger. Companies may have ambitious mission statements and communicate lofty goals to their employees, but people respond mostly to specific incentives. In the context of corporations, the incentives are primarily financial, but reputational and aspirational incentives cannot be ignored. For example, Buffett's annual letter has become a powerful tool for recognizing publicly the contributions of executives who may not respond solely to financial incentives. For many of Berkshire Hathaway's top managers, gaining and maintaining Buffett's confidence represents a reward in its own right.

In the context of screening for companies with close alignment of interests between management and shareholders, we rely on two readily available proxies: stock ownership and insider buying activity.

PROXY ONE: STOCK OWNERSHIP Ownership of common stock by key executives may be the best gauge of the alignment of incentives. If the chief executive has significantly more value tied up in company shares than in compensation, the executive may act not only as a manager but also as a shareholder. Daniel Gladiš points to incentives as a key reason for investing in family-controlled businesses: "If a family has half or three-quarters of its assets invested in this particular business, they're probably going to take care of it better than a management for hire that comes and goes in three or four years."[23]

Our experience suggests that when the market value of common stock owned outright by the CEO—leaving aside stock options—exceeds annual total compensation by six or seven times, the CEO may approach decision making from the viewpoint of a principal rather than an agent. Unfortunately, few stock screeners include data on the annual total compensation of the chief executive, making it difficult to screen for the relationship between ownership and pay.

As a crude approximation, we might assume annual pay of $1 million, implying a minimum screening requirement of $7 million in stock owned by the CEO. This value requirement can be converted into percentage ownership of the company, providing a basis for a mechanical screen. For example, in the case of a company with a $350 million equity market value, we may require the CEO to own at least 2 percent of stock. Once again, we may need to compromise, as most stock screeners include data on insider ownership in aggregate. If we require insiders to own at least 2 percent of stock, we may be implicitly setting a lower hurdle for CEO stock ownership. As a result, we may decide to increase the screening hurdle from 2 to 3 percent in this example.

Sometimes investors screen for insider ownership of at least 10 percent, reasoning that such a level of ownership would deliver a better list of investment candidates. We need to answer two questions in this context: How long a list of potential investments are we looking for? And are we willing to focus our search on smaller-cap opportunities? The latter will inevitably become the focus if we set a 10 percent or higher insider ownership hurdle, as the executives and directors of large-cap public companies rarely own more than 10 percent of stock. For this reason, we may alternatively screen for companies at which insider ownership in percentage terms exceeds the division of $1 billion by the equity market value. In this example, we would require insiders to own at least 10 percent of a company with a market value of $100 million, at least 1 percent of a company with a market value of $1 billion, and at least 0.1 percent of a company with a market value of $10 billion. To shorten the list of candidates, we might increase the numerator from $1 billion to $2 billion or even $5 billion. The higher we set the numerator, the more small companies we will eliminate from consideration.

PROXY TWO: INSIDER BUYING ACTIVITY   Many services track the purchase and sale of stock by corporate managers and directors. In the United States, the SEC requires such transactions to be reported shortly after they take place, typically on Form 4. In other countries, reporting requirements vary widely, with information on trading activity usually available on the websites of public companies, stock exchanges, or other regulatory bodies. Investors typically view insider transactions as a timing signal for entering or exiting a stock, reasoning that managers may buy or sell due to anticipated catalysts in the not-too-distant future.

While insider trading may indeed serve primarily as a short-term indicator, insider purchases also create an incentive for managers. A recency bias may be at play in making executives care disproportionately about their latest decisions, including stock purchases. Additionally, even if recent trades do not significantly augment a CEO's overall holdings of stock, the fact that the executive made a conscious decision to invest money may bind the executive emotionally to the interests of shareholders. The bulk of many executives' stock holdings stems from restricted stock awards or stock option exercises, which might be viewed by some managers as akin to playing with the house's money. When CEOs deploy their own capital—money that could be invested in or spent on many other things—the executive makes an affirmative decision in favor of the equity.

Depending on the stock screener we use, stock ownership and buying activity may be the only mechanical ways of gauging the alignment of interests between management and shareholders. Other considerations include the terms of executive compensation packages, the presence of a major nonmanagement shareholder on the board of directors, and the existence of a viable takeover alternative if current management fails to create equity value.

Capital Allocation Ability

At the extremes, little skill may be required to assess capital allocators. If a CEO has been running a company for decades, a look at the long-term stock price chart should suffice. Consider the long-term value creation by companies such as Berkshire Hathaway, Fairfax Financial, and Markel Corporation. Only the most cynical of investors would find it hard to conclude that Warren Buffett, Prem Watsa, and Tom Gayner are skilled capital allocators. It helps that each of the three men has articulated a philosophy of investment that makes economic sense. Occasionally, we come across executives who seem to be great capital allocators but falter when the circumstances change. Think of Angelo Mozilo at Countrywide Financial or even Hank Greenberg at AIG.

Between the extremes of excellent and poor capital allocators is a world of mediocrity, in which managements often view reinvestment of capital in their operating businesses as the default option, giving little consideration to the alternatives. Amit Wadhwaney, founding manager of the Third Avenue International Value Fund, shares an example of a Japanese company that "has done everything right except for one of the most important things. Mitsui Fudosan is a magnificent real estate company. . . . The rub is the following. You're building buildings there with cap rates of 5 percent when you can repurchase shares at high single digits, like 9–10 percent. To my mind it's not a very big leap of imagination that gets you there. Yet, for the last number of years they visited us here, for the last number of years we asked them, 'Why do you not do that?' They said, 'No, no, no, we have to grow the business.'"[24]

As investors, we strive toward some way of screening the public company universe for businesses run by skilled capital allocators. No quantitative screen will be perfect in this regard, but the following approaches could yield lists of companies to consider for further research.

PROXY ONE: SHARE REPURCHASES When companies buy their own stock at prices below intrinsic value, the latter increases on a per-share basis. It is little wonder that repurchases have become somewhat of a rallying cry for investors if we consider that investors usually buy the stocks they perceive as undervalued. In this sense, investors self-select into companies they believe should repurchase shares. Buybacks are no panacea, however, as buyback activity does not necessarily translate into greater equity value per share. We try to screen for companies at which an inverse relationship exists between repurchase activity and the stock price. When the price goes down, we want management to repurchase shares more aggressively than it did when the stock traded higher. Unfortunately, many CEOs behave just like stock market participants—they get exuberant at the top and despondent at the bottom. Witness the progressively lower repurchase activity at Apollo Group and ITT Educational Services as their stock prices declined during 2012.

Most stock screening tools include time series data on shares outstanding, making it possible to look for repurchasers even if data on buyback activity is not explicitly provided. A decline in the number of basic shares outstanding usually serves as a good proxy for the number of shares repurchased. If we consider a quarterly series over several years, we may be able to develop insight into the relationship between repurchase activity and stock price changes. We may also be able to identify one or more key points at which management bought back shares particularly aggressively. With the benefit of hindsight, we can determine whether it overpaid for the shares, at least in the subsequent judgment of Mr. Market.

This last caveat is important: We cannot expect CEOs to pick the bottom when buying back stock. CEOs add value by repurchasing shares below fair value, even if the stock price declines following those repurchases. Since we may not be in a position to estimate the intrinsic value of a company at various points in the past, we resort to the current market price as a proxy, but only if we allow for the passage of time. In our experience, a two- to three-year horizon is the minimum amount of time required to judge the soundness of a repurchase decision.

PROXY TWO: DIVIDENDS Those who studied economics may recall the Modigliani-Miller theorem, an implication of which is that, leaving aside tax considerations, dividends do not matter. Yogi Berra might agree. More likely, he might observe, "In theory there is no difference between theory and practice. In practice there is." Franco Modigliani and Merton Miller may not have surveyed corporate executives when formulating their mathematically sound theorem. Managements exhibit a tendency toward spending the money at their disposal. If an amount of capital is retained rather than paid out as a dividend, the excess capital may find a way into general and administrative expenses—without a commensurate increase in revenue.

In Yogi Berra's practice, there have also been quite a few value-destructive acquisitions done by management teams with too much capital at their disposal. Those acquisitions were not rational deals that turned sour later, but rather deals a rational observer might have identified as destructive ex ante. We recall cringing on two separate occasions when the highly pedigreed management team of Hewlett-Packard decided to allocate billions of shareholder capital to Compaq and, some years later, to a software company called Autonomy.

Dividends not only remove some capital from management, giving investors many allocation options, but they also impose a certain discipline on management. Periodic dividend checks, even if sent only electronically, remind executives and directors of the true owners. When a company adopts a dividend-paying policy, the board becomes more acutely aware of the capital allocation choices available to it. Suddenly, spinning the wheels may not seem like the only option. If management cannot identify compelling reinvestment opportunities, it may let the shareholders redeploy cash in more productive ways.

Beyond Screening: Building a Rolodex of Great Managers

It is lonely at the top. Greatness is quite rare among corporate managers, despite their impressive pedigrees. Managers are but a product of their time and environment, with conformity a driving force in executive suites and boardrooms. For every Steve Jobs, there might be a thousand John Scullys. This is true with regard to business leadership, but it is even more striking with regard to capital allocation. Many business school graduates aspire to be great business leaders. Few aspire to be great capital allocators. Business leadership is associated with winning in the marketplace, taking share from competitors, launching innovative products, attracting the best talent, and growing the company. No wonder many CEOs prefer to talk about market share or revenue growth rather than returns on capital or the growth in per-share equity value. A CEO might be recognized as a great business leader virtually overnight— a groundbreaking product or a major acquisition might suffice. It takes longer for the effects of great capital allocation to become apparent. One of the greatest capital allocators of the twentieth century, Henry Singleton of Teledyne, never achieved the public status of a Michael Eisner or Jack Welch, although former Teledyne shareholders would no doubt recognize the true corporate hero among those three managers.

Due to the distinction we draw between business leadership and capital allocation, we keep two lists of great managers. The list of great businessmen is considerably longer. While few names earn a spot on both lists, great capital allocators are rarely terrible business leaders. Their major perceived failing seems to be their zealous focus on returns on capital, which has caused some of them to starve their operating businesses of cash. Most famously, Warren Buffett turned Berkshire Hathaway into a multibusiness compounding machine, letting the original textile business fade into oblivion. More recently, Eddie Lampert of Sears Holdings has been accused of starving the retail business by keeping inventories low and minimizing store expenditures. Lampert has prioritized sound capital allocation, and rightfully so.

Building a list of great capital allocators represents a continuous process of discovery and curation. Corporate executives come and go, and seemingly great managers may reveal themselves as not so great over time. Still, we find the process of building a Rolodex a rewarding exercise. We do focus more on the list of capital allocators, as the list of great business leaders tends to correlate less with great investment opportunities. The stocks of companies whose executives earn accolades from the business press tend to be quite popular with the investment community, rendering most of them at least fairly valued. By contrast, great capital allocators either operate in relative obscurity, or they occasionally earn less-than-flattering profiles by the business press. Consider again the often harsh media coverage of Eddie Lampert's efforts to grow shareholder value at Sears.

We get to know the capital allocation tendencies of managers particularly well when we own shares of stock. As shareholders, we form certain expectations or conceptualize an ideal course of action. We may expect dividend increases or wish for share repurchases. This gives us a basis for judging management actions in real time. The managers who perform most in accordance with our views as informed shareholders may deserve a place on our list of good capital allocators. Unfortunately, experience shows it may be easier to build a list of bad capital allocators. It could take a lifetime to develop a meaningful list of great capital allocators from personal experience alone. Even then, the list might become outdated due to management turnover. It therefore becomes crucial to enlist the help of fellow investors in identifying great executives. *Fellow* is the operative word here, as only like-minded investors may judge capital allocation skill in a way congruent with our approach.

We draw on the following sources for building a list of capital allocators:

- *13F-HR filings by like-minded investors* (sec.gov): Many prominent value investors have expressed a strong preference for companies run by shareholder-friendly management teams. In the periodical edition of *The Manual of Ideas*, we monitor the quarterly SEC filings of more than 50 respected value-oriented investment firms, including Berkshire Hathaway, Fairfax Financial, Markel Corporation, Leucadia National, and Fairholme Capital Management. The portfolios of these firms are packed with companies whose managers have an above-average capital allocation record. Occasionally, however, these investors may buy stock in a company in which another investor has amassed a large position in order to put pressure on an underperforming management team. Such exceptions highlight the importance of conducting independent due diligence, even if we learn of a CEO from a superinvestor.
- *Corner of Berkshire & Fairfax* (cornerofberkshireandfairfax.ca): This message board has been moderated by Sanjeev Parsad, chairman and president of Corner Market Capital, for several years. We have found the interaction with like-minded investors helpful in learning about companies that employ value-maximizing capital allocation policies.
- *Value Investors Club* (valueinvestorsclub.com): This members-only community of investors regularly includes discussion of the incentives, conflicts, and actions of CEOs and boards of directors. Nonmembers can sign up for a free account that offers delayed access to content.
- *Interviews with like-minded investors* (manualofideas.com, valueconferences.com, and greatinvestors.tv): Conversations with thought-leading fund managers frequently reveal nuggets about great capital allocators or ways to look for them.

Table 5.2 names executives who may be appropriate additions to a list of great capital allocators (in alphabetical order).

TABLE 5.2 Selected Public Company Jockeys

Name	Company	Year of Birth	Year Joined Firm	Top Job Since	Stock Price When Joined	Price When Assumed Top Job	Recent Stock Price
Michael Ashner	Winthrop Realty	1953	2003	2004	$2.16	$2.76	$12.34
Raymond Barrette	White Mountains	1951	1997	2007	117.64	579.70	567.34
Warren Buffett	Berkshire Hathaway	1930	1965	1965	18	18	152,000
Patrick Byrne	Overstock.com	1962	1999	1999	13.03	13.03	12.52
Ian Cumming	Leucadia National	1941	1978	1978	0.05	0.05	28.16
David Einhorn	Greenlight Capital Re	1968	2004	2004	24.03	24.03	24.78
Charlie Ergen	EchoStar	1953	1980	1980	18.83	18.83	38.36
Bruce Flatt	Brookfield Asset	1966	1990	2002	10.45	19.65	37.80
Martin Franklin	Jarden Corporation	1965	2001	2001	2.44	2.44	59.66
Thomas Gayner	Markel Corporation	1962	2001	2010	164.75	345.55	491.79
Weston Hicks	Alleghany	1957	2002	2004	180.50	285.25	377.33
Edward Lampert	Sears Holdings	1962	2005	2005	132.52	132.52	47.19
John Malone	Liberty Media	1941	1990	1990	n/m	n/m	107.14
Joe Steinberg	Leucadia National	1944	1978	1979	0.03	0.04	28.16
Kenneth Peak	Contango Oil & Gas	1945	1999	1999	1.50	1.50	41.70

Michael Smith	MFC Industrial	1948	1986	2010	11.75	13.15	10.07
William Stiritz	Post Holdings	1934	2012	2012	26.89	26.89	38.29
James Tisch	Loews	1953	1986	1999	4.56	16.32	43.68
Jeffery Tonken	Birchcliff Energy	1957	2004	2004	0.30	0.30	7.67
Kyle Washington	Seaspan	1970	1994	2005	21.30	21.30	19.33
Prem Watsa	Fairfax Financial	1950	1985	1985	3.25	3.25	393.50

International jockeys not shown above include Bernard Arnault of LVMH (assumed top position in 1989), Albert Frère of Pargesa (1981), Guangchang Guo of Fosun International (1992), Brian Joffe of Bidvest Group (1988), Li Ka-shing of Cheung Kong (1950), Stanley Ma of MTY Food Group (1979), and Larry Rossy of Dollarama (1973).

Note: Recent stock prices are closing prices as of February 22, 2013. *Berkshire Hathaway*: Warren Buffett became chairman in 1970. However, Buffett became a director and effectively took control of Berkshire in 1965. The $18 stock price in 1965 is based on the closing price on May 10, 1965 when Buffett took control (source: http://brkticker.com/brk-chap1.html). Overstock.com: Historical stock prices based on IPO in May 2002. *Greenlight Capital Re*: Historical stock prices based on IPO in May 2007. *EchoStar*: Historical stock prices based on IPO in December 2007. *Sears*: Historical stock prices based on March 24, 2005, the completion date of the merger transaction involving Kmart Holding Corporation and Sears, Roebuck and Co. *Liberty Media*: Historical prices are not meaningful due to various corporate restructurings. *Seaspan*: Historical prices based on IPO in August 2005.

Sources: SEC filings, other publicly available data sources, *The Manual of Ideas* analysis.

Asking the Right Questions of Management

Some institutional investors used to gain an edge simply by sitting down with public company CEOs and asking them how business was going. In the case of long-standing relationships between executives and investors, much could be said that escaped the strict definition of inside information but nonetheless provided a meaningful advantage. Sometimes institutional investors needed to pull together and interpret a few disparate pieces of information shared by management to arrive at a material insight. At other times, managements could reveal much through body language, especially if the investors involved possessed context due to multiple prior meetings with the same management team.

Regulation FD (full disclosure) changed the nature of management-investor communications, as companies are no longer permitted to disclose new information selectively. While this has not stopped investors from probing for news and interpreting the body language of executives, it has become more difficult to obtain an informational edge through management meetings. Such meetings increasingly serve to inform investor judgment on management's mastery of the business, forthrightness of communications, and views on capital allocation. In this sense, investors may still derive value from meetings with corporate executives.

Some investors place little emphasis on face-to-face meetings with management teams, and a small number of successful fund managers even avoid meetings as a matter of policy. A risk is that such meetings introduce selection bias, as investors are physically able to meet with only a subset of companies worthy of such meetings. While meetings can serve to disqualify an investment candidate, they are more likely than not to elevate the company a notch above firms with which no meeting is possible. Some investors rightfully fear they could be unduly influenced by articulate CEOs whose skilled salesmanship may have little to do with the actual prospects of a business. Corporate executives generally do not rise to the top because they provide the most evenhanded assessment of their operations. Executives are more likely to become CEOs because they have a positive vision for the business and are skilled at articulating that vision to their coworkers. They also possess above-average interpersonal skills, equipping them well for persuasion but perhaps less well for unbiased reflection.

Investors who eschew management meetings generally focus on the information available in company filings when evaluating the track record, incentives, and stated intentions of management. Any forward-looking assessment tends to be speculative, but investors can improve their intuition by analyzing many managements and by following the actions of those teams over time. The historical record and incentives may reveal quite a bit about the path an executive team may pursue with regard to capital reinvestment choices, acquisitions, share repurchases, and dividends.

Evaluating the track record of a chief executive may be more difficult than it looks because no CEO operates in a vacuum. Most companies had been in existence for many years before the current CEO assumed the role, and the businesses were moving along a certain trajectory at the time of the appointment. During an executive's tenure, many external factors may conspire to influence the performance of the business—for better or worse. Rarely do investors face a situation as clear-cut as Steve Jobs's influence on Apple. More typically, we evaluate CEOs like Jeff Immelt at General Electric or Muhtar Kent at Coca-Cola. These are perfectly capable executives, but their impact on the corporate giants they lead may not quite match the impact of a Jack Welch or Roberto Goizueta. In the case of Jeff Immelt, for instance, we might assess GE's return on capital, market position, and stock price performance in relation to comparable companies. The analysis would benefit from disaggregation of GE into the major components, as the financial crisis of 2008 affected the performance of GE Capital differently than that of some other units, such as GE Aviation.

If management's track record is one side of the coin, incentives are the other side. The importance of incentives can hardly be overstated. Warns Charlie Munger: "Never, ever, think about something else when you should be thinking about the power of incentives." Anyone but the most wide-eyed idealist understands that humans respond to incentives. Capitalism works and communism fails largely due to incentives. As investors, we want the agents (corporate managers) to act in the interest of the principals (the owners). To accomplish this as well as possible in light of the principal-agent conflict in modern corporations, shareholders act through the boards of directors to put in place proper incentives. CEOs typically find ways to exert influence on boards, implying that, at least to some degree, executives set their own incentives. The types of incentives executives choose for themselves reveal much about their regard for shareholders and their confidence in driving positive performance. One of the most constructive steps an incoming CEO can take is to purchase a large chunk of common stock with personal capital. Such a move not only signals the executive's confidence in the future of the business but also casts the CEO in the role of agent as well as principal.

Subjective assessment of management in a one-on-one meeting likely adds value to the investment process, assuming the investor is aware of the biases involved and judges correctly that awareness will render inconsequential any such biases. Awareness of biases may also inform an investor's agenda for a meeting with management. The investor may focus the discussion less on topics that give the CEO an opportunity to sound persuasive in an area in which the investor is on shaky ground. Envision a non-tech-savvy investor asking John Chambers, chief executive officer of Cisco Systems, how well Cisco products compete with those of Juniper. Chambers could put forth an argument, the veracity of which would be nearly impossible for the investor to judge. On the other hand, if the investor poses a question about Chambers's plans for Cisco's anticipated free cash flow over the next 12 months, the investor may have a solid basis for evaluating Chambers's response.

Brian Bares, chief executive officer of Bares Capital Management and author of *The Small-Cap Advantage*, has met with hundreds of managers over the years. He covers a wide range of topics in conversations with corporate managers, while staying aware of potential biases.

> *We can usually spot exceptional managerial talent. But experience has also taught us that personalities vary widely, and we are very careful not to let likability or other traits bias our assessment of their capability as managers. Our focus in these meetings is on better understanding the business, products, and competitive dynamics. Once we feel like we have a good handle on the business, we move on to discussions about incentives, and how management has executed against what they said they would do. We also like to focus on how managers think about capital allocation. Will they invest internally or use capital for acquisitions? Asking management about*

their board's thinking on dividends versus buybacks is often a
very insightful conversation.[25]

Nick Kirrage, fund manager of Specialist Value UK Equities at
Schroders, prioritizes the following questions: "How do you allocate
capital? If I gave you a blank check tomorrow for £1 billion or £10
million or £1 million, what would you do with that? How would
you appraise what to do with that?"[26]

In addition to selecting a proper focus for a management meeting, investors may want to prioritize meetings likely to produce
incremental, differentiated insights. Hundreds of portfolio managers and analysts have probably met with Jeff Immelt or attended
small analyst gatherings with him in recent years. It seems unlikely
a one-on-one meeting with Immelt would reveal anything the market does not already know, about either GE or him as a manager.
On the other hand, a meeting with a small company CEO could
provide a differentiated view into the company, the limitations of
Reg FD notwithstanding.

Ori Eyal, portfolio manager of Emerging Value Capital
Management, shares an anecdote about the value of differentiated
interactions and highlights some of the traits that make one-on-one
meetings useful to superinvestor Guy Spier of Aquamarine Capital:

> *At one point, Guy and I traveled to Israel together and we*
> *went to visit and research about 15 undiscovered companies*
> *in Israel. In some cases I think we were the first international*
> *investors that had ever visited them. Watching Guy interact*
> *with the management teams of these companies was a key*
> *learning event for me. He has the ability to quickly develop*
> *rapport with everyone in the room and get to the main busi-*
> *ness issues that each company faces. By the time the meet-*
> *ing is over, Guy has a better understanding of the business*
> *than the company management team does. Furthermore,*
> *Guy intuitively understands the people running the company,*
> *their motives, and their likely future behavior.*[27]

Most investors combine a study of publicly available objective
information with subjective impressions gleaned from a meeting in
their investment processes. States Paul Johnson, portfolio manager

of Nicusa Capital: "We rarely invest in a company unless we can develop a strong relationship with management and they share our views on corporate governance."[28] Investors may also take a cue from Lisa Rapuano, who derives value from the way she sequences meetings during the idea evaluation process. "You can learn a lot about managements by not talking to them until you've analyzed the financials," states Rapuano.[29] Prior study of the objective data may help investors see through the salesmanship of bad executives:

> *Managements who truly understand shareholder value usually have been successful in creating it over time, whether they say all the right things or not. One of the absolute worst CEOs I ever knew . . . talked about ROIC and free cash flow and shareholder friendliness extremely well, but when you looked at his record the company rarely earned its cost of capital, had made stupid, expensive value-destroying acquisitions, had a terrible rubber stamp board of directors and had compensation packages that enriched him and his minions whether they did a good job or not. But, if you met the CEO in person he made you feel good about their processes. So, what I'm saying is judge a management by what they do, not by what they say. Good returns, smart capital allocation and sensible, goal-oriented compensation are the cornerstones.*[30]

Key Takeaways

Here are our top 10 takeaways from this chapter:

1. Chief executives can distinguish themselves in two major ways: business value creation and smart capital allocation.
2. We need to distinguish between business performance and the stock price. It may be a foregone conclusion that better management results in better business outcomes. Whether it also results in market-beating stock performance depends not only on the actions of management but also on the market's quotation at the time of investment.
3. Charlie Munger's advice to invert serves us well when analyzing managers—not in identifying the greatest jockeys but rather in eliminating the bad actors, even when those individuals

are esteemed by the business establishment. An acid test is compensation.

4. Several factors reflect directly upon a CEO's attitude toward the owners of the business. Are the CEO's communications with shareholders open and honest? What is the composition of the board of directors? What does financial leverage tell us about the management?

5. Determinations like shareholder friendliness, alignment of interests, and the ability to run a business not only involve many variables but also an element of judgment. While we cannot exactly screen for jockey stocks, we can use screens to move a step closer toward identifying companies with good management.

6. In the context of screening for companies with close alignment of interests between management and shareholders, we rely on two readily available proxies: stock ownership and insider buying activity.

7. Between the extremes of excellent and poor capital allocators is a world of mediocrity, in which managements often view reinvestment of capital as the default option, giving little consideration to the alternatives.

8. Building a list of great capital allocators represents a continuous process of discovery and curation. Corporate executives come and go, and seemingly great managers may reveal themselves as not so great over time.

9. Subjective assessment of management in a one-on-one meeting likely adds value to the investment process, assuming the investor is aware of the biases involved and judges correctly that awareness will render inconsequential any biases.

10. In addition to selecting a proper focus for a management meeting, investors may want to prioritize meetings likely to produce incremental, differentiated insights.

Notes

1. *The Manual of Ideas*, July 2012, 26.
2. *The Manual of Ideas*, July 2012, 18.
3. *The Manual of Ideas*, January 2012, 6.
4. *The Manual of Ideas*, March 2012, 7.

5. *The Manual of Ideas*, March 2012, 7.
6. John Mihaljevic, "The Manual of Ideas on Business Leader Henry Singleton, Founder of Teledyne," www.youtube.com/watch?v=3Beq IrpnmT8, accessed on January 22, 2013.
7. Quoted from John Brooks, *Once in Golconda: A True Drama of Wall Street, 1920–1938* (New York: Harper & Row, 1969), 272.
8. *The Manual of Ideas*, March 2012, 7.
9. *The Manual of Ideas*, November 2011, 8.
10. *The Manual of Ideas*, May 2011, 15–16.
11. *The Manual of Ideas*, September 2011, 13.
12. *The Manual of Ideas* interview with Pavel Begun and Cory Bailey, 2012.
13. *The Manual of Ideas*, January 2012, 9.
14. *The Manual of Ideas* interview with Pavel Begun and Cory Bailey, 2012.
15. See Fama and Jensen (1983).
16. See Coffee, Lowenstein, and Rose-Ackerman (1988).
17. *The Manual of Ideas*, September 2011, 13.
18. See Morgenson (2004).
19. See Schwed (1995).
20. *The Manual of Ideas*, September 2011, 13.
21. *The Manual of Ideas*, December 2011, 67–68.
22. Dell 3Q FY13 Performance Review, November 15, 2012, 12, http://i .dell.com/sites/doccontent/corporate/secure/en/Documents/ jkhgff133qsldeck.pdf.
23. *The Manual of Ideas* interview with Daniel Gladiš, Zurich, Switzerland, February 2012.
24. *The Manual of Ideas*, November 2012, 6–7.
25. *The Manual of Ideas*, August 2009, 31.
26. *The Manual of Ideas* interview with Kevin Murphy and Nick Kirrage, Schroders, London, 2012.
27. *The Manual of Ideas*, February 2012, 34.
28. *The Manual of Ideas*, August 2011, 15.
29. *The Manual of Ideas*, September 2011, 13.
30. Ibid.

CHAPTER 6

Follow the Leaders

Finding Opportunity in Superinvestor Portfolios

Strive not to be a success, but rather to be of value.
—Albert Einstein

Have you ever invested in a company simply because a famous investor bought stock in it, or have ever you been tempted to do so? If you answered yes, you would be neither alone nor misguided. Ever since some investment managers have gained superstar status in the media, following the moves of those investors has become somewhat of a sport in the investment industry.

One of the best pieces of advice in investing goes something like this: "Do your own work, and don't trust the tips of others." Nonetheless, following the moves of superinvestors can be both smart and profitable, if done correctly. After all, most so-called superinvestors have attained their status by virtue of superior investment performance over a long period of time. Warren Buffett, perhaps more than any other investor, has defied the academic notion of efficient markets. When Buffett buys a stock, is there really just a 50-50 chance that the stock will outperform the market? Investors who source ideas by tracking the activity of successful fund managers are putting themselves on fertile ground. Success is not assured, but it is more likely.

Superinvestors Are Super for a Reason

As we conducted more than 100 interviews with investment managers while researching this book, we realized that the best investors not only share the distinction of having superior long-term investment returns but also tend to exhibit a number of other traits: clear thinking, lucid communication, a visible passion for the process of investing, and a surprisingly humble attitude toward success. Warren Buffett has attributed his success ultimately to having won the "ovarian lottery," a lucky outcome completely outside his control. Buffett is undoubtedly aware of his skill and the dedication it has taken to keep improving even at the ripe age of 80+. However, Buffett is also aware of the danger of overconfidence, a bias that has led to the downfall of many almost-great investors.

When we sat down with Guy Spier of Aquamarine Fund at his offices in Zurich, Switzerland, it quickly became obvious why Spier has enjoyed much success since starting his fund in 1997. Lacking the sense of ego commonly associated with market-beating hedge fund managers, Spier attributes his success to the teachings of Warren Buffett and Mohnish Pabrai, another superinvestor in the value investing tradition. A few years earlier, Spier and Pabrai teamed up to bid on a charity lunch with the Berkshire Hathaway chairman to express their gratitude through a $650,000 donation to a nonprofit organization handpicked by Buffett—the Glide Foundation of San Francisco. When we asked Spier why he so readily attributed his success to others, he said his father had once told him that giving credit to others never diminishes ourselves. In fact, it usually enhances our standing.

Another trait we observed with Spier was his willingness to say, "I don't know." Imagine confronting an economist or investment pundit with the following query during the European debt crisis of 2011: "It's a lovely day, but not all is well in Europe. What's going on?" Such an open-ended question would usually provoke a response that shows off the pundit's expertise. Meanwhile, Spier's response was "If the likes of you and I knew exactly what was going on, we would probably be able to invest a lot better."[1] By acknowledging the impenetrable complexity of the European debt situation, Spier put himself in a stronger position as an investor. Rather than delude himself into thinking that he had a handle

on the eventual outcome of the crisis, he forced himself to identify investments that could outperform under a number of different
scenarios. Contrast this with the approach of investment managers who might have felt compelled to guess the potential outcome
of the crisis and then position their portfolios accordingly. If the
wrong outcome materialized, those investors would stand to suffer
material losses.

Finally, Spier exuded a passion for investing that Buffett has
echoed in his comments about "tap dancing to work." Spier frequently describes himself as one of the luckiest people he knows,
not because he has built a successful investment business with considerable assets under management, but rather because he feels he
has arranged his life in a way that allows him to pursue his passion
for investing without the distractions of constant marketing meetings, adversarial relations with corporate executives, or the need
to handhold investing clients. Spier frequently says no to potential
clients who may not be a good fit with his value-oriented, long-
term approach to investing. In a review of Youngme Moon's book
Different, Spier writes,

> *One of the simple messages I took from the book is that you
> can achieve a lot of success in business by making a strategic
> choice to say "no" to the customer. Twitter, for example, only
> allows 140 characters in a message. If someone wants to write
> more, they need to use a different service: Facebook, LinkedIn,
> or a blog. When it comes to purchasing assembled furniture,
> Ikea also says "no." Furniture at Ikea comes flat packed and
> has to be self-assembled. In saying "no" to the vast majority
> of people, these businesses ensure that the only people who
> become customers are those who will value and appreciate the
> specific configuration the company is set up to provide.*[2]

Superinvestors like Buffett, Pabrai, and Spier are the first to
admit their losing investments and to warn investors against blindly
following them into stocks. Nonetheless, sourcing ideas from these
and other great investors should be a part of every serious investor's idea process. The not-invented-here syndrome has no place in
investing. After all, an investment idea cannot be copyrighted, nor
are investors copying the moves of others obligated to pay any kind

of royalty. Sometimes, the best things in life—and in investing—really are free.

How Superinvestors Add Real Value to Companies

One of the facts often missed by market participants who view stocks as squiggly lines on a computer screen is that some investors do not simply try to anticipate which way a stock's price will move. Instead, those investors view themselves as what they are legally—part-owners of a real-life business. As co-owners, investors employ corporate managers. If a CEO is squandering capital on expensive acquisitions or reinvesting in a dying business, shareholders have every right to express their views on capital allocation. If the board of directors is unresponsive, shareholders can attempt to elect their own slate of directors through a proxy fight. If successful, shareholders may decide to fire the CEO or compel him or her to allocate capital in a value-enhancing way.

Most superinvestors view themselves as employers of management, and they are generally not shy about voicing their views on how existing equity value can be unlocked or new value created. For example, shareholders may push management to repurchase undervalued shares, pay a dividend, or refrain from empire-building but value-destructive acquisitions. While investors may be familiar with activists like Bill Ackman and Carl Icahn, many superinvestors prefer to work behind the scenes, quietly cajoling management into doing the right thing.

Prominent examples of superinvestors using their status as co-owners to help companies improve their capital allocation decisions include Warren Buffett at the Washington Post Company, Eddie Lampert at AutoZone, and Ted Weschler at WSFS Financial. In recent years, Bill Ackman became constructively involved with J.C. Penney, and Canadian superinvestor Prem Watsa joined the board of Research in Motion.

Have Superinvestor Disclosures Been Arbitraged Away?

Even if we accept that superinvestors are likely to outperform the market, it is not entirely clear that copying superinvestors also leads to outperformance. After all, if too many investors pile into a super-investor position once it becomes public knowledge, we may not be quick enough to buy before others do so, or we may be unable to buy at a reasonable price. Moreover, a superinvestor's outperformance may stem from acting in a certain way at a specific point in time. Add a delay to each trade, and it may no longer represent a winning proposition.

Opposed to this reasoning is the real-world observation that the price of a stock purchased by a superinvestor rarely goes up materially or permanently following disclosure of the purchase. The most striking example is purchases disclosed by Berkshire Hathaway. Despite Buffett's long-term record of outperformance, the market does not immediately revalue stocks bought by Berkshire. A 2008 study by Gerald S. Martin of American University and John Puthenpurackal of the University of Nevada found that "the market appears to under-react to the news of a Berkshire Hathaway stock investment since a hypothetical portfolio that mimics the investments at the beginning of the following month after they are publicly disclosed also earns significantly positive abnormal returns of 10.75 percent over the S&P 500 Index." As the Berkshire Hathaway portfolio outperformed the S&P 500 by 11.14 percent annually over the same period of time, we conclude that the drag of delayed copying of Buffett's actions was quite small compared to the performance advantage realized. While the numbers could look quite different for other superinvestors, the Berkshire-related evidence suggests that any alpha associated with superinvestor tracking has not been arbitraged away.

Uses and Misuses of Superinvestor Tracking

One of the dangers of tracking superinvestors is our propensity to elevate them to hero status. Superinvestors are neither heroes nor infallible. The specific idea we might be copying could turn out to be the one investment in a superinvestor's portfolio that becomes a complete write-off. As a result, cherry-picking an investor's portfolio may be a sound strategy only if the chosen ideas survive our normal idea evaluation process. Investors interested in passively tracking a superinvestor's portfolio may be better off simply allocating some capital to that investor's vehicle.

When the Going Gets Tough, Where Is the Conviction?

Many investors have learned the hard way that relying on someone else's work to justify an investment often results in an undesirable outcome. The problem is not only that all investors make mistakes but also that our ability to stick with an investment is diminished if we have not done the research to give ourselves a certain level of conviction. Few investments go straight up. As a result, obtaining a satisfactory outcome often depends on an ability to remain invested in a downturn. When a stock goes down in price, all kinds of plausible-sounding reasons start emerging as to why the stock will stay down permanently or decline further. Without conviction in the soundness of the original investment decision, we may well end up selling at the most inopportune moment.

The Importance of Context: Why, Not Just What

Some superinvestor purchases are fairly straightforward in their context and reasoning; others may have been made for reasons that render copying inappropriate. Mohnish Pabrai's purchase of Bank of America probably reflects a judgment that the shares are undervalued and that they will appreciate over time as the bank's financial strength and earning power become clear to other investors. Meanwhile, a multistrategy hedge fund manager's purchase of the same stock may not represent an unconditional endorsement of the common stock. The same fund manager may own Bank of America derivatives or may even be short another major bank, giving the manager a more nuanced payoff profile.

Consider the following extreme scenario of a superinvestor owning a corporate bond but acting in a way that helps destroy the value of that bond. Imagine that an investor spends $10 million on the bonds of Company X, a cyclical business that has just breached a covenant specified in their indenture. The company needs the investor's agreement to waive the covenant temporarily to avoid a damaging bankruptcy filing. Most bondholders in this situation would waive the covenant, perhaps in exchange for an increase in the interest rate or, if the company is in more serious distress, in exchange for warrants to buy the common stock.

A bondholder would not really have an incentive to put the company into bankruptcy—unless the investor also sneakily purchased credit default swaps (CDS), which are essentially low-cost insurance contracts that pay off in the case of a specified event, such as a bankruptcy filing. The investor might have bought CDS on Company X even after learning of the covenant breach. The price of the CDS may have gone up somewhat after the covenant breach, but this does not deter the investor who can still make 10x on the CDS trade if the company files for bankruptcy.

What is neat about this hypothetical situation is that the buyer of the CDS has the power to put Company X into bankruptcy by refusing to waive the covenant breach. Even if the investor loses $10 million on the bond investment, the CDS trade might pay out $100 million when the company files for bankruptcy protection. Not a bad position to be in—and it's apparently perfectly legal. Forget about the fact that the bondholder has inside information about what she will do with regard to the covenant breach—the SEC doesn't care. Forget about the fact that the investor will hurt other bondholders and shareholders—she is out for herself. Forget about the fact that the company's business will be harmed by a bankruptcy filing and employees will be fired. The investor stands to make a cool $100 million on the CDS, just by using her $10 million bond investment as the vehicle for getting there.

A similar scenario may have unfolded in the bankruptcy filings of AbitibiBowater and General Motors in April and June 2009, respectively. Those companies might have gone bankrupt anyway, especially in the case of GM. But that is not the point. There might have been bondholders of AbitibiBowater and General Motors who wanted the companies bankrupt because they had side deals with payoffs that were far sweeter than any potential return on their bond investments. Those folks might have put the companies into bankruptcy even if the remaining bondholders had wanted to find a compromise solution. Imagine if you had followed the bondholders and CDS holders into the debt of AbitibiBowater or General Motors, only to find out later that those bondholders never intended to make money on their bonds.

While the foregoing example illustrates rather strikingly the fact that following the moves of some investors can be difficult at best, less exceptional examples of noise in institutional investor filings abound. One scenario that plays out quite often among equity investors is their desire to invest in a macro theme or political outcome. To do so, the investor may purchase a basket of stocks that express the high-level thesis. The investor may have much conviction in the basket but little conviction in each stock individually. It would be a mistake for an observer to view such stock purchases as endorsements of the underlying equity value of the stocks involved. This is one of the reasons why tracking the equity investments of a macro-driven investor like George Soros may be less rewarding in terms of idea generation than tracking those of a bottom-up investor like Warren Buffett.

Another common source of noise in portfolio filings is many investment managers' desire to closet index, that is, closely mimic the composition of a relevant benchmark index. Such managers deviate from their performance benchmarks in ways that allow them to outperform slightly and prevent them from underperforming materially. *Closet indexers* is an apt term because such managers rarely admit their portfolios deliberately hug a benchmark in that their clients might as well choose cheaper index funds.

In *Simple But Not Easy*, Richard Oldfield tells the story of a British pension fund that had a 5 percent allocation limit for individual equities. Following Vodafone's acquisition of Mannesmann in 2000, Vodafone represented 14 percent of the benchmark FTSE 100 index. Even though the pension fund's investment manager was rather cautious on the outlook for Vodafone shares, he requested the investment committee to remove the 5 percent limit so he could buy more shares of Vodafone to bring his allocation to 12 percent, slightly below the benchmark allocation. An outside investor seeing purchases of Vodafone shares by said fund manager would have been wrong to conclude that the purchases represented a high level of conviction in the outlook for Vodafone.[3]

Screening for Companies Owned by Superinvestors

Screening for superinvestor stocks is not as straightforward as screening for stocks that may be cheap on specific quantitative metrics. Traditional databases lack an ability to screen by a specific investor or group of investors. To set up an efficient process for tracking the buy-and-sell activity of selected investors, we need to get a bit creative.

Deciding Which Superinvestors to Track—and Which to Ignore

The first step in setting up a superinvestor tracking system involves choosing the investors we wish to track. Several factors figure into this decision, including the concentration of an investor's portfolio, average portfolio turnover, propensity to employ short selling, and the congruence between one's investment approach and that of a specific superinvestor.

The more concentrated a portfolio, the more significant a single holding is likely to be. Investors with highly concentrated portfolios typically have high conviction in their holdings, while managers with broadly diversified portfolios may include securities based on quantitative criteria or a desire to expose their portfolios to macro trends, such as emerging markets growth, an aging population, or accelerating inflation. In addition, a superinvestor with a highly concentrated portfolio is less likely to ignore management's bad capital allocation decisions or a board's abuse of its fiduciary duty. If a company's stock price declines due to the actions of insiders, an investor with a large holding is more likely to act aggressively in defense of shareholder interests than an investor for whom the company represents an immaterial portfolio allocation.

Turnover is an important consideration because as outside observers we receive only delayed notice of other investors' buy-and-sell activity. The higher the turnover of a superinvestor's portfolio, the higher the chance that an investor is considering selling an equity by the time we consider buying it. For example, following the moves of one of the most successful quantitative funds, Renaissance Technologies, based on the firm's SEC filings is a futile activity because Renaissance often exploits small short-term disparities in securities prices. A quarterly snapshot of the portfolio of Renaissance holds little useful information, even if the snapshot were available to us in real time. Add a 45-day filing delay, and the firm's 13F-HR filing becomes useless for outside investors.

A consideration related to turnover is a superinvestor's propensity to stick with underperforming stocks. While investors like Paul Tudor Jones and Bruce Kovner may close out a losing position at a minimum possible loss, investors like Bruce Berkowitz and Prem Watsa may buy more of a stock that has declined in price. The former investors tend to enter into many trades and abandon those trades if the market does not start rewarding them quickly; the latter enter only into situations in which they are likely to put more capital to work if the investments get even cheaper. Both investment strategies can work if executed well, but outside investors will find it easier to follow the moves of investors who are likely to add to their positions when stock prices decline.

A superinvestor's propensity to employ short selling can be a factor in deciding whether to follow the investor's portfolio moves, because as outside investors we may miss one side of the story. If a superinvestor does not short stocks, we can rely on the long positions as a complete expression of the investor's investment judgment. However, if an investor uses short-selling strategies to a considerable degree, a long position may not represent an unqualified endorsement. Instead, a position in Company L, the company being bought, could simply reflect a judgment that it will outperform Company S, the company being sold short. Emulating the pair trades of successful investors is virtually impossible because investment firms are not required to disclose their short positions in SEC filings. In other words, when we review the disclosed portfolio of an investor who also shorts stocks, we cannot be sure whether a long position represents a high-conviction call on the merits of a specific investment or whether it simply represents the long side of a pair trade. Similarly, investors who engage in certain risk arbitrage trading strategies may have long positions for reasons that have little to do with the long-term investment merits of a company.

Congruence between one's investment approach and that of a particular superinvestor is perhaps the most important criterion for deciding how closely to follow a particular investor's activity. It makes little sense for a day trader to track the activity of Warren Buffett or for a value-oriented investor to track the activity of Jim Cramer. Ultimately, whichever idea we adopt from a superinvestor should become no less our own than an idea we identified from a quantitative screen or from reading the newspaper. We are much more likely to understand and agree with the investment rationale of a superinvestor who has an approach we understand and embrace.

The Superinvestors of Buffettsville

In 1984, Ben Graham's former student Warren Buffett gave a speech at his alma mater, Columbia Business School, in which he marked the fiftieth anniversary of the publication of Graham and Dodd's *Security Analysis*. Entitled "The Superinvestors of Graham-and-Doddsville," the article published in *Hermes*, the Columbia Business School magazine, presented long-term performance tables for seven investment operations run by students of Graham: Walter J. Schloss, Tweedy Browne, Buffett Partnership, Sequoia Fund, Charlie Munger's partnership, Rick Guerin's Pacific Partners, and Perlmeter Investments.[4] Buffett did not select those investors with the benefit of hindsight; he had identified them at least 15 years earlier as likely to outperform the broader market. Those investors' subsequent long-term outperformance challenged the efficient markets hypothesis, as the superinvestors of Graham-and-Doddsville shared the same intellectual origin: the teachings of Ben Graham.

Today, it may be appropriate to speak of the superinvestors of Buffettsville—fund managers whose intellectual origin can be traced primarily to the teachings of Buffett, as eloquently articulated in his annual letters, communicated in meetings with business school students, and shared at Berkshire Hathaway annual meetings in Omaha. Many of the disciples of Buffett have moved on from Graham's focus on dirt cheap but potentially inferior businesses to Buffett's focus on fairly priced superior businesses. The latter generally exhibit high returns on capital, an ability to reinvest capital at high rates of return, and a sustainable competitive moat.

While the media have sometimes attempted to anoint the next Warren Buffett, even Berkshire Hathaway is likely to have at least two investment managers with decision-making authority in a post-Buffett era. Rather than engage in the futile exercise of trying to find the next Buffett, investors may want to assemble a tracking portfolio of a dozen or so superinvestors of Buffettsville, thereby gaining a good view into investment ideas that may meet Buffett's criteria for high quality at an attractive price. When building such a tracking list, we may wish to consider adding the following investors (shown in alphabetical order), some of whom are well-known, while others have tended to keep a low profile.

- **Bill Ackman, Pershing Square Capital Management**. Ackman is a value-oriented activist investor. He runs a concentrated portfolio with the largest 10 equity investments accounting for the vast majority of his long book. Before the credit crunch developed into a full-blown economic crisis, Ackman made a strong case for why MBIA and AMBAC were overvalued and fundamentally more distressed than the market judged at the time. On the long side, Ackman has approached large companies, including McDonald's and Target, with proposals for unlocking value.

- **François Badelon, Amiral Gestion**. French superinvestor Francois Badelon, manager of the Sextant PEA fund at Paris-based Amiral Gestion, has found success by applying value investing principles to areas that have been mostly out of the view of U.S.-based fund managers. Badelon places a premium on good management, viewing it as "an essential net asset for any mid-sized company." Badelon states the following regarding the genesis of his firm: "With the support of Didier Le Ménestrel, the manager of the famous Agressor fund, I launched Sextant PEA in January 2002. . . ."[5]

- **Brian Bares, Bares Capital Management**. Bares started his firm in 2000, focusing initially on micro-cap public companies. The firm launched a small-cap institutional strategy in 2001 and now manages assets in two value-oriented strategies. Bares Capital Management is differentiated in the institutional asset management world, as it has adhered to a strategy of limiting the growth of assets under management to benefit investment performance. Bares is author of *The Small-Cap Advantage*.

- **Bruce Berkowitz, Fairholme Capital Management**. Berkowitz was one of the most successful value-oriented investors of the decade from 2000 to 2010. He is a contrarian who favors companies with strong free cash flow generation, as well as companies that are deeply undervalued based on assets. The Fairholme Fund runs a concentrated, high-conviction portfolio.

- **David Einhorn, Greenlight Capital**. Einhorn is the founder of Greenlight, a value-oriented, research-driven investment firm with a market-beating long-term track record. Since inception in 1996, Greenlight has reported a compounded annual return, net of fees and expenses, of close to 20 percent. Einhorn is author of *Fooling Some of the People All of the Time*.

- **Tom Gayner, Markel Corporation**. Gayner has been president of Markel Gayner Asset Management since 1990 and EVP and CIO of Markel, a Richmond, Virginia-based international property and casualty insurance holding company, since 2004. Tom has been a disciplined steward of capital on behalf of Markel shareholders, and his long-term investment record is one of the best in the business.
- **Joel Greenblatt, Gotham Asset Management**. Greenblatt famously achieved a 50 percent compounded annual return during the 10 years he managed outside capital starting in 1985. Since then, Greenblatt has continued a successful investing career that includes an association with Formula Investing, which offers investment strategies based on Greenblatt's magic formula concept. The latter is explained in *The Little Book That Beats the Market*.
- **Mason Hawkins, Southeastern Asset Management**. Hawkins is chairman and chief executive of Southeastern, a firm he founded in 1975. Southeastern serves as investment advisor to the Longleaf Partners value-oriented mutual funds.
- **Eddie Lampert, ESL Investments**. Lampert is a value investor who started out under Bob Rubin at the arbitrage desk of Goldman Sachs. When he left Goldman to start ESL in 1988, he received the support of Texas investor Richard Rainwater. Lampert compounded ESL's capital at rates of more than 20 percent per annum for many years. His largest investment was the much-publicized taking control of Kmart during the bankruptcy process in 2002. Lampert engineered the merger of Kmart and Sears in 2004. He is chairman and chief capital allocator of the combined firm, Sears Holdings. He also still manages a concentrated investment portfolio at ESL.
- **John Lewis, Osmium Partners**. John Lewis started Osmium in 2002 and has generated a market-beating record by investing in small- and micro-cap equities. Lewis focuses on high-quality businesses in underfollowed and undervalued segments of the market. He also frequently engages with management to drive shareholder value.
- **Mohnish Pabrai, Pabrai Investment Funds**. Pabrai manages value-oriented investment partnerships with a fee structure similar to that of the Buffett Partnerships (no management fee,

25 percent performance fee above 6 percent annual hurdle
rate). Pabrai Funds have a long-term track record superior to
that of the S&P 500 Index. Pabrai embraces an approach built
on the principles of Graham, Buffett, and Greenblatt.

- **Francisco García Paramés and Álvaro Guzmán de Lázaro
  Mateos, Bestinver**. Based in Spain, these two value investors rank among Europe's most successful long-term investors.
  According to Parames, "Any undervalued company that is a
  good business, [has] a competitive edge over its rivals, with a
  strong management team and transparent information can represent an opportunity for us."[6]
- **Chuck Royce, Royce Funds**. Royce is a small-cap value-
  investing pioneer whose Royce Funds have outperformed over
  long periods of time due to their research-driven value investment approach.
- **Guy Spier, Aquamarine Capital**. Spier's fund has outperformed the market indices since its inception in 1997. The
  Aquamarine Fund was inspired by the original 1950s Buffett
  Partnerships and has a similar fee structure. Spier seeks out
  equities with strong economics trading at a price that affords a
  large margin of safety.

Scouring News and SEC Filings for Superinvestor Activity

Some of our favorite superinvestors are shown in alphabetical order
(by last name) in the following lists. We have slotted each investor
in only one category, but note that most investors would fit into
more than one. We also show the Central Index Key (CIK) numbers
by which you may find SEC filings associated with each superinvestor. To do so, visit sec.gov and search by CIK number.

Large-Cap Value: Top 10 Superinvestors to Follow
1. Bill Ackman, Pershing Square Capital Management, CIK 0001336528
2. Warren Buffett, Berkshire Hathaway, CIK 0001067983
3. Tom Gayner, Markel Corporation, CIK 0001096343
4. Tony Guerrerio and David Rolfe, Wedgewood Partners, CIK
   0000859804
5. Mason Hawkins, Southeastern Asset Management, CIK 0000807985

6. Sandy Nairn, Edinburgh Partners, CIK 0001313926
7. John Paulson, Paulson & Co., CIK 0001035674
8. Prem Watsa, Fairfax Financial Holdings, CIK 0000915191
9. Wally Weitz, Wallace R. Weitz & Company, CIK 0000883965
10. David Winters, Wintergreen Advisers, CIK 0001360079

Mid-Cap Value: Top 10 Superinvestors to Follow

1. Richard Breeden, Breeden Capital Management, CIK 0001376259
2. Charles de Vaulx, International Value Advisers, CIK 0001456417
3. David Einhorn, Greenlight Capital, CIK 0001079114
4. Eddie Lampert, ESL Investments, CIK 0000860585
5. Dan Loeb, Third Point, CIK 0001040273
6. Mick McGuire, Marcato Capital, CIK 0001541996
7. Mohnish Pabrai, Pabrai Investment Funds, CIK 0001173334
8. Larry Robbins, Glenview Capital Management, CIK 0001138995
9. Jeffrey Ubben, ValueAct Holdings, CIK 0001418814
10. Ed Wachenheim, Greenhaven Associates, CIK 0000846222

Small-Cap Value: Top 10 Superinvestors to Follow

1. Brian Bares, Bares Capital Management, CIK 0001340807
2. Ian Cumming and Joe Steinberg, Leucadia National, CIK 0000096223
3. Glenn Fuhrman and John Phelan, MSD Capital, CIK 0001105497
4. Jeffrey Gates, Gates Capital Management, CIK 0001312908
5. Rehan Jaffer and Usman Nabi, H Partners, CIK 0001364412
6. Paul O'Leary, Raffles Associates, CIK 0001169581
7. Lisa Rapuano, Lane Five Capital Management, CIK 0001410352
8. Clifton Robbins, Blue Harbour Group, CIK 0001325256
9. Robert Robotti, Robotti & Company, CIK 0001105838
10. Meryl Witmer, Eagle Value Partners, CIK 0001469209

Graham-Style Deep Value: Top 10 Superinvestors to Follow

1. Zeke Ashton, Centaur Capital, CIK 0001453039
2. Bruce Berkowitz, Fairholme Capital Management, CIK 0001056831
3. Francis Chou, Chou Associates Management, CIK 0001389403
4. Mark Gallogly and Jeffrey Aronson, Centerbridge Partners, CIK 0001484836
5. Carl Icahn, Icahn Capital, CIK 0001412093

6. Robert Jaffe, Force Capital Management, CIK 0001317601
7. Seth Klarman, Baupost Group, CIK 0001061768
8. Rich Pzena, Pzena Investment Management, 0001027796
9. Wilbur Ross, WL Ross, CIK 0001128452
10. David Tepper, Appaloosa Management, CIK 0001006438

Buffett/Greenblatt-Style Quality Value: Top 10 Superinvestors to Follow

1. Chuck Akre, Akre Capital Management, CIK 0001112520
2. Jonathan Auerbach, Hound Partners, CIK 0001353316
3. James Crichton, Scout Capital Management, CIK 0001134406
4. Boykin Curry, Eagle Capital Management, CIK 0000945631
5. Hassan Elmasry, Independent Franchise Partners, CIK 0001483866
6. Alan Fournier, Pennant Capital Management, CIK 0001168664
7. Glenn Greenberg, Brave Warrior Capital, 0000789920
8. John Griffin, Blue Ridge Capital, CIK 0001056258
9. Allan Mecham, Arlington Value Management, CIK 0001568820
10. Alexander Roepers, Atlantic Investment Management, CIK 0001063296

Highly Concentrated Portfolios: Top 10 Superinvestors to Follow

1. Ian Cumming and Joe Steinberg, Leucadia National, CIK 0000096223
2. Ed Gilhuly and Scott Stuart, Sageview Capital, CIK 0001389563
3. Glenn Greenberg, Brave Warrior Capital, 0000789920
4. Chris Hohn, The Children's Investment Fund, CIK 0001362598
5. Robert Karr, Joho Capital, CIK 0001106500
6. Paul Orfalea and Lance Helfert, West Coast Asset Management, CIK 0001276537
7. Mark Rachesky, MHR Fund Management, CIK 0001277742
8. Wilbur Ross, WL Ross, CIK 0001128452
9. Toby Symonds, Altai Capital Management, CIK 0001478982
10. Steve Tananbaum, GoldenTree Asset Management, CIK 0001278951

A Few Industry Specialists Worth Following

- Energy: Boone Pickens, BP Capital, CIK 0001218269
- Financials: Tom Brown, Second Curve Capital, CIK 0001136704
- Pharma: Will Edwards, Palo Alto Investors, CIK 0001306923
- Technology: Charles Coleman, Tiger Global, CIK 0001167483

A Few Hard-to-Follow Superinvestors

The following list includes tips on how to track selected investors who do not file forms 13F-HR with the SEC.

- *Guy Spier, Aquamarine Capital.* Request access to the Aquamarine website and investor letters at aquamarinefund.com.
- *Daniel Gladiš, Vltava Fund.* Read quarterly letters at vltavafund. com. Our interview with Gladiš is available at http://youtube/ fO8MNy-kwSI.
- *John Lewis, Osmium Partners.* Search for CIK 0001316729 at sec.gov.
- *Lloyd Miller III.* Miller is one of the most astute private investors in cash-laden micro-cap equities. Search for CIK 0000949119 at sec.gov.
- *Stephen Clearman and Tushar Shah, Kinderhook Partners.* Kinderhook runs a concentrated portfolio of small- and micro-cap companies that might be regarded as compounding machines. Search for CIK 0001220338 at sec.gov.

Homing in on High-Conviction Ideas

Tracking superinvestor activity can be quite daunting because of the sheer volume of data to process if you wish to follow more than just a handful of investors. The goal, of course, is to quickly ascertain which ideas a superinvestor is likely to be most excited about at any given time. While position size is often a good indicator of the level of conviction, what if an investor's largest position has increased as a percentage of the portfolio but decreased in terms of the number of shares owned? Would this top holding represent the investor's best current idea? Unlikely, as the position's quoted value may have increased due to a rise in the stock price, prompting the investor to start selling shares. Such a position would hardly be the kind of investment we would want to consider adding to our portfolio.

Similar complications abound when we try to determine which superinvestor holdings have the most *signal value*, a term we use to distinguish noteworthy investments from the noise that exists in SEC filings. For example, what if a position ranks only as an investor's fifteenth-largest holding, but it reflects the investor's purchase of 19.9 percent of a company that has a 20 percent poison pill threshold? This position may well represent the investor's highest-conviction investment. Developing a methodology that lets an investor's fifteenth-largest holding bubble up to the top of the list can be challenging but also rewarding. As we cannot get into the mind of a superinvestor, we cannot know with certainty which investments the investor would consider to be his or her best at any given time. However, we can develop a ranking system to focus our effort on the most promising superinvestor ideas.

Here are factors that help us estimate an investor's likely conviction level:

- *Position size within the superinvestor's portfolio.*
- *Type of change in the number of shares owned:* new, increased, or reduced position. In the case of a new position, is it only an initial dabble, or is it already a major holding?
- *Holding as a percentage of the subject company's equity:* less than 5 percent, more than 5 percent, or more than 10 percent. The numbers are significant because they represent SEC filing thresholds. Fund managers like to stay under the filing thresholds to preserve their ability to trim a position without triggering a filing obligation. In addition, some companies make it infeasible for an investor to acquire more than a specified ownership percentage by putting in place a poison pill. Other considerations may also limit an investor to a certain ownership number. For example, some companies have large net operating loss carryforwards that might become impaired if there is too much turnover in the company's 5+ percent shareholders. As a result, even if a superinvestor would like to acquire more than 5 percent of an NOL-rich company, the investor may opt to stay under the threshold to preserve equity value.
- *Stock price change since the filing date:* As value-oriented investors, we are likely to prefer superinvestor ideas that have declined in price, giving us an opportunity to pay less than a respected investor might have paid only a couple of months ago. One important caveat exists in this regard: If major negative news has been released since a superinvestor acquired the shares, we should be more skeptical, even if the stock price has declined.
- *Time lapse since filing date:* The informational value of SEC filings tends to depreciate rapidly. Investors' quarterly 13F-HR

filings show portfolio snapshots with a delay of up to 45 days. Add to this the difference between the filing date and the date we access the filing, and we may be looking at a two- or three-month-old portfolio. Form 4 filings are more useful in this regard because they are generally filed within a day or two of the trade that triggered the filing obligation. Unfortunately, Form 4 is only required if an investor owns more than 10 percent of a class of securities or is a member of the board of directors.

- *Relevant investor commentary:* Occasionally, superinvestors share their theses on specific holdings in their letters or media appearances. Such commentary can be a useful qualitative input into a signal value ranking methodology.

Beyond Screening: What Makes a Company Attractive to Superinvestors?

When we study great investors, the near-term goal may be to figure out which equities they embrace and why they do so. The long-term goal, however, may have less to do with specific ideas and more with the thought processes of those fund managers. Pavel Begun, managing partner of 3G Capital Management, reflects on his background: "I started looking at the world's most successful investors, and I tried to reverse-engineer all of the ideas that they invested in. I tried to see if there was a common denominator to all of those ideas. . . . I came up with the three G's: good business, good management, and good price. . . ."[7]

One Step Ahead: Anticipating Superinvestor Moves

If you've been around investment managers long enough, you're probably aware of one of their favorite boasts—having bought a stock that was subsequently also purchased by Berkshire Hathaway. The listener is inevitably expected to arrive at the inescapable conclusion: Great minds think alike. More often than not, however, such front running of Buffett is little more than coincidence. Investors who believe they can anticipate the moves of superinvestors may have been fooled by randomness.

Buying a stock ahead of a superinvestor's purchase is likely to be more profitable than following the moves of the superinvestor, so is there a legitimate way to anticipate such moves? Is it possible to consistently find ideas superinvestors are likely to buy?

Ultimately, superinvestors deserve the title only if their investments, on average, outperform the market indices. Anticipating superinvestor moves essentially means choosing market-beating investments. The latter, not the former, should be the goal for investors. If we can develop an approach that outperforms, we will have achieved our primary objective. Coincidentally uncovering an investment opportunity before Buffett does so should be a nice bonus for dinner party conversation.

It may be fair to state that most superinvestors achieve success by finding high-quality businesses at attractive prices. A high-quality business typically has several key attributes, including high returns on capital employed, an ability to reinvest capital at a high rate of return, an ability to sustain high rates of return through durable competitive advantage, a balance sheet that affords the company strategic flexibility, and a management team that is both capable and shareholder-friendly. An attractive price is easier to gauge, as it typically implies a high yield based on earnings or free cash flow to market value. In rare instances of market distress, high-quality businesses may also trade at a discount to tangible book value.

Assuming agreement on these typical superinvestor criteria, the challenge becomes identifying companies that meet those criteria. The genius of Buffett lies more in his ability to identify suitable businesses than in his possession of any special mix of investment criteria. Buffett's highly successful investment in the Coca-Cola Company reflected superior judgment in Coke's ability to reinvest capital at high rates of return over a long period of time due to the potential for per-capita consumption growth globally and the durability of Coke's competitive advantage.

It is anything but easy to make the type of correct judgment Buffett made in the case of Coca-Cola. At various points in time, investors may have thought of some of the following companies as possessing high incremental returns on capital and sustainable competitive advantage: Microsoft, Morgan Stanley, the New York Times, Nokia, and Sony. While a company like Microsoft may still be able to sustain its competitive advantage in operating systems, it seems to be no longer in a position to reinvest meaningful amounts of capital at high rates of return. Does a company like Apple meet the twin criteria of Buffett's investment in Coke? Perhaps, but the ability to reinvest capital at high returns inversely correlates with the size of a business. If a cash flow machine such as Apple were able to reinvest large amounts of capital organically, management would almost certainly opt to have less cash on hand. In this sense, a buildup of net cash materially in excess of the seasonal cash needs of a company reflects a paucity of reinvestment opportunities.

Know Your Superinvestors—Defining Style Buckets

Sometimes how you say something matters more than what you say. The context and nonverbal communication surrounding the spoken word may be key to understanding whether someone is employing sarcasm or expressing a genuine feeling. One of the often-cited shortfalls of e-mail communication is an inability to add context to the written word. As a result, e-mails sometimes seem impolite or sensational, even if neither is intended.

Context is paramount when assessing the purchase and sale activity of superinvestors. Imagine three investors, each of whom has invested 5 percent of their respective equity portfolios in Bank of America. It would be wrong to infer that each investor's position has comparable significance for our purposes. The first investor might be Tom Brown of Second Curve, a firm that focuses on the financial services sector. On the one hand, Brown's investment may be significant because he is a sector expert. On the other hand, Brown invests his equity portfolio in financial stocks even when better opportunities might be available in other sectors. Meanwhile, the second investor might be Glenn Surowiec of GDS Investments, a deep value firm that invests across multiple sectors. Surowiec's investment might be significant because it represents a judgment that even in nonfinancial sectors, no company represents a better opportunity than Bank of America. Finally, the third investor might be Seth Klarman. If Klarman invested 5 percent of his equity portfolio in Bank of America, the significance of the move might be lessened by the fact that the vast majority of Klarman's fund tends to be invested in nonequity securities. As a result, a 5 percent allocation disclosed on Form 13F-HR would likely represent a smaller allocation in Baupost's overall portfolio.

It is also beneficial to understand the relative strengths and weaknesses of superinvestors when assessing their portfolio activity. In times of market euphoria or despair, investment managers are tempted to act uncharacteristically to accentuate gains or preserve capital. A small-cap investor may invest in large-cap stocks due to sharp declines in small-cap market indices, negating the investor's traditional advantage associated with uncovering under-followed companies. A value investor may invest in more expensive growth stocks due to client pressure or a perceived market preference for such companies, putting the investor in an unfamiliar position of trying to determine whether an expensive company is experiencing sustainable or faddish growth. During the market downturn of late 2008 and early 2009, some equity investors sold their equity holdings in favor of bonds that were yielding 15 to 20 percent. While such a return is attractive at almost any time, implied yields on equity investments were significantly higher in early 2009. As a result, equity investors who were suddenly moving up the capital structure to capture safer returns were doing so at precisely the wrong time.

Guy Spier has emphasized the importance of context: "As I look at other people's portfolios, I look to understand what their biases are and what particular chinks in their armor they may have. They may have a predilection for small-cap stocks or they may have a predilection for niche companies with niche ideas. Ultimately, what I can say for myself, I have had a bias towards low-capital invested, high-ROE businesses."[8] Knowing the biases or specialties of different investors can help us put their investment decisions in the proper context.

Letters to investors represent a great source of learning about fund managers' approaches to investing and their idiosyncrasies. While Buffett's letters to shareholders are famous and eagerly anticipated by thousands of investors, many investment managers write thoughtful, idea-rich letters. Reading those letters not only makes it easier to interpret investors' portfolio moves but also comes with side benefits, such as learning from the successes and failures of great investors. Fund managers whose letters tend to be available to those who seek them out online include Bill Ackman, Bruce Berkowitz, David Einhorn, Dan Loeb, and Guy Spier. An excellent free resource for finding letters by managers of private partnerships is Hedge Fund Letters (hedgefundletters.com).

Does It Ever Pay to Go against Superinvestor Herds?

Great investors are generally not afraid to go against the crowd and invest in unloved, even hated, companies. Still, it is not as lonely at the top as one might think. Most of the great investors we have interviewed do indeed exchange ideas and opinions with fellow fund managers. As a result, it is not unusual to find well-known investors clustered in some of the same equities. Occasionally, even the smartest investors succumb to the pitfalls of groupthink, finding themselves in agreement with the consensus of their peers when independent analysis might warrant a variant view.

Some superinvestors are known for doing especially thorough primary research on individual companies; others may be better known for making macro calls. Bruce Berkowitz and David Einhorn are widely regarded as doing their homework. As a result, when one of them initiates a position, their peers may be inclined to do so as well, in part relying on the research already done by Berkowitz or Einhorn. So, what may look like five superinvestors exhibiting a high level of conviction may actually be a case of four superinvestors following one of their peers. If the thesis turn out to be incorrect, all five investors might be saddled with losses, potentially prompting an exodus from the stock. Few companies' share prices will remain unaffected by a scenario in which five superinvestors wish to dispose of the same security at the same time.

Key Takeaways

Here are our top 10 takeaways from this chapter:

1. One of the best pieces of advice in investing goes something like this: "Do your own work, and don't trust the tips of others." Nonetheless, following the moves of superinvestors can be both smart and profitable, if done correctly.

2. As we conducted more than 100 interviews with investment managers while researching this book, we realized that the best investors not only share the distinction of having superior investment returns but also exhibit a number of other traits: clear thinking, lucid communication, a visible passion for the process of investing, and a surprisingly humble attitude toward success.

3. Most superinvestors view themselves as employers of management, and they are generally not shy about voicing their views on how existing equity value can be unlocked or new value created.

4. Even if we accept that superinvestors are likely to outperform the market, it is not entirely clear that copying superinvestors also leads to outperformance.

5. One of the dangers of tracking superinvestors is our propensity to elevate them to hero status. Superinvestors are neither heroes nor infallible. The specific idea we might be copying could turn out to be the one investment that becomes a complete write-off.

6. The problem is not only that all investors make mistakes but also that our ability to stick with an investment is diminished if we have not done the research to give ourselves a certain level of conviction in an idea.

7. One scenario that plays out quite often among equity investors is their desire to invest in a macro theme or political outcome. To do so, the investor may purchase a number of stocks that express the high-level thesis. The investor may have much conviction in the latter but little conviction in each stock individually. It would be a mistake for an observer to view such stock purchases as endorsements of the underlying equity value of the stocks involved.

8. The first step in setting up a superinvestor tracking system is deciding which investors to track. Several factors figure into this decision, including the concentration of an investor's portfolio, average portfolio turnover, propensity to employ short selling, and the congruence between one's own investment approach and that of a superinvestor.

9. Turnover is an important consideration because as outside observers we receive only delayed notice of other investors' buy-and-sell activity. The higher the turnover of a superinvestor's portfolio, the higher the chance that an investor is considering selling a holding by the time we consider buying it.

10. Context is paramount when assessing the purchase and sale activity of superinvestors. Imagine three investors, each of whom has invested 5 percent of their respective equity portfolios in Bank of America. It would be wrong to infer that each investor's position has comparable significance for our purposes.

Notes

1. www.youtube.com/watch?v=YSkJzBoAGC4, accessed May 4, 2012.
2. *The Manual of Ideas*, April 2012, "A Message from Guy Spier," 39.
3. Oldfield (2007), 94–96.
4. www.tilsonfunds.com/superinvestors.pdf.
5. Amiral Gestion website, accessed on February 24, 2013, www.amiral gestion.fr/ENG/Presentation/our-team.php.
6. www.valuewalk.com/francisco-garcia-parames-resource-page/.
7. *The Manual of Ideas* interview with Pavel Begun, 2012.
8. *The Manual of Ideas*, July 2009, 13.

CHAPTER 7

Small Stocks, Big Returns?

The Opportunity in Underfollowed Small- and Micro-Caps

All truths are easy to understand once they are discovered;
the point is to discover them.

—Galileo Galilei

Small public companies are implicitly discussed in each of the other idea categories in this book, yet we find several reasons to devote a chapter to small caps. First, misconceptions exist about small stocks, with many investors shunning them due to a perception that such securities are more likely to be manipulated or fraudulent. Although various pump-and-dump schemes and revelations such as the high fraud rate of U.S.-listed Chinese small caps have hurt investors, small equities as a group have offered attractive returns over long periods of time. Second, we approach screening for small-cap ideas differently than we might screen for large stocks, as we indeed regard a large percentage of small companies as uninvestable, whether due to infrequent reporting, liquidity considerations, or the speculative nature of the underlying businesses. We apply an investability screen prior to considering individual small-cap opportunities. Finally, we find that the approach to analyzing small companies differs sufficiently from analysis of large-cap equities that it makes sense to outline the distinct process in this chapter.

The Approach: Why It Works

Virtually everyone has heard of Microsoft, and many smart and resourceful people have an opinion as to what it is worth. Neither of these statements applies to Cybex International, a formerly Nasdaq-listed company that traded at a market value of just $13 million in March 2011. Given the huge disparity in the amount of investor attention each company receives, it seems reasonable that Microsoft's market value should more accurately reflect the company's underlying fundamentals than may be the case for Cybex. This thesis sums up the opportunity in small and micro caps: As there is less competition for analyzing the intrinsic worth of small companies, pricing inefficiencies in that part of the market are more likely and potentially bigger in relative magnitude, making it easier for knowledgeable investors to find bargains.

Sources of Inefficiency in Small-Cap Investing

Several key developments have created opportunities for small-stock investors. First, the explosion of institutionalized investment has led to an increase in the size of portfolios managed by mutual funds, pension funds, and hedge funds. This development forces established firms to impose on themselves arbitrary market value cutoffs, as companies that are too small offer insufficient liquidity. Second, an escalation of compensation expectations by experienced analysts and portfolio managers means that the best talent is almost exclusively employed by funds with enough size to generate the fees necessary to support large bonuses. Finally, stocks with market values of less than $100 million are excluded from virtually every stock market index, making them irrelevant to the benchmarking of the performance of the vast majority of investment professionals. They have little incentive to pay attention to the relative performance of micro-cap stocks.

According to investment manager Fred Speece Jr., "The concentration of assets . . . is a significant change that creates more opportunity to add value. The money management community is obviously consolidating, and as the consolidation occurs, liquidity becomes a major obstacle. That liquidity barrier creates opportunities in the mid- to small-cap sector of the market for those who can effectively manage around the liquidity issue and take advantage of it." This opportunity may be amplified in the international arena, where liquidity and access are constrained, even in the case of American depositary receipts (ADRs) with fairly large market caps. Notes investment manager Andrew Williams of Philadelphia International Advisors, "Transaction costs and market impact costs . . . for international stocks can almost cut . . . return in half."

We asked institutional investor Brian Bares to explain the source of structural inefficiencies in small-cap investing. According to Bares, "Successful professionals who operate in small caps tend to attract assets and graduate to mid and large caps, while their unsuccessful peers leave the business. Wall Street firms dependent on investment banking, trading, and other fees shy away from the space for profitability reasons, and their research departments tend to focus on the largest companies. The resulting vacuum in participation provides a real opportunity for individuals and small firms focused on doing their own homework."[1]

With regards to the rewards of in-depth fundamental research, Bares notes: "Our investment process mandates a comprehensive understanding of our portfolio companies. It is much more likely that we can profit from this understanding in small caps, where information scarcity allows for opportunity."[2]

Steering a Speedboat Rather Than a Cruise Ship

Outperformance by small-cap equities may also have something to do with the significant positive influence key shareholders and capable management can have on franchise value. Small-cap CEOs could be seen in charge of a speedboat, whereas the CEOs of Dow 30 companies may be viewed akin to cruise ship captains. Changing course to capture a sudden opportunity or avoid a sudden danger is more difficult for a cruise ship than a speedboat. Similarly, a cruise ship has elaborate navigation systems and a bridge crew in place, limiting the impact of the captain on the overall operations of the cruise ship. Meanwhile, the person steering a speedboat is in charge of all major aspects of the journey at all times. Actions are punished or rewarded instantly. While cruise ships are generally stuck on prescribed routes and need large harbors to dock, speedboats can embrace new, more rewarding routes and dock almost anywhere.

Major shareholders may have more influence on small-company CEOs than they do on their large-company counterparts, as more investment firms can credibly put small companies in play if management fails to act in the best interest of shareholders. One exception is the instance when company insiders own a sufficiently large block of stock to give themselves de facto control. This scenario is more likely among small companies, some of which may be little more than publicly traded family businesses. In this case, however, management may still heed the advice of sophisticated long-term shareholders, as value-enhancing actions would also create value for the owner-operators of the business. For example, a small-company board of directors may be unsophisticated when it comes to thinking about capital allocation. The directors may want to do what is best for shareholders, but they have grown to believe that the best path is to reinvest in the business in hopes of making it better. If an outside shareholder can develop a constructive dialogue that includes a cost-benefit analysis on a per-share basis of actions such as reinvestment in the business, payment of dividends, or repurchase of stock, insiders may well agree that buying back undervalued shares represents the best use of capital. In such instances, the outside shareholder and management would have created incremental per-share value.

The fact that activism and management quality may have a greater relative impact on small-company performance leads to another conclusion: The variability in the fortunes of small companies should be greater because the variability in management quality has a more direct effect on intrinsic value. As a result, even if we regard the speedboat versus cruise ship dichotomy as misplaced in terms of explaining the outperformance of small-cap equities overall, the dichotomy implies that top-quartile CEOs and top-quartile investors may outperform their competitors by a wide margin. The long-term experience of investors like Brian Bares, John Lewis, David Nierenberg, Paul O'Leary, and Lisa Rapuano supports this view. The corollary, unfortunately, is that despite the likely outperformance of small-cap equities overall, we may still reap disappointing results. In this regard, we communicate the idea generation strategies of top-quartile investors to assist you in achieving improved performance.

The Numbers Don't Lie: Small Is Beautiful

If we take a retrospective look, we find that small stocks outperform large caps by a statistically significant margin over time. While the results differ for various historical time periods and due to differences in defining the two universes, the verdict is clearly in favor of small stocks. UBS Financial Services published one of the more aggressive performance statistics we could find, arguing that small caps had outperformed large caps by roughly five percentage points annually over the long term.[3] Meanwhile, research by Jeremy Grantham shows that illiquid stocks outperformed liquid equities by two percentage points annually over four decades.[4] Value investment firm Tweedy Browne has further shown that the outperformance of small stocks persists across geographies. In the booklet *What Has Worked in Investing*, Tweedy Browne found consistent results in the countries it examined, including historical data for Australia, Canada, France, Germany, Japan, and the United Kingdom.[5]

In the book *What Works on Wall Street*, James O'Shaughnessy examines the long-term historical returns of various investment strategies. Using U.S. stock market data from 1927 through 2009, he calculates a compounded annual return of 9.7 percent for large stocks and 10.8 percent for small stocks.[6] While this may seem like a minor difference, the cumulative impact over a long period is quite large. According to O'Shaughnessy, $10,000 invested in large and small stocks in 1927 would have grown to $22 million and $51 million, respectively, by the end of 2009. O'Shaughnessy's small-stock category excludes micro-cap stocks, which outperformed by a much wider margin but are considered noninvestable due to their lack of trading liquidity. Based on Compustat data from 1964 to 2009, O'Shaughnessy calculates a compounded annual return of 28 percent for microcap stocks initially trading for at least $1 per share.[7] Based on our experience and the performance of professional investors who focus on micro-cap equities, we concur with O'Shaughnessy that published returns on micro-cap stocks are nearly impossible to achieve in reality, due to higher trading commissions, wider bid-ask spreads, greater market impact costs, and other factors.

Defenders of the efficient market hypothesis have tried to explain the small-stock phenomenon by arguing that smaller stocks are riskier (as judged by price volatility) and must compensate investors with a higher expected return. Adherents of the efficient market hypothesis use the same logic to explain the outperformance of value versus growth stocks. Neither argument is plausible, as many considerations other than pure investment risk drive equity valuations. In the case of value versus growth, an argument can be made that value stocks are actually less risky than growth stocks, as value investors generally require a greater margin of safety than do growth investors. It seems that whenever empirical data show that one group of stocks outperforms another over the long term, theorists conclude that the better-performing group must be riskier. They apparently assume the validity of the efficient market hypothesis to refute empirical challenges to the increasingly discredited concept.

Figure 7.1 illustrates the annual gap in investment return between small-cap and large-cap stocks in the United States from 1927 to 2012, as compiled by Kenneth French. The outperformance of small stocks, while not without exception, predominates the historical experience.

There is no guarantee that small or illiquid stocks will continue to outperform, and if they do, it seems reasonable to expect that

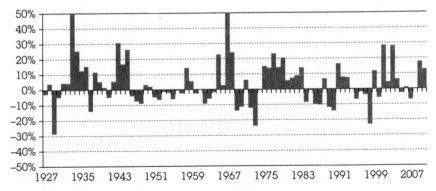

FIGURE 7.1 Annual Performance Difference between Small-Cap and Large-Cap Stocks in the United States, 1927–2012
Source: Kenneth French.[8]

the margin of outperformance will narrow. However, even if small caps as a group do not outperform, the differential between top and bottom performers should continue to be greater in the case of smaller stocks, providing opportunity for research-driven investors.

Uses and Misuses of Investing in Small Companies

Many market participants dismiss the small-cap equity universe as the Wild West of the investing world. This view is unjustified, although small companies occasionally do get away with shareholder-damaging actions that might not be tolerated at larger companies. If significant institutional capital is not at stake, CEOs who do not take their fiduciary responsibility seriously may conclude, often correctly, that they can get away with enriching themselves at the expense of shareholders. CEOs may do so on their own by pillaging assets to fund exorbitant cash compensation, or they may collude with outside or related parties to steal equity from shareholders by issuing stock and warrants on preferential terms.

Another tactic of the smallest public companies is to go dark, that is, deregister with the SEC and therefore stop making public disclosures about their financial affairs. Companies with fewer than 300 shareholders and in some cases with fewer than 500 holders cease to have filing obligations with the SEC.[9] While shareholders may conceptually favor going dark to eliminate the significant ongoing expense of being a public company, our experience shows that shareholders almost always lose when companies stop reporting to the SEC. Call it value destruction due to a lack of accountability.

The Underfollowed-Equals-Inefficient Fallacy

While underfollowed situations generally offer fertile ground for research-driven investors, it is not always necessary that many people consider an investment for pricing inefficiency to be eliminated. If the value of something is obvious, it will be efficiently priced, even if only a few people analyze it. If we stood on a street corner and auctioned off $20 bills, it would take only two bidders to eliminate the possibility of either of them obtaining a bargain.

The corollary is that the biggest opportunity for outsize gains may be found in situations in which value is a subjective judgment rather than the result of straightforward quantitative appraisal. What if instead of auctioning off a $20 bill, we sold a 1 percent share of our future income? Some passersby would pay nothing, and others might pay quite a bit more than $20. The winning bidder could end up with an excellent or terrible investment. Small caps may offer more opportunities of this nature than do large caps because, by virtue of their size, small companies have more potential for sustaining superior growth over the long term (identifying future winners ex ante, however, is an entirely different matter).

In fairness to large investment funds, which are forced to shun small stocks because of their illiquidity, the stock market does offer plenty of opportunity for judgment-driven investments in large stocks. Buffett has repeatedly displayed superior judgment in the case of large companies, resulting in impressive performance even as Berkshire Hathaway's investable assets have mushroomed. Google exemplifies a large cap whose value appraisal depends quite a bit on the subjective judgment of the appraiser. Superior judgment is likely to be more profitable in the case of Google than in the case of a company like Procter & Gamble, which has a relatively stable business model with predictable long-term performance drivers.

Another corollary of the fact that no bargains can be found in $20 bills is that simple quantitative strategies tend to become commoditized over time, leaving investors with little ability to outperform without additional risk. For example, pure arbitrage has already virtually disappeared from financial markets, even among small companies that may trade on more than one exchange. So-called risk arbitrage has become more competitive, particularly in the arena of straightforward mergers and acquisitions. By straightforward, we mean situations in which few things can upset the applecart. These situations typically have low risk of regulator roadblocks, a high probability of shareholder approval (perhaps because the majority have already consented), deal consideration the value of which is easily determinable, high confidence with regard to completion timeframe, low downside if the transactions were to unravel, and other features that allow for quantitative appraisal.

Looking beyond risk arbitrage, the next layer of strategies that may offer limited opportunity for superior risk-adjusted returns consists of strategies based on simple screens, such as the Fama-French portfolios, whose components are mechanically selected based on company size and book-to-market ratios. These types of quantitative portfolios may outperform because of investors' systematic tendency to prefer glamour stocks with low book-to-market ratios. However, simple quantitative strategies are easy to emulate and, therefore, easily commoditized. This is why the most successful investment approaches are not doctrinal when it comes to any one financial ratio but are instead built on common sense and an intuition for value.

In the small-cap arena, moving beyond quantitative screens is valuable because few professional investors are willing to start at *A* and work through *Z* in their appraisal of the qualitative value drivers of small companies. Paul Sonkin explains how he fishes for ideas where most other funds do not: "I've seen a lot of companies [in the micro-cap space]. There are companies that I'll look at for 5 or 10 years before I even own a share. . . . I read through their press releases, and if the stock price falls to a level that becomes extremely attractive, or there is some corporate event, then it moves to the top of the inbox."[10]

A Chance to Know What You Own

One of the main arguments against the notion that small stocks represent the Wild West of investing is that small companies listed on the NYSE, the Nasdaq, or the American Stock Exchange have nearly identical SEC reporting requirements as do large corporations. At the same time, small companies typically operate simpler businesses and have less sophisticated accounting practices. The latter is actually a good thing, as sophistication in accounting may tempt chief financial officers to massage the numbers to meet or exceed investor expectations. Smaller companies with no consensus earnings estimates have less of an incentive to use management's discretion in accounting matters to bump up short-term results.

Business simplicity is also a key difference between large and small companies. Consider the choices among Dow 30 components: Can we truly understand the underlying risk exposures of companies like Bank of America, J.P. Morgan, Travelers, General Electric, or American Express? Those companies are so large and their balance sheets so unwieldy that we inevitably rely on multiple layers of abstraction and financial aggregation. When Jamie Dimon has trouble understanding the risk exposures of the megabank he runs, you can be sure those investing in J.P. Morgan are acting at least in part on faith rather than hard data.

Meanwhile, research-oriented investors do stand a chance of understanding the inner workings of many small companies. Their balance sheets and financial footnotes are generally easier to read and understand. They may operate a straightforward business of the type in which more customers means more revenue, and more revenue means more profit. If you have focused your investment activities on large-cap stocks, you might enjoy picking up a 10-K filed by a sub-$100 million market cap company. You might be pleased by the simplicity and transparency of the disclosures.

We may also pick up the phone and dial a small company's main number. Chances are decent we will succeed in getting through to the company's CEO or CFO, allowing us to build a direct relationship with the key decision makers. Small-company executives are also generally more forthcoming than are corporate executives, whose ability to communicate spontaneously has been lawyered into oblivion. Ask a small-company CEO how business is going, and you might get an answer. Ask a large-company CEO the same question, and you might hear a disclaimer. We are not talking about the disclosure of inside information here but rather the willingness of CEOs to explain their business in plain language to current and potential shareholders.

If You Might Need the Money, Mind the Liquidity

One well-known drawback of small-stock investing is the at times severely constrained trading liquidity of smaller companies. With fewer shares traded, investors deploying anything more than token amounts of capital must consider carefully the process of building and unwinding an investment. Wider bid-ask spreads, greater market impact, and perhaps greater trading commissions conspire to make entering and exiting the equity of small companies a costly affair. It is only justified if the investor intends to hold onto a position for a relatively long time. Actually, intent is one thing, while the potential need to sell at an inopportune time is an entirely different matter. Unfortunately, the realized selling price of a small stock may be far from the quoted market price if multiple investors attempt to sell at the same time. As a result, intent to hold for the long term is generally insufficient; an ability to do so regardless of the market environment is critical.

Illiquidity is not an unambiguous negative, however, as institutional investors appear willing to pay dearly for liquidity. The option to exit a position at a moment's notice has gained value in the eyes of many market participants following the crisis of 2008. This provides an opportunity for long-term-minded investors, as the potential rewards to illiquidity have increased. Not everyone can take advantage of these rewards. Many institutions are structurally prevented from doing so, due to the size of assets under management, an open-ended fund structure, a limiting investment mandate, benchmarking, or other considerations. However, for those of us who deploy quasi-permanent capital without leverage, the assumption of illiquidity in exchange for higher expected returns should be a viable alternative for a portion of the equity portfolio. After all, trading illiquidity is neither a business-specific nor an industry risk, so the intrinsic quality of an investment opportunity is rarely diminished by illiquidity. It represents a transactional risk, one that is more manageable for some investors than for others.

Screening for Promising Small- and Micro-Caps

The small-stock space offers fertile hunting ground for investment opportunities, but how do we separate the wheat from the chaff? The first step involves narrowing down the field of potential investments to companies we might consider investable. For practical screening reasons, we use purely quantitative criteria to make this determination. This is an imperfect process, and we want to embrace a generous definition of investability to eliminate only truly undesirable companies. Once we arrive at an investable universe, we are ready for step two, which involves running one or more additional screens to arrive at manageable lists of stocks for further analysis.

Removing the Chaff with a Basic Investability Screen

Every investor will have a different definition of investability. However, since we are trying to define a universe of small stocks, it might make sense for all investors to start the process by deciding what market cap range they consider appropriate. The high end of the range might be a reflection of an investor's deployable capital or a desire to include fairly substantial companies in the small-cap definition. It is not uncommon for investors to consider all companies with a market value of less than $2 billion as small or micro caps. (When we refer to small caps, we automatically include micro caps, as the latter exhibit the attributes commonly associated with small-cap stocks to an even stronger degree.) We view $2 billion as a maximum upper limit for any definition of small caps. In fact, we prefer to use $1 billion because most companies with market values of more than $1 billion should be quite well known to at least some sophisticated equity funds. Bargains among companies with $1+ billion market caps are simply harder to obtain than are bargains among sub-$1 billion companies.

The more important cutoff, however, might be the lower limit of the small-cap range. We want to set the limit high enough to eliminate tiny companies and low enough to give ourselves an opportunity to identify stocks that could grow their market cap 10-fold and still be considered small. Eliminating the tiniest of companies make sense for a number of reasons: Insiders rarely own enough stock (in terms of market value) to care more about ownership than their cash compensation and perks. The number of shareholders may be less than 300, heightening the risk of management deciding to go dark. Market impact costs can be prohibitive. Finally, the 5 percent SEC filing threshold for Form 13D might be triggered by a relatively small investment. However, since we enjoy browsing through tiny companies, we generally set the lower market cap limit at $10 million, though most investors might set it at $25 million, $50 million, $100 million, or even higher.

The next investability requirement might be that a company is current in its SEC filing obligations, or, if we are generous, no more than one quarter late on those obligations. The relaxed condition should be used with caution, however, as many companies that are a few months late on their filing obligations have actually stopped filing due to recent deregistration of their stock with the SEC. If we allow companies to be late, we will need to go through the offenders to determine which ones are likely to resume on-time filings. Adding the on-time condition to a quantitative screen is a simple matter of requiring that the date of the most recent quarterly filing is no more than three to six months earlier than the today's date.

Next we like to eliminate companies with no employees or with fewer than an arbitrary low number of employees—for example, 10. While there are some legitimate companies with no employees due to unusual corporate structures, such structures can in the best of scenarios create conflicts of interests for insiders who might be employees of a related company but not the entity in which public shareholders hold a stake. In the worst of scenarios, an employee number of fewer than 10 simply reflects the absence of a real business. It may not necessarily reflect fraud, but shell companies rarely deliver superior returns, except in the rare cases in which they trade in line with or at a discount to net cash *and* the management has a reputation for deploying cash through value-accretive acquisitions. We do believe requiring some minimum number of employees helps us avoid many unsuitable companies while only rarely eliminating an interesting company from consideration.

Another suitability requirement is that insiders collectively own a minimum amount of stock, which can be as low as 1 percent or as high as 5 percent. While this requirement would be inappropriate for Dow 30 companies, it makes perfect sense for stocks in which 1 percent ownership can be purchased for $1 million or less. We would set the limit at 1 percent so as not to exclude companies in which insiders may not own much stock but are still acting in the best interests of shareholders. Meanwhile, we get rid of companies in which insiders are clearly in a position to free ride off shareholders without having any of their own capital at risk. Setting an upper limit on insider ownership does not make sense in this context, as some controlled small caps are likely to do well for minority shareholders. In general, we prefer management to own no more than 25 percent to remain accountable, but we do not require it as a starting condition.

A controversial requirement but one we like is that the investable universe exclude Chinese companies that have gone public in the United States via reverse merger. Many of these companies have been exposed as frauds, rendering the group uninvestable, in our view. Some may object, perhaps rightfully so, that many Chinese reverse-merger companies are legitimate businesses and that their market valuations may be too low to ignore. We have been burned in this regard and have lost our appetite for trying to determine which company is legitimate and which is not. Unfortunately, most quantitative screeners cannot exclude reverse mergers only; instead, we are forced to exclude all small companies domiciled in China and traded on a U.S. exchange. Still, we believe the benefit of doing so outweighs any lost opportunities.

Another controversial requirement is that each company should have some minimum amount of annual revenue, perhaps $10 million. We have found that the vast majority of small companies with no revenue are doomed to shareholder value destruction. While a small subset of companies have no revenue but do have much intrinsic value, we are once again willing to pass up a few potential opportunities in favor of saving ourselves many potential issues.

We do not have any other minimum performance requirements, which might come with too high a cost in missed opportunities. Companies with negative tangible book value may simply be great businesses that keep repurchasing stock. Companies with recent operating losses may have hit a bump in the road, only to soon revert to their former profit-making ways. Companies with lots of debt could represent equity stubs with a highly attractive risk-reward trade-off. Companies with declining revenue may have correctly opted to forgo value-destructive acquisitions in favor of milking a cash-generative legacy business and returning cash to shareholders.

As Table 7.1 shows, by applying these criteria, we are able to go from 10,068 public companies traded on U.S. exchanges to 1,456 investable small caps. We believe this is accomplished without excluding a material number of compelling investments. While 1,456 remains too large a number for us to become familiar with each company, it is quite manageable if we layer additional screens on top of this investable universe. Some of the screens might be as simple as narrowing down the market cap range or excluding certain industries that fall outside our circle of competence. Each investor will have different preferences in this regard.

Let us assume we want to narrow the small-cap investable universe further to be in a position to analyze all qualifying companies, thereby eliminating the need for additional screens. Table 7.2 shows the criteria we might add to the previous screen. It also shows that we are now starting to cut into the meat of what might be considered investable opportunities.

We have shrunk the investable universe by requiring a larger minimum market value, eliminating companies traded on the Pink

TABLE 7.1 U.S. Companies Passing Selected Small-Cap Investability Criteria

Screening Criteria	Companies (cumulative)
All U.S.-listed public companies	10,068
Market value of less than $1 billion	7,980
Market value of more than $20 million	4,015
Financial statement date no older than six months	3,204
Number of employees is 10 or more	2,828
Insider ownership of 1% or more	1,581
Country not equal to China	1,571
Trailing revenue of at least $10 million	1,456

Source: AAII Stock Investor Pro, based on database update as of June 1, 2012.

TABLE 7.2 U.S. Companies Passing Tightened Small-Cap Investability Criteria

Screening Criteria	Companies (cumulative)
Companies passing criteria in previous table	1,456
Market value of more than $50 million	1,261
Stock exchange not equal to Pink Sheets	1,218
Industry not equal to Gold & Silver	1,216
Industry not equal to Metal Mining	1,212
Industry not equal to Tobacco	1,212
Industry not equal to Biotechnology	1,166
Industry not equal to Semiconductors	1,116
Industry not equal to Airlines	1,113
Average daily trading volume of at least $500,000	756

Source: AAII Stock Investor Pro, based on database update as of June 1, 2012.

Sheets, and excluding industries we consider outside our circle of competence. We also require average daily trading volume of at least $500,000. We are thus left with 756 investable small-cap stocks. This number is still a bit unwieldy, but ambitious investors could choose to narrow this universe down further over a period of two to three years, during which they devote one day of analysis to each company. Such an exercise could leave the investor with a manageable tracking list of perhaps 200 to 250 small companies.

Zeroing in on Investable Companies Meeting Specific Criteria

Like many investors who run quantitative stock screens as part of their research process, we like to rank stocks based on a variety of performance or asset value criteria. The goal of these screens is to narrow the field of companies meriting further analysis. The downside of any mechanical screen is that we might miss good opportunities while devoting time to companies that are cheap for good reason. These drawbacks have prompted David Einhorn to embrace a slightly different approach to idea screening: "We take the traditional value investor's process and just flip it around a little bit. The traditional value investor asks 'Is this cheap?' and then 'Why is it cheap?' We start by identifying a reason something might be mispriced, and then if we find a reason why something is likely mispriced, then we make a determination whether it's cheap."[11]

The following are a few ways we might screen for compelling opportunities within our previously defined investable small-cap universe.

SAMPLE STOCK SCREEN: DEEP VALUE **Screening criteria:** price to tangible book below 1.1; debt to equity below 0.2.

This screen seeks to identify micro caps with a strong balance sheet (high book value and low debt) without regard for profitability. By screening for stocks that trade at or below book value, we boost the likelihood of finding companies that can be bought for less than replacement cost. As for book value, we are interested in tangible book rather than total book. Tangible book is a more appropriate measure in the case of statistically cheap companies because they are more likely to have intangibles whose carrying values exceed their true worth. We want the cheap companies that pass our screen to have low financial leverage and therefore a lower likelihood of going bankrupt.

Profitability is obviously a desirable characteristic, but by excluding a profit requirement from the screen, we hope to identify some companies for which we can ascertain that current losses are likely transitory and that profitability may be restored in the not-too-distant future. If you prefer to narrow your results from the start, add a profitability requirement to the initial screen, such as a P/E (price/earnings) multiple above zero. This will leave you with companies that are not losing money, even if their profitability is currently severely depressed.

SAMPLE STOCK SCREEN: ACTIVIST TARGETS **Screening criteria:** price to tangible book value below 0.5; current assets minus total liabilities above 50 percent of market value; insider ownership below 20 percent.

This screen seeks to identify companies that may unlock value through a corporate event, such as a sale, liquidation, or recapitalization. Companies ranking highly meet Ben Graham's net net criteria, raising the possibility of a discount to liquidation value. Requiring insider ownership of not more than 20 percent is crucial because an outside catalyst is usually needed when management chooses to sit on significant balance sheet liquidity without creating value. Outsiders can put pressure on management to do the right thing by threatening a proxy fight or takeover bid.

In some cases, companies meeting these criteria also have material net operating loss carryforwards that could be used to offset future income taxes. Such NOL assets usually come with a valuation allowance in the case of companies meeting net net valuation criteria, suggesting that the stated balance sheet may underestimate true asset value. In addition to requiring strong liquidity, the screen also focuses on companies trading at steep discounts to tangible book value. This condition ensures that shareholders stand a good chance of not losing money, and perhaps have an opportunity to make money, in a liquidation scenario.

Liquidations are difficult propositions for the creation of equity value, as the carrying value of assets might be impaired while the carrying value of liabilities typically remains unchanged in a liquidation. Often, additional expenses and liabilities arise for legal fees, severance costs, asset retirement obligations, and other items that do not exist in a going-concern scenario. As a result, a strategic sale or recapitalization is usually preferable to an outright liquidation.

SAMPLE STOCK SCREEN: MARGIN UPSIDE POTENTIAL **Screening criteria:** enterprise value to sales below 1.5; debt to equity below 0.3.

This screen seeks to identify small stocks with a large revenue base relative to enterprise value. Such firms may be more likely to have margin leverage opportunities than firms trading at a high multiple of revenue. Firms that trade at a high sales multiple typically have higher current operating and net margins, so that their P/E-based valuation may be reasonably low. Firms that have higher profit margins, however, may be less likely to grow their margins than firms that have lower margins, hence our focus on companies with a low multiple of revenue and, implicitly, lower current margins. Since most free online screeners look for price-to-revenue rather than enterprise value-to-revenue multiples, we add a requirement that all results have low financial leverage (debt-to-equity ratio below 0.3). This requirement eliminates most companies with a large discrepancy between price to revenue and enterprise value to revenue, as net debt represents the difference between the two numerators.

A caveat regarding this stock screen: As we look for low enterprise value-to-revenue stocks, we may unfairly favor companies in industries that tend to have low normalized profit margins, including retailers, distributors, and other businesses whose products or services may be highly commoditized. Companies with low normalized margins may not have more margin upside potential than companies in industries with high normalized margins. A better screen for identifying margin upside potential may be one that considers each company's current operating margin relative to other companies in the same industry. Still, studies have shown that revenue-based valuation metrics are quite useful in identifying potential outperformers among small-cap stocks.

SAMPLE STOCK SCREEN: GROWTH AT A REASONABLE PRICE **Screening criteria:** price to book below 2; debt to equity below 0.5; P/E below 15; revenue growth above 10 percent; optional: dividend yield above 0.5 percent.

Our top-line growth requirement is only 10 percent, so a key focus of follow-up research should be whether the revenue growth of the identified companies is likely to accelerate or decelerate. Accelerating double-digit top-line growth and a P/E below 15 might be a winning formula. The next step in vetting the companies that meet these two criteria might be to consider likely margin performance. Companies that grow revenue at the expense of profit margins are less attractive because their profit growth will trail revenue growth. Since profit growth is ultimately more important, we want to be comfortable that the company in question is well positioned to accelerate revenue growth while keeping margins constant or, better yet, while expanding margins.

We add the price-to-book requirement to eliminate firms whose underlying low net equity base may at some point make it more difficult to ward off competitors, thereby negatively affecting profitability. We add the debt-to-equity requirement to eliminate firms whose strong bottom-line performance is primarily a result of financial leverage. We eschew these because it cuts both ways—when times get tough, the pain shareholders endure may significantly exceed the difficulties of the underlying business. Prudent investors seek to avoid such arrangements.

Beyond Screening: Other Ways of Finding Compelling Small- and Micro-Cap Ideas

Many of the best small-stock opportunities elude discovery by quantitative screens. The reasons include rapid change in company fundamentals, the disproportionate impact of management quality on value, and the tendency of small companies to lump nonrecurring items into financial reports without showing results on an adjusted basis. Quantitative screens, no matter how well designed, remain crude tools for finding interesting ideas. We use them primarily when the field of potential candidates is too large to allow analysis of each individual security. But what if there was a middle ground between screening and laboring from A to Z? Once we have defined an investable universe of perhaps 1,000 U.S.-listed small stocks or a few thousand globally, how do we focus our attention on a manageable number of promising candidates while avoiding the limitations of screens? The following tactics go beyond quantitative screening and focus on other ways of generating ideas.

Big to Small, Small to Small, or Small to Big: Where Is This Company Going?

Historical context helps us understand how a company has developed over time. Attractive small stocks generally either succeed in reinvesting capital at high returns over long periods of time, or they send capital to shareholders in the form of dividends or repurchases when reinvestment returns are unattractive. In the former scenario, a company should get bigger over time, putting itself on a trajectory to outgrow the definition of micro cap or even small cap. In the second scenario, a company may not grow much in size, but it may return significant capital to shareholders, providing them with an attractive total return on investment. The problem for long-term investors typically lies with companies that may be cheap but whose management teams keep sinking new capital into projects that offer only mediocre returns. In such cases, an attractive earnings yield may not translate into an attractive long-term return for shareholders as cash is put to suboptimal use.

Another category includes small stocks that might have been considered mid caps or even large caps but have fallen from grace. If we view the fall as indicative of the forward-looking trajectory of the underlying businesses, we will be inclined to pass on an investment. However, as the famous Horace saying goes, "Many shall be restored that are now fallen and many shall fall that are now in honor."[12] Horace was actually referring to words rather than people or institutions, but the statement captures the concept of mean reversion so well that it has become widely cited in investment literature. Many investment thought leaders, including Ben Graham and Jeremy Grantham, have highlighted mean reversion as a central concept in investing.

It would be foolish to dismiss out of hand companies whose recent stock price decline qualifies them as small stocks, yet some small-cap investors may be doing just that, as they find it difficult to stray from the investment universe they have built over time. Investors who like to track companies for a long time to build up a sufficient level of comfort may incur an opportunity cost. While tracking small companies for a long time before investing is generally desirable, investors can also benefit from acting decisively on new small-cap opportunities resulting from fear or a short-term disappointment of investor expectations. During the market downturn of late 2008 and early 2009, companies like Boise, Crocs, Pier 1 Imports, Select Comfort, and many credit-sensitive businesses fell into small- or micro-cap range, only to rebound 10-fold or more in price over the following couple of years. Those who bought into such new small and micro caps heeded the proverbial advice to buy when there is blood in the streets—and they were richly rewarded for doing so. Of course, this is not an unconditional endorsement of buying into financially distressed businesses trading at near-bankruptcy valuations, as many such companies do end up bankrupting or diluting the interests of shareholders.

How do we distinguish between a fallen angel doomed to irrelevance or worse and one likely to take off again? This is an extremely difficult question but also one to which a correct answer could have tremendous value. Situations in which we are confronted with a fallen angel are almost by definition high-uncertainty scenarios, unless the worst case has already materialized and the distressed equity has become almost certainly worthless. High-uncertainty situations typically involve a wide range of potential outcomes and highly subjective probabilities associated with those outcomes. We are not only rolling a die, but the die is so imperfect that we are forced to guess the probabilities associated with six outcomes that are in turn anything but clear-cut. To paraphrase a former U.S. defense secretary, we are dealing with known unknowns and unknown unknowns, each of which may occur with an unknown probability. As a result, judgment informed by past experience becomes crucial, though perhaps the most profitable judgment would be to place the fallen angel into the too hard pile and move on.

The enterprising investor willing to accept enormous uncertainty and the possibility of capital loss may consider the following factors when judging whether a fallen angel will fly again. First, it helps to know why a stock has collapsed. If it is the result of a long-term blow to the business model, as was the case with video rental chains or newspaper publishers, management will find it difficult to restore the business to former glory. However, if the stock collapse resulted from the existence of distressed sellers, a liquidity rather than a solvency issue, or a business going through a cyclical industry trough, the stock price may rebound under certain circumstances. Graham Cunningham once told us about the case of United Rentals, an equipment-leasing company whose stock price collapsed under the cloud of a perceived liquidity issue during the crisis of 2008–2009. The market quotation of the equity was decidedly too pessimistic, unless the liquidity issue forced the company into bankruptcy. Cunningham assessed the situation in this context, so when major shareholder Bruce Berkowitz publicly stated that the Fairholme Fund would support the company through any liquidity crunch, Cunningham's investment case was complete. With Fairholme firmly behind United Rentals, market concern around the perceived liquidity issue receded, putting the equity on a path to revaluation in line with long-term intrinsic value.

Situations in which a major investor can serve as the value-unlocking catalyst have not gone unnoticed by aggressive funds willing to exploit the misfortune of companies and their shareholders. As a result, distressed equities occasionally become targets of funds looking to inject equity capital on preferential terms, thereby diluting other shareholders and impairing their ability to recover unrealized losses. To avoid becoming victims of such schemes, we weigh heavily insider ownership of common stock in distressed companies. It is easy for a beleaguered management team to give away equity on the cheap to prop up the balance sheet and secure their jobs, unless the CEO owns a large equity stake. In that case, the CEO will be likely to explore every alternative before considering a dilutive equity offering.

Hidden Inflection Points and How to Uncover Them

Hundreds of public companies are likely to find themselves in an exciting place at any given time: They are experiencing a major positive inflection point in their businesses. While the past may have been one of stagnation or operating losses, the future for these companies looks bright. A biotech company may stand at such an inflection point because it has just received FDA approval for a major drug. A satellite radio company may be at an inflection point because it has just signed deals to have its system preinstalled by major auto manufacturers. A technology company may have just acquired a start-up with a highly promising product. Whatever the scenario, a positive inflection point produces a hockey-stick improvement in operating performance, creating a potentially rewarding situation for investors.

Unfortunately, the market is pretty good at anticipating inflection points, and valuations reflect this fact. Legions of biotech analysts closely follow the FDA approval progress of various drugs. There is also no shortage of investors envisioning fledgling companies changing the world someday. XM Satellite Radio lost hundreds of millions of dollars in 2005, but investors valued it at several billion dollars. The reason? They anticipated—it turns out wrongly— a major positive inflection point. Disciplined investors resist the impulse to invest when everyone anticipates an inflection point. The challenge is to uncover situations that remain underappreciated or misunderstood. Naturally, these kinds of situations are most often found in the arena of small public companies.

The rewards are substantial, but how do we find such opportunities? We may be able to uncover hidden inflection points by scouring the small-cap landscape for companies with two or more businesses, one of which is typically a large, declining legacy business. If the other business is a profitable growth business, we may have found a gold mine. The reason is that, at a company level, operating performance probably appears lackluster. States value investor Aaron Edelheit: "I'm looking for . . . special situations, such as a company with two divisions, in which the poor division is masking the other division that is very attractive." As most investors find small, underfollowed companies via quantitative stock screens, a company that at the corporate level shows stagnant revenue growth and poor earnings will fail the test, often resulting in a low market value. By reading earnings releases and regulatory filings of small companies, we put ourselves in a position to find stocks that look like duds but actually hide a valuable growth engine. If we are lucky, the market quotation of the entire company will be less than our estimate of the value of the most promising business segment alone.

Dissecting companies with multiple segments is not the only way to uncover hidden inflection points. Occasionally, simply reading the public filings of a small- or micro-cap company can yield surprising insights. Eric Khrom, managing partner of Khrom Capital Management, tells the story of how he was able to act on a valuable piece of information in an 8-K filing by Patient Safety Technologies, a company that sells surgical sponges with a barcode on them, thereby addressing the costly issue of sponges accidentally remaining inside a patient following surgery. According to Khrom, "There is a lot of time pressure in the operating room, and there are 32 million procedures done annually . . . there are about 4,000 retained sponges" at a cost to the industry of $1.7 billion. "So, this is a very serious need this company is providing. All the hospitals that have so far used their system have had zero retained sponges." Khrom takes us back to the moment he uncovered a likely inflection point: "I'm reading the 8-K, and I notice that this company is still at its infancy. They have about 80 hospitals, and they are about break-even. . . . Reading the 8-K was very interesting because they pretty much announced in one sentence that they signed on the second-largest hospital operator in the United States. They went from having about 80 hospitals to immediately having 255 hospitals."[13]

PT INDOSAT CASE STUDY: HITTING A MOBILE PENETRATION INFLECTION POINT This number-two Indonesian phone service provider stood at a major positive inflection point at the beginning of 2002. The company's cellular business was taking off. However, because Indosat's core international long-distance business stagnated due to competition, investors shunned the stock. At the end of 2001, Indosat had a market value of $916 million (stock price of $8.85) and was trading at 1.1x tangible book value, 5.2x trailing earnings, and 2.2x enterprise value to revenue. Political risks notwithstanding, such a valuation would have been justified only for a company in rapid decline.

Meanwhile, Indosat faced a bright future in 2002. Its Satelindo subsidiary was the second-largest mobile phone service provider in Indonesia, a country with cellular penetration of 5 percent at the time, significantly below that of similar Asian countries. Indosat's mobile business was highly profitable and was growing by ~30 percent annually. It was also rapidly becoming a significant slice of the company's overall revenue and profits, with sustained growth in the mobile business likely to translate into accelerating growth at the company level.

Indosat's mobile business went on to contribute 62 percent of revenue in 2003, up from 48 percent in 2002 and 34 percent in 2001. This growth fueled overall revenue increases from 5.1 billion rupiah in 2001 to 8.2 billion in 2003. Operating income grew from 1.8 billion rupiah in 2001 to 2.3 billion in 2003. By the time Indosat

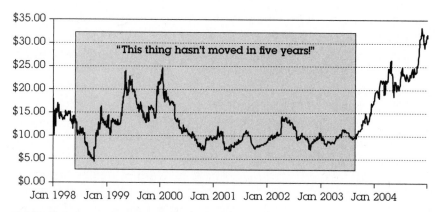

FIGURE 7.2 Indosat Stock Price Chart

filed an annual report on Form 20-F in mid-2004, the stock had climbed to $21.20, up 140 percent from year-end 2001. The total return was sweetened by a meaningful dividend yield.

In retrospect, we may wonder how the market could possibly value Indosat at just five times trailing earnings in 2002 and 2003 when the mobile subsidiary was already showing strong growth and was quickly becoming a large piece of the business. Given the wide availability of public information on Indosat, behavioral factors might have played at least as important a role in keeping investors from embracing Indosat shares as did the fact that Indosat was underfollowed. Quite simply, many investors seem to lack confidence in their own reasoning unless others agree with them. When I pitched Indosat to a few colleagues in the financial services industry in 2002, they seemed to doubt their judgment in deference to the market's apparent negative verdict, as expressed in Indosat's low stock price. A typical excuse for not investing was "This thing hasn't moved in five years!" Figure 7.2 illustrates why relying on a historical price chart has little relevance in investing, especially if a fundamental inflection point is at hand.

MEADOW VALLEY CASE STUDY: GROWTH BUSINESS MASKED BY LEGACY LOSSES Meadow Valley Corporation would have shown up on some micro-cap screens in early 2004. If we looked for companies with a low ratio of enterprise value to revenue and a high ratio of tangible book value to market value, we might have come across the company. It was neither highly leveraged nor losing money. Meadow Valley, a Phoenix, Arizona-based provider of heavy construction services and materials, had the financial attributes summarized in Table 7.3.

The company had revenue in excess of $150 million and an enterprise value of only $16 million, quite a statistical find for a company that was not losing money. It was not exactly minting money either, however. Net income for the 12 months ended September 30, 2003, was slightly more than half a million dollars, a dismal net margin. It turned out that Meadow Valley was in a highly competitive business with razor-thin gross margins (4.8 percent for the first nine months of 2003). Most investors eschew companies with such low margins, but even low-margin businesses can be good investments under the right circumstances. If Meadow Valley could expand its net margin by just one percentage point, net income would jump by $1.5 million. At roughly $2 million in net income, even a low-quality business such as Meadow Valley's road construction business would likely be worth no less than $15 million, a 75 percent return based on a market value of $8.6 million in early 2004.

A look under the surface would have revealed that future margin improvement might not just be wishful thinking, for Meadow Valley was hiding a major fundamental inflection point. Consider the performance of the company's two businesses, as shown in Table 7.4.

Construction services was the dog, but the materials business was fast-growing and boasted a gross margin of close to 10 percent, significantly above the company's overall gross margin. Materials was quickly becoming a large piece of the pie, and it seemed only a matter of time until the undiscovered engine started accelerating the performance of the entire company.

An analysis of the materials business would have shown that the segment alone was worth quite a bit more than the market was valuing the entire company. With materials revenue growing by more than 20 percent and segment net income exceeding $1 million, rational investors might have been willing to pay a P/E multiple of 10 to 15× for the materials business. This alone would have resulted in a market value of $10 to 15 million.

A risk existed that the construction services segment would worsen and smother the performance of the materials segment

TABLE 7.3 Meadow Valley Corp. Selected Financial Data, as of February 20, 2004

Trading Data		Valuation Metrics	
Price (2/20/2004)	$2.40	Tangible book/market value	1.4x
Shares out (mn)	3.6	Price/LTM EPS	11.9x
Market value	$8.6	Enterprise value/LTM revenue	0.1x
Enterprise value	$16.1		

	Fiscal Year Ended			Nine Months Ended	
Operating Data	12/31/2000	12/31/2001	12/31/2002	9/30/2002	9/30/2003
Revenue	$163.6	$174.1	$151.0	$114.5	$117.0
Operating income	($2.1)	($3.4)	$0.9	$0.9	$0.6
Net income	($1.6)	($2.5)	$0.7	$0.5	$0.4
EPS	($0.44)	($0.71)	$0.21	$0.13	$0.12

Source: Company data, The Manual of Ideas analysis.

TABLE 7.4 Meadow Valley Corp. Selected Financial Data by Division

($ in millions)	Fiscal Year Ended				Nine Months Ended	
	12/31/2000	12/31/2001	12/31/2002		9/30/2002	9/30/2003
Revenue						
Construction Services	$144.6	$143.1	$114.2		$87.9	$84.1
Construction Materials	$19.0	$31.0	$36.8		$26.6	$33.0
Gross Profit						
Construction Services	$3.9	$3.1	$3.6		$2.5	$2.5
Construction Materials	($0.6)	$0.0	$1.8		$2.7	$3.2
Net Income						
Construction Services	($0.7)	($1.9)	($0.5)		($0.3)	($0.3)
Construction Materials	($0.8)	($0.6)	$1.3		$0.8	$0.8

Source: Company data, The Manual of Ideas analysis.

for a long time. However, as we would have learned from reading the company's SEC filings, losses on one specific project in Utah accounted for the entire loss of the construction segment—and then some. Meadow Valley appeared to be losing roughly $2 million on that project per year. However, there was a high likelihood that losses would be lower in the future, and the project seemed to be nearing completion anyway.

Other idiosyncrasies made an investment in Meadow Valley even more attractive. For instance, the company was still fighting in court to receive payment of millions of dollars in project work the company had performed for governmental agencies. At issue were disputes over who should carry the burden of major cost overruns. In early 2004, Meadow Valley settled one of the claims and received a $7 million cash payment.

Last but not least, investors reaching out to Meadow Valley CEO Brad Larson might have been impressed by his open and honest communication regarding the challenges facing the company. Larson seemed to care about shareholders, even if the company's past stock performance had been dismal.

What happened? In December 2004, Meadow Valley announced the spin-off of its materials business in an IPO. In February 2005, the company disclosed that one million shares, comprising 40 percent postdeal ownership of the materials subsidiary, would be sold in a firm commitment underwritten offering at $12 per share, implying an $18 million value for Meadow Valley's 60 percent majority stake in the materials business. Meadow Valley shares closed at $5.10 on the day of the announcement of tentative IPO terms, implying a market value of $18 million, a 113 percent return in one year. Figure 7.3 shows the progression of the company's stock price in the context of key corporate events.

Asking the Right Questions of Small-Cap Prospects

When we use screening as a first step in the idea generation process, the kind of stock screen we run will affect our follow-up research, as each screen produces a list of companies with a different set of issues.

FIGURE 7.3 Meadow Valley Corporation Annotated Stock Price Chart

If we run a deep value screen, we will be looking at companies that may be going through a downturn in their businesses, perhaps causing their stock prices to languish below tangible book value per share. In such a case, we will be most concerned about the screened companies' ability to survive and turn around operations. To gauge survivability, we may focus on liquidity requirements, the ratio of debt to equity, financial covenants, and the near-term profit outlook for the business.

Contrast this with the research we may do after running a screen for companies meeting selected criteria for growth at a reasonable price. Our primary goal will be not to gauge survivability but rather to ascertain the prospects for continued revenue growth and margin expansion. Adjustments in analytical focus notwithstanding, we may structure the research process to answer several initial questions, followed by in-depth analysis and, ultimately, a judgment call on whether an investment makes sense.

Did a Company Pass the Right Screen for the Wrong Reason?

Anytime we use quantitative screening as the first step in the idea generation process, we may want to determine if there is an obvious reason that a company should not be considered further. This allows us to eliminate bad investments quickly and move on. To do so, we check if the financial data used in a stock screen are still up-to-date, as some companies passing small- or micro-cap screens may have missed their filing deadlines or stopped reporting altogether. We also ascertain whether a company has passed a screen due to a one-time financial benefit or another nonrepeatable factor. We check if any recent news is likely to have a major negative impact on future operations, as companies passing value-oriented screens may have issued bad news not yet reflected in their financial statements.

Do the Financial Statements Raise Any Red Flags?

We conduct a cursory review of each screened company's financial statements to develop a general feel for the numbers. We want to detect key historical trends in revenue, gross profit, and operating profit. We also check historical cash flow statements to ensure that cash realization over time does not significantly deviate from reported income. We look for red flags such as rapid and sustained growth in receivables as a percentage of sales or inventories as a percentage of cost of goods. We also look for postponement of expenses via line items such as software capitalization.

We probe the most recent balance sheet for the quality of assets—the more readily they are turned into cash, the better. We review the types of major liabilities—deferred revenue is good, while debt with a near-term maturity may be bad. We also check whether the shareholders' equity section includes preferred stock. As common stock investors, we exclude preferred stock from shareholders' equity and treat it as similar to debt. This is important because many stock-screening tools include preferred stock in equity, raising the possibility that the true price-to-book multiple is higher than shown. Such a scenario would make a company more expensive than it appears to be.

Who Has Been Buying and Selling the Shares?

We review recent insider transactions and a list of major institutional shareholders. Insider selling may be a big negative in the small- and micro-cap arena, as greater informational asymmetry between insiders and investors exists in this underfollowed part of the market. Insider buying, of course, is a positive, especially if insiders have purchased stock recently at prices higher than the current price. Getting a sense for the institutions owning a stock can also be helpful, especially if we have context around the investment approach of those institutions and their rationale for owning the company under consideration.

What Is Management's Attitude toward Outside Shareholders?

When gauging the friendliness of management, we want to see relatively low cash compensation and no bonuses if corporate performance has been lacking. Other cash compensation, such as car allowances, is an acid test we frequently use. CEOs who receive a car allowance (especially if it is more than $1,000 a month) are more likely to be preoccupied with getting reimbursed for every little expense than those who forgo such compensation. Some proxy statements do not disclose the amount of other compensation but state that such compensation amounts to less than 10 percent of total compensation. Such lack of disclosure may be even more alarming. Stock option awards also sometimes run amok at small companies, and it is important to verify that shareholders are not turning over several percentage points of equity to insiders each year. Such pillaging of value can significantly lower returns over time.

We like to see senior management own a sizable portion of a company, but not too much. We consider insider ownership of about 20 percent as ideal, with insiders owning enough to care but not so much that they are immune to potential shareholder action. Insiders can make themselves immune, however, even without majority ownership—via devices such as a staggered board of directors, poison pills, insider ownership of a supervoting class of common stock, or generous severance packages in case of a change in control. We also check the proxy statement for related-party transactions, sometimes also referred to as certain transactions. Such transactions can be innocuous, or they can represent sweetheart deals for insiders that are emblematic of a general disregard for shareholders. One of the worst kinds of related-party transactions is money lent to insiders to purchase company stock. Very often in the past, such loans were forgiven if the stock price declined subsequent to the purchase by insiders.

Paul Sonkin shares an interesting perspective:

One of the documents we spend a lot of time on is the proxy statement. It discusses the compensation, the board, and has the "certain transactions" section, which is where you find the insider skullduggery that's going on. With a lot of these companies, you'll find that the CEO owns the building and leases it back to the company; or what expenses are being paid for by the company. Usually, you're trying to separate the wheat from the chaff with these small companies. If you have an owner-operator, it's usually preferential to an operator. But we've seen different cases—we've seen cases where management owns a lot of stock and they still take big salaries and they treat the company like their own piggybank.[14]

Where Are the Shares Relative to Their Historical Range?

If a company's stock price chart shows that the shares trade near multiyear highs, we may require greater proof that the stock is indeed undervalued. If a company has in the past traded substantially below the current price, we want to know why it traded so low to minimize the possibility of missing an important risk, such as the cyclical nature of a business. Unlike technical analysts, we use charts for historical context, not as predictive tools. A price chart does not figure into our final verdict on the attractiveness of an equity investment. It merely represents a contextual tool for helping determine where the burden of proof should lie during further analysis of a potential opportunity.

The per-share trading range of a stock generally tells us less than does a trading range modified for certain operating data. For example, when we analyze how a company's current forward P/E ratio compares to the company's historical range of forward P/E ratios, we can quickly gauge how the market's perception of a company's earnings growth prospects has changed over time. Also useful might be comparing the P/E ratio percentile rank of a company within its industry to the historical percentile rank. This might reveal how a company is perceived relative to other companies in the same industry. The P/E ratios can be highly volatile, as annual profitability for all but the most stable businesses also tends to be volatile. As a result, plotting a historical chart of enterprise value to revenue, in absolute terms and as a percentile rank, could give us more meaningful insights.

Moving on to the Subjective Qualities of a Business

If the preceding checks give us comfort that we are dealing with a shareholder-friendly and statistically cheap company, we may launch into a more qualitative assessment of a company's business model and long-term prospects. As part of this second-step analysis, we scrutinize the company's most recent annual and quarterly reports. We also read other historical reports to see how management's commentary has evolved over the years. We try to judge the quality and competitiveness of the company's products and services, as well as the likely durability of any advantage the company may have.

At this point in the idea assessment process, we may spend a lot of time and effort analyzing a company's position in the industry, as well as the prospects of that industry. We may speak with the company, competitors, customers, suppliers, and anyone else who can help us answer specific research questions. It is not always possible to get information from the right people when analyzing a small company, so the amount of due diligence that is practicable for a passive investor may vary greatly by company.

The final decision to purchase a stock will be the result of subjective judgment. This is where it becomes clearest that investing is art rather than science. No treatise on investing can spell out how to make a decision on every potential opportunity. However, throughout this book, we have sought to share insights into making sensible investment decisions.

Key Takeaways

Here are our top 10 takeaways from this chapter:

1. Several key developments have created opportunities for small-stock investors, including an increase in the size of institutional portfolios, an escalation of compensation expectations,

exclusion of small stocks from major market indices, and scant research coverage by sell-side firms.

2. Major shareholders may have more influence on small-company CEOs than they do on their large-company counterparts, as more investment firms can credibly put small companies in play.

3. We find that small stocks outperform large stocks by a statistically significant margin over time. While the results differ based on the time periods examined and the definitions used, the verdict is clearly in favor of small stocks.

4. Even if small caps as a group stop outperforming large caps, the differential between top and bottom performers should continue to be greater in the case of smaller stocks, providing opportunities for research-driven investors.

5. While underfollowed situations generally offer fertile ground for research-driven investors, it is not always necessary that many people analyze an investment for pricing inefficiency to be eliminated.

6. In the small-cap arena, moving beyond quantitative screens is valuable because few professional investors are willing to start at *A* and work through *Z* in their appraisal of the qualitative value drivers of small companies.

7. Small-company executives are also generally more forthcoming than are corporate executives whose ability to communicate spontaneously has been lawyered into oblivion. Ask a small-company CEO how business is going, and you might get an answer.

8. One well-known drawback of small-stock investing is the, at times, severely constrained trading liquidity of smaller companies. Wider bid-ask spreads, greater market impact, and perhaps greater trading commissions conspire to make entering and exiting the equity of small companies a costly affair.

9. Many of the best small-stock opportunities elude discovery by quantitative screens. The reasons include rapid change in company fundamentals, the disproportionate impact of management quality on value, and the tendency of small companies to lump nonrecurring items into financial reports.

10. We may be able to uncover hidden inflection points by scouring the small-cap landscape for companies with two or more businesses, one of which is typically a large, declining legacy business. If the other business is a profitable growth business, we may have found a compelling opportunity.

Notes

1. *The Manual of Ideas*, February 2011, 9.
2. *The Manual of Ideas*, August 2009, 29.
3. UBS Financial Services Inc., "Revenge of the Large Caps," http://finan
   cialservicesinc.ubs.com/Home/PWSmain/0,,SE3424-EN3424,00.html,
   accessed October 31, 2005.
4. Curt Morrison, "Find Your Investing Edge," Morningstar.com, March
   30, 2005, http://news.morningstar.com/doc/article/0,1,130088,00.html?
   asection=archive.
5. Tweedy Browne, "What Has Worked in Investing," http://www.tweedy
   .com/resources/library_docs/papers/WhatHasWorkedFundVersionWeb
   .pdf, 42–45, accessed on June 1, 2012.
6. O'Shaughnessy (2012), 71.
7. Ibid., 68.
8. Up-to-date data available online at http://mba.tuck.dartmouth.edu/
   pages/faculty/ken.french/data_library.html.
9. Ellenoff, Douglas S., "Going Dark: What Companies Need to Know,"
   www.egsllp.com/GoingDark.ppt, accessed on June 1, 2012.
10. *The Manual of Ideas*, November 2009, 37.
11. Interview with David Einhorn, Value Investor Insight, March 23, 2005,
    2, www.valueinvestorinsight.com.
12. Horace, *Ars Poetica*.
13. *The Manual of Ideas* interview with Eric Khrom, New York, 2012.
14. *The Manual of Ideas*, November 2009, 36.

CHAPTER 8

Special Situations

Uncovering Opportunity in Event-Driven Investments

Simplicity is the ultimate sophistication.

—Leonardo da Vinci

So much to discuss, so little space. This sums up our predicament in this chapter, as the sprawling topic of special-situation investments can hardly be confined to the available pages. That said, if we succeed only in demystifying the subject and sharing a few overarching thoughts, you may find it a bit easier to progress on the path toward acquiring expertise in the special situation categories you find most intriguing. Kenneth Shubin Stein, portfolio manager of Spencer Capital Management, frames the topic as follows: "For us, special situations run the gamut from companies that are in distress, in bankruptcy, are in turnaround situations, companies that are doing spinoffs or debt recapitalization or large share repurchases or are experiencing significant short-term events that are impairing their earnings power but don't impair the long-term intrinsic value of the company."[1]

Framed even more broadly, special situations encompass equities whose near- to medium-term stock price performance is largely independent of the performance of equity markets in general. In this context, stock price performance refers to the total investment return, including dividends, other cash payouts, and noncash value that may accrue to investors. Notice we refer neither to the performance of the business itself nor to long-term performance. Business performance, as distinct from the stock price, may be independent of market performance, even for companies that do not find themselves in a special situation.

Meanwhile, every security might be considered a special situation, given a long-enough time horizon. The long-term stock price reflects the market's role as a weighing machine rather than a voting machine. Since we wish to examine special-situation investments as distinct from normal-situation investments, we avoid a definition that includes substantially all companies. We therefore limit the time horizon to roughly two years, while allowing for exceptions.

Some investors refer to special situations as event-driven investments, highlighting the fact that one or more near-term corporate events are likely to drive the investment return. We do not view potential acquisition targets as special-situation investments, despite the fact that an acquisition may qualify as a material event. Rumored acquisitions appear too speculative in this context. Event-driven opportunities typically allow the investor to conceive of a timetable according to which the strategic event(s) may unfold. In the case of major corporate actions, such as spin-offs or recapitalizations, management may lay out an anticipated timetable, aiding the analytical process of equity investors.

The Approach: Why It Works

The category of special situations overlaps with the definitions of other types of equity investments. A proportion of small-cap equities may be dealing with special events at any given time. Deep value equities become special situations when they start liquidating assets, paying special dividends, or pursuing other strategic actions. The line is blurred in many cases, but this should not discourage us. Any framing of the topic of special situations should offer not a rigid framework, but rather a loose guide to qualifying opportunities.

Numerous academic studies confirm the outperformance of special-situation investments over time, but a distinction is needed between the various types of situations that fall into this category. The relative performance dynamics evolve materially over time, making reliance on historical studies inappropriate. For example, following the publication of Joel Greenblatt's ground-breaking book on special situations, *You Can Be a Stock Market Genius*, in 1997, many would-be geniuses embraced areas such as spin-offs, rights offerings, restructurings, recapitalizations, and risk arbitrage. The flood of talent and capital took these areas from obscurity to popularity, reducing prospective investment returns. While large institutional investors may not devote much attention to special situations, the rise of go-anywhere hedge funds provides a basis for sustained interest in these types of securities.

In Table 8.1, we summarize some of the types of situations that may create opportunity for equity investors. Not all of these situations fit the definition of event-driven investments, but they all represent areas of potential inefficiency.

The Rewards of Obscurity

The more obscure a market niche, the higher the likelihood that diligent investors will generate market-beating returns. Sahm Adrangi, portfolio manager of Kerrisdale Capital Management, points to an area of outperformance for his firm: "We've made some of our best investments by becoming experts in weird and unusual areas of the public markets, and using that deep understanding to our advantage. For instance, we generated strong returns on SPAC [special purpose acquisition company] warrants in the second half of 2009, and accomplished that by becoming experts on how SPACs operated."[2] Greater investor interest in SPACs, partly due to the experience of firms like Kerrisdale, may have reduced forward-looking prospects for investors in this area. Moreover, SPACs also illustrate the ebb and flow of special opportunities, as various factors conspire to change the supply of such situations. In the case of SPACs, they may have peaked in late 2007, when Liberty Acquisition Corp. raised $900 million in a related offering. The ensuing financial crisis appears to have impacted the ability of SPACs to obtain funding. It is unclear whether SPAC vehicles will regain the position they enjoyed briefly as an alternative to private equity vehicles.

As the residential real estate upturn accelerated in the United States in the mid-2000s, the emergence of new financial products created a whole slew of obscure special-situation opportunities.

TABLE 8.1   Potential Sources of Opportunity in the Stock Market

What?	Why?
End-of-year tax selling	Value of tax shield impacts sell decision.
Deletion from index	Index funds must sell regardless of investment merit.
Dividend cancellation	Income funds and other yield seekers likely to sell.
Distressed seller	Near-term liquidity more important to seller than full value.
Spin-off	Holders of parent may sell spin-off without regard for merit.
Rights offering	Distressed companies recapitalize in shareholder-friendly way.
Growth disappointment	Growth investors sell; value investors not yet ready to buy.
High fear factor	Buyers likely doing more due diligence than sellers.
High greed factor	Short sellers likely doing more due diligence than buyers.
High judgment factor	Value not evident from book or earnings; answer years away.
Extrapolation of fad	Analysts extrapolate faddish growth too far into the future.
Friendly management	Investors underestimate benefits of good capital allocation.
Valuable intangibles	Brand, distribution, etc., not reflected on balance sheet.
1x book, low EPS, no debt	High-ROC firm with strong asset value temporarily depressed.
Recency bias	Investors overweight recent experience, misjudging situation.
Promotional company	Sell-side support and PR can keep stocks artificially high.
Multiple assets	Sum-of-the-parts value may exceed market value.

Source: The Manual of Ideas.

Those willing and able to work through thousands of pages of mortgage-related security prospectuses might have gained insights similar to those of Michael Burry. This huge but short-lived opportunity to generate outsize returns was dubbed *The Big Short* by Michael Lewis. While many investors look back at the chance missed in the subprime mortgage bust, Burry has moved on to other atypical financial investments, including farmland.

Adrangi's experience in SPACs preceded his even more rewarding interest in so-called Chinese RTOs—companies based in China but publicly listed on a U.S. stock exchange via reverse merger. Scores of RTOs were introduced to U.S. investors over the previous decade, mostly by third-tier brokerage firms looking to satisfy investors' appetite for tapping into China's economic growth. The niche of Chinese reverse-merger companies qualified as an obscure market phenomenon, one enabled by financial services industry greed, investor hope, and the willingness of many Chinese executives to perpetrate fraud. The short-selling of reverse-merger stocks may not have technically met the definition of special-situation investing. However, the swiftness with which many of the frauds were exposed, and the resulting decoupling of their stock price performance from that of the market, enabled Adrangi to generate outsize investment returns. In the case of RTOs, the success of the short investment thesis literally killed this opportunity by pushing the offending companies into oblivion.

Informational and Analytical Inefficiencies

The obscurity of many special-situation investments goes hand in hand with the factors that make it difficult for many investors to incorporate such ideas into their investment process. According to Jake Rosser, "Informational inefficiencies are often present in spinoff situations, busted IPOs or post re-org opportunities."[3] The hurdles to obtaining the information needed for proper analysis constitute one driver of opportunity. Just like small-cap equities may present informational challenges, data on strategic events such as spin-offs tend to be less readily available than data on earnings releases and other periodic events. Spin-off data do not fit neatly into most public company databases, forcing investors to access specialized databases or piece together the relevant data from company filings and news releases. In markets that exhibit informational inefficiency, rewards may accrue to those who make the effort to obtain timely, accurate, and relevant information.

Analytical inefficiencies may play an even greater role in driving outperformance in special situations. Information is generally publicly available and may be obtained by investors willing to dig for it. However, many market participants struggle to overcome analytical hurdles. Some special situations may seem daunting: In a spin-off, how do we value the newly created entity, and what does this imply for a shareholder of the still-combined entity? In a debt-financed recapitalization, what does the assumption of new debt mean for the shareholders, and how should we treat the potential introduction of dilutive securities? The questions are nearly endless—and it sometimes seems that the more questions we ask, the more confused we become. To make money in special situations, we need to move beyond semantics and address the value drivers of such opportunities.

Uses and Misuses of Investing in Special Situations

We may put ourselves in an unenviable position if we use the experience of investors like Joel Greenblatt, Michael Burry, and Sahm Adrangi as the primary motivation for allocating capital to special situations. This area alternatively offers outsize gains and capital losses, with the two sometimes separated by a thin line. Vastly different outcomes may hinge on timing, security selection, trade execution, and fees.

In the instance of Chinese reverse-merger equities, investors who acted on the research published by short sellers would have lost money if they entered too late and exited too early, even if the short thesis was correct. This is not a far-fetched scenario, as the affected equities frequently gapped down in price following a well-founded accusation of fraud. Having missed the major price decline, some investors might have shorted the shares anyway. After all, if a company was a total fraud, the stock was worthless. Unfortunately, the routine assessment of negative rebates on heavily shorted securities meant that investors could lose money even if the stock price kept declining but did so at a slow pace. Worse still, many of the frauds were initially strongly denied by the affected companies and the U.S. brokerage firms making markets in those stocks. The battered stocks often received a reprieve following the denials. If an investor started doubting the short thesis just as the stock price rebounded, the temptation to cover might have been overwhelming.

Passive investment in special situations carries with it significantly greater risk than does passive investment in equities overall. If we buy into a high-quality, well-financed company like Procter & Gamble, Johnson & Johnson, or Coca-Cola, we have the option of letting the passage of time erase a temporary mark-to-market loss. However, in the case of a special situation, investing in the wrong security may result in forced realization of loss. The high turnover that may be expected in most special situations heightens the impact of systematic errors, as a large number of investment decisions may be made in a short time. Whenever we are unsure of our edge in an investment, it makes sense to slow down or opt for investments whose outcome is likely to benefit from the passage of time.

The Danger of Robotic Analysis

I do not recall many things from the five years spent in elementary school in communist Yugoslavia in the 1980s, but I do remember dreading memorization exercises. We had to commit to memory many silly things, such as the dates of communist victories during World War II and the birth dates of political leaders. My family's escape from the Yugoslav system of indoctrination enabled me to develop analytical thinking skills and creativity. However, growing up in the West did not render me immune to mindless memorization either. How often have we heard the lament that kids memorize information to score well on a test while learning little in the process? Investing is a different kind of test, one for which mindless memorization does not equip us well.

Some structure is necessary, even for art to reach its full potential. If you know the rules and process, you make a statement by choosing to ignore specific prescriptions. Twenty-first-century philosopher king Arnold Schwarzenegger advises us to "break the rules, not the law." The distinction is instructive, both in life and investing. When we refer to the laws of investing, we do not mean government-imposed restrictions. Instead, we focus on truths that cannot be ignored if we desire long-term success. For example, repeatedly investing all of our capital in one idea will result in total loss of capital, given a long enough time horizon. If we use excessive recourse leverage of the portfolio level, the long-term result will be similar. If we day-trade securities with large bid-ask spreads, the speed with which we surrender our capital becomes a function of the speed with which we turn over the portfolio.

Investing rules, as distinct from laws, need to be broken occasionally in the pursuit of investment excellence. In this context, rules include the financial formulas we have memorized along the way, including selected measures of operating performance, returns on capital, and valuation ratios. If we have memorized enterprise value as market value plus net debt, and if we apply this definition mechanically in every investment situation, we will be prone to certain errors of judgment.

Assume that a company has a market value of $50 million, with $200 million of cash, $150 million of debt, and $250 million of prepaid liabilities, such as ticket sales, magazine subscriptions, or tuition receipts. The standard enterprise value formula tells us to start with the market value of $50 million, add debt of $150 million, and subtract cash of $200 million. This implies an enterprise value of zero, a number that will tilt any valuation exercise that involves enterprise value toward a favorable conclusion.

However, is the market really valuing the enterprise at zero in this case? Could this company use $150 million of cash to pay off debt and send shareholders a $50 million dividend, reducing their cost basis to zero? This seems highly unlikely, as the company may need to keep cash on hand to satisfy the obligations implicit in the large amount of prepaid liabilities. The limitation is especially acute if the company's business is eroding, as the normally desirable negative working capital position turns into a cash-sucking feature of the business model.

Some investors act like robots when using a popular operating performance measure, EBITDA, in security analysis. The formula for EBITDA flows straight from the acronym—earnings before interest, taxes, depreciation, and amortization. We have no quarrel with the formula itself but rather with its use as an authoritative measure of leverage-adjusted profitability or cash flow. The DA in EBITDA gives a company credit for depreciation and amortization, a non-cash expense. Adding D&A to operating income may indeed provide a worthwhile view into a distressed company's ability to keep paying interest. If management can curtail capital expenditures, cash generation may exceed GAAP income, implying a stronger financial position than might be suggested by reported profitability. This commonsense use of EBITDA appears to have evolved into an overly broad application of the measure. If we analyze a telecom services company as a going concern, and the firm's maintenance capital expenditures approximate depreciation and amortization, EBITDA may obscure rather than illuminate owner earnings.

Special-situation investing seems prone to robotic analysis, as different types of situations come with their own rules, jargon, and acronyms. Investors may find it hard enough to memorize the key equations and concepts that apply in various special situations. Questioning the accepted rules may seem like too much to ask. Yet, unquestioning adherence to the mechanics may bias investors toward opportunities that appear most compelling in a textbook sense but contain a major flaw.

Experience teaches us when to bend the rules and when to break them—but only if we invest with eyes wide open. Deliberate practice, in the parlance of Anders Ericsson and Malcolm Gladwell, constitutes the difference between continuous improvement and eventual stagnation. According to Ericsson, "Nobody becomes an outstanding professional without experience, but extensive experience does not invariably lead people to become experts."[4] By asking why and what if—rather than settling at how—we start a process of inquiry. Just like a picture may be worth a thousand words, a real-time investment experience may be worth a thousand insights. The more questions we ask along the way, the more of those insights we are bound to capture.

Some insights can be gained only if we launch the process of inquiry at the relevant point in time. If we do so, we can still enrich the process with new insights at a later date, but if we fail to launch the process at the right time, we may never capture all the available insights. This is somewhat analogous to the rationale for point-in-time databases, which allow investors to test certain hypotheses against the data available at the time at which an investment might have been made. For example, a company may restate past profits, presenting investors interested in backtesting their hypotheses with a dilemma—whether to use the restated numbers or the figures as they were reported initially. If the investor is backtesting an approach that requires simulating decisions at specific points in time, it makes sense to use the data reported at the time when a decision would have been made.

To foster deliberate practice over time, we may want to catalogue our investment experiences, including decisions to forgo specific investments. By recording the reasons for each decision, we form a basis for reevaluation in the future. We also forestall the temptation to revise history to avoid regret or the admission of mistakes. According to James Montier, "Keeping a diary of your investment ideas is a powerful aid memoir when it comes to behavioral biases, as you can see what you were thinking in real time, and then evaluate your process in the cold light of day provided by the distance of time. The downside of this approach is obviously that it takes time to build up a catalogue of mistakes to learn from."[5] Montier's last point may be as crucial as it is innocuous. A small sample can teach us the wrong lessons, as bad outcomes sometimes follow good decisions. Poker players know that playing a single hand well may not produce the desired outcome. One bad outcome should not be sufficient justification for modifying our approach. If we assume that the batting average of successful investors is modestly above 50 percent, it becomes clear that it may take quite a few outcomes before we can draw lessons with some conviction.

We may avoid an overly mechanistic approach to investing by considering the outside view in addition to the inside view. Explains Michael Mauboussin, chief investment strategist of Legg Mason Capital Management and chairman of the Santa Fe Institute:

> *The core idea is that when you make a prediction, you can consider the individual circumstances of the case and/or the base rate. In the first case, you're taking the information you have and combining it with your own view of things. Psychologists call this the "inside view." Consideration of the base rate basically means you ask the question: "when others have been in this situation before, what happened?" This is known as the "outside view." Kahneman and Tversky showed that for most decisions, people rely too much on the inside view and not enough on the outside view.*[6]

A robot might be quite good at applying a rigid process or crunching numbers, but considering the actions of others might be more difficult. We include the incentives of others in this context as well. Special situations may feature a game-theoretic interplay of multiple parties. By using experience and judgment in considering the interests and potential actions of the players involved, we elevate our thesis well beyond the realm of a computing device.

Timing as a Driver of Annualized Returns

Special situations are one of the few investment areas in which it makes sense to pay at least as much attention to the time component of annualized return as to the absolute return expected in a particular situation. The importance of timing may be reflected in the term *event-driven investing*, as timing represents a key feature of any event. In risk arbitrage, including trades designed to capture the spread in announced mergers and acquisitions, the expected return may be quite low. However, when the time to realization is compressed, the annualized return increases markedly. As the relatively small absolute return heightens the sensitivity of the annualized return to changes in timing, analysis of the time variable becomes critical.

The importance of timing in event-driven opportunities may necessitate a shift in mind-set for value-oriented investors, as so-called time arbitrage has long been a component of value investors' edge. By arbitraging time, value investors profit from the compressed investment time horizons of other market participants. If most investors pass on ideas that may take several years to play out—whether due to impatience or an institutional imperative—an opportunity exists for patient investors to acquire assets well below fair value. The gap between price and value, sometimes referred to as the margin of safety, tends to predominate in value investment theses. The time it may take for the gap to close seems too speculative a basis for investment. Additionally, a large margin of safety, as opposed to a compressed time horizon, favors return *of* capital over return *on* capital. That said, event-driven investments correlate less closely with market indices than do general equities in the short to medium term. If volatility is your (or your client's) barometer of risk, special situations may qualify as less risky than investments exhibiting a wider margin of safety.

Timing is an area in which knowledge of the rules of special situations holds particular value. In merger arbitrage, familiarity with the typical sequence of events helps us estimate the time until deal completion. While management may disclose a target for deal completion, the insider estimate may be influenced by a desire to speed up the process. Investors should be in a position to verify the management estimate or derive an alternative projection. In cases in which our informed judgment differs materially from management guidance, an attractive investment opportunity may exist. Both theoretical study and real-life experience may boost our knowledge of merger process timelines.

Analogous but distinct expertise may be developed in the areas of spin-offs, bankruptcies, and liquidations. In case of liquidations, the wide range of potential timelines, sometimes stretching out years into the future, results in a wide range of annualized return scenarios. As a result, an investor's superior knowledge of liquidations in general and the likely course of the particular liquidation under consideration may result in superior investment performance—or may help the investor avoid an inferior result. For example, some liquidations may look straightforward at first glance due to a highly liquid balance sheet. However, on closer examination, an investor may notice contingent liabilities that are likely to delay cash distributions.

Positive Spillover Effects

It may be tempting to dismiss special situations entirely as an investment area that does not offer a commensurate return on the time required to gain expertise. If we focus primarily on identifying great businesses and buying them when they are cheap, spin-offs or liquidations may seem like unwelcome distractions. Event-driven investments are anything but buy-and-hold propositions. If successful, special situations will come to an end, leaving us with a new pile of cash to invest. The steep initial learning curve, coupled with relatively high turnover, implies a need for an ongoing research effort. Not all investors may wish to expend such effort when their core investment approach yields satisfactory results.

Despite the legitimate objections to dabbling in special situations, we believe the positive spillover effects of event-driven investing justify the effort. Just as learning to kick the ball with the left foot may improve a soccer player's right kick, doing the perhaps uncomfortable work involved in evaluating special situations may build overall investment skill. Newtonian physics seemed coherent when contained within itself, but Einstein's theory of relativity gave us an alternative view into several areas of physics. By seeking to understand the drivers of value in various types of special situations, we may glean insights that also improve our core expertise. How specifically each of us may gain is impossible to predict.

Special situations may inform our investment philosophy in several ways: First, event-driven investments are neither popular nor momentum-driven, forcing us to independently assess the investment merits. As many special situations may be considered off the beaten path, we learn to build and sustain an investment thesis in the absence of a constant flow of news.

Second, special situations crystallize the meaning of value. In a liquidation, value is determined solely by when and how much cash we will receive in exchange for the cash we give up today. When no terminal value remains, we cannot base the investment thesis on what other investors might pay for a business. The opinion of other investors is irrelevant in a typical liquidation scenario, a valuable insight even for those of us who consider ourselves disciplined value investors.

Finally, the importance of timing in special situations makes us more cognizant of this component of annualized return. Rather than insist on maximizing the gap between value and price, we may learn to appreciate that a smaller gap can result in a strong outcome if a catalyst exists for the realization of fair value. That said, few investors need additional awareness of timing, as most of us are no strangers to impatience. On balance, we find that a disciplined approach to time arbitrage tends to be harder to sustain, but also more profitable, than an approach focused on identifying catalytic events.

Uncovering Special Situations

The nature of event-driven investing makes quantitative screening largely ineffective. Many special-situation opportunities arise after a corporate event has been announced but not yet consummated, with the pro forma data unavailable in traditional screening tools. Even in the case of completed deals, it may take some time for databases to reflect the new reality. When post-deal financials do enter screening databases, we may still find it difficult to separate special situations from other companies that happen to meet our screening criteria.

Hacking Traditional Screeners to Identify Special Opportunities

If we insist on using a quantitative screening tool to find companies that have recently completed a special event, we may apply a few hacks. For instance, we may undertake a broad screen, perhaps limited only by market capitalization, and then ask the screening tool to show data on the stock price change of all passing companies over the past 1, 3, or 12 months. Companies that have recently gone public, whether in a traditional initial public offering or via spin-off, will show no applicable stock price change over the relevant period. As most screeners include reliable data on historical stock prices, the absence of a recent stock price suggests strongly that the company was not yet listed as of the relevant date. We may then go to the company's filings or investor relations website to examine the circumstances in which it became publicly listed.

Another hack involves screening for slow-growth companies that have experienced an apparently inorganic jump in revenue. Such companies may have just completed a transformational acquisition. While M&A often destroys value, synergistic deals completed at reasonable prices can have the opposite effect. Unfortunately, companies experiencing large increases in sales rarely fly below the radar screen of most investors, although many investors terminate their search as soon as they realize that the revenue increase is due to a strategic event rather than organic growth.

Yet another hack focuses on the number of shares outstanding. A large drop in the share count is usually desirable and may reflect a large repurchase that effectively recapitalizes the balance sheet. If we determine that the shares were bought back at a price materially below estimated fair value, we may have uncovered an interesting opportunity. On the other end of the spectrum are companies whose share count has increased materially in the latest reporting period. While an increase in shares outstanding is undesirable ceteris paribus, scenarios exist in which such an increase points to an event that deserves scrutiny. For example, a company may have acquired a competitor recently, paying an attractive price in cash and stock (or all stock) while consolidating the market and creating synergies. If the stock price of the company under consideration has declined since the combination, we have an implicit opportunity to buy the acquired business at a cost below the recent acquisition price. Another example may involve a distressed equity whose price had declined precipitously due to a high likelihood of dilution. As the degree of dilution needed to shore up the balance sheet was uncertain, the downward momentum of the stock price continued unabated. A recent jump in shares outstanding may indicate that the dilutive event is now behind the company, allowing us to appraise value using the new share count. If the equity remains materially undervalued following the recapitalization, we may have uncovered an interesting opportunity.

Other Ways of Building a Pipeline of Event-Driven Ideas

Several alternatives exist to rather deficient quantitative screens when it comes to identifying special situations. The financial media love to cover strategic corporate events, making regular consumption of news and related feature stories quite useful. In addition to typical sources such as the *Wall Street Journal*, the *Financial Times*, and the *Economist*, we also derive value from online media and blogs, including the following:

- Tadas Viskanta's *Abnormal Returns* (abnormalreturns.com)
- Ryan O'Connor's *Above Average Odds* (aboveaverageodds.com)
- David Merkel's *Aleph Blog* (alephblog.com)
- Saj Karsan's *Barel Karsan* (barelkarsan.com)
- Jonathan Heller's *Cheap Stocks* (stocksbelowncav.blogspot.com)
- Andrew Ross Sorkin's *DealBook* (dealbook.com)
- Toby Carlisle's *Greenbackd* (greenbackd.com)
- Greg Speicher's *Ideas for Intelligent Investing* (gregspeicher.com)
- John DiStanislao's *ShadowStock* (shadowstock.blogspot.com)
- Tariq Ali's *Street Capitalist* (streetcapitalist.com)
- Ravi Nagarajan's *The Rational Walk* (rationalwalk.com)
- Wes Gray's *Turnkey Analyst* (turnkeyanalyst.com)
- Joe Koster's *Value Investing World* (valueinvestingworld.com)
- Todd Sullivan's *ValuePlays* (valueplays.net)
- Jacob Wolinsky's *ValueWalk* (valuewalk.com)
- Mebane Faber's *World Beta* (mebanefaber.com)

Specialized newsletters, such as Bill Mitchell's *Spinoff & Reorg Profiles*, provide systematic data and analysis of the special-situation pipeline. We also find online discussion forums, such as *The Corner of Berkshire and Fairfax*, moderated by Sanjeev Parsad, an excellent source of special-situation ideas that have caught the eye of fellow investors. Customizable Google news alerts provide another mechanism for tracking announced special situations.

Finally, the full-text search feature of the SEC website (sec.gov) allows U.S.-focused investors to search for relevant filings, such as Form 10, and for specific words within filings. The SEC filings of selected superinvestors on Form 13F-HR may also reveal intriguing event-driven investments. Fund managers who have made special situation investments include Bill Ackman, Sahm Adrangi, David Einhorn, Carl Icahn, Dan Loeb, John Paulson, and Mark Rachesky.

If we decide to build a pipeline of opportunities in a particular event-driven niche, we may embrace a format that fosters not only current analysis but also future assessment of performance. For example, rather than tracking ideas in a way that makes data on completed events of little use, it makes sense to expand the pipeline into a quasi-journal, allowing us to keep track of our point-in-time assessment of each situation. By recording our thoughts in real time, we create a basis for evaluating the decision-making process as situations play out. The greater the number of situations we have considered, the higher the likelihood that we will identify patterns to help us improve the subjective assessment of probabilities and payoffs in specific types of situations.

A Step Ahead: Uncovering Equities That May Become Special Situations

Activist investors often pressure boards of directors into action by making the case that a strategic event would unlock value for shareholders. The mere announcement of an intended spin-off or recapitalization can send the price of an equity higher as investors anticipate that a source of hidden value may be revealed to the market at large. If we can identify companies most likely to pursue a value-unlocking strategic event, we might be in a position to generate returns that exceed those available in announced or completed special situations.

Our search for equities likely to announce a strategic event steers us toward undervalued companies. Only such companies actually possess value that needs highlighting, though not all undervalued equities have hidden components of value. In some cases, value exists in plain sight, but investors refuse to see it, usually due to fear. In yet other cases, an overvalued company may decide to spin off a noncore business, potentially creating an interesting situation—not necessarily to invest in the overvalued parent but in the spin-off entity instead. Our quantitative search for companies that may be in a position to expose hidden value focuses on readily ascertainable asset values rather than earning power values. Asset values are somewhat easier to identify with a mechanical screen, and they may be subject to less debate than are intangible values.

In one of the 10 quantitative screens featured in the periodical edition of *The Manual of Ideas*, we focus on companies with large net liquid assets as a proportion of market value. Such companies tend to possess one or more obvious paths toward value creation, such as using liquid assets to repurchase stock, pay a special dividend, or pursue a sale or liquidation. For whatever reason, management at most of those companies has not taken the steps needed to unlock value; otherwise, the stock price might be materially higher in some cases. As a result, a special situation may arise primarily as a result of shareholder pressure or an unsolicited bid by a competitor or financial sponsor. To focus the search on equities ripe for strategic action, we eliminate companies at which management has de facto control, whether through a large economic stake, ownership of a supervoting class of stock, or tactics that serve to discourage a change of control, such as a poison pill or staggered board.

Asking the Right Questions of Special Situations

Each event-driven investment opportunity typically prompts a multitude of situation-specific questions. These inquiries help us understand the nature of a situation, thereby revealing the key drivers of value. Once we identify the drivers, we may assess them to estimate value, providing an informed basis for an investment decision.

What Is the Source of Potential Inefficiency?

The reasons for undervaluation may have little to do with the fundamental merits of an investment. It helps to consider the factors causing an equity to trade at a price materially different from intrinsic value. In the absence of identifiable drivers of inefficiency, the probability may be higher that our appraisal of value contains an oversight or flaw. If we can identify a non-fundamental factor that explains the low valuation of a security, we justifiably gain confidence in an estimate of value that differs from the market price. As a result, we like to know the story of how a special situation came into being and what is driving the supply-and-demand dynamic in the shares.

One of the more widely accepted views with regard to spin-offs seems to be that inefficiency is more likely in situations in which the entity to be spun off is considerably smaller than the remaining entity. In such cases, the size of the spun-off entity may be so small in terms of market value that the investors who receive the spin-off shares decide to sell them for the non-fundamental reason that the spin-off would be too small to move the needle in the context of a broader portfolio. The stock price pressure created by the non-fundamental selling could create an opportunity for investors willing to appraise the value of the spin-off entity—and to hold the shares in their portfolio.

Unfortunately, the factors that in the past may have caused a category of special-situation investments to be undervalued may not be significant factors going forward. Indeed, the fact that a certain type of inefficiency has existed may make it more likely that the same factor fails to persist because it has become appreciated by the investment community. For example, the realization that small spin-offs may be dumped by large funds may have prompted some investors to focus on small spin-offs. The corresponding increase in demand for small spin-offs may have altered the supply-demand balance in a way that eliminates the inefficiency. If investors fail to realize that the influx of similarly minded investors impacts the odds of success, demand could increase to the point at which a previously attractive type of special situation becomes an underperforming category. The opportunity in spin-offs may have diminished somewhat in the years following the publication of Joel Greenblatt's *You Can Be a Stock Market Genius.*

We consider two layers of potential pricing inefficiency. First, we assess the general drivers of inefficiency given the type of situation under consideration. According to Christopher Detweiler, relatively low trading volume may have driven potential inefficiency in the pricing of South Korean preferred stocks in early 2013. The lower the trading volume, the fewer investors opt for the preferred shares, the greater the pricing discrepancy between the common and preferred stocks. This dynamic creates a self-reinforcing cycle that persists until the magnitude of the relative undervaluation of the preferred shares becomes large enough to attract an influx of value-seeking investors. In the case of spin-offs, general drivers of inefficiency include a lack of visibility while the shares trade on a when-issued basis, a shorter history of public disclosure of financial results, and various factors that make investors transact for nonfundamental reasons.

Second, we consider security-specific drivers of inefficiency. The more specific the factors we identify, the higher the likelihood that inefficiency does indeed exist. General causes may be so well understood that their impact has become de minimis, unless the category is quite new or has received little investor attention to date. In the case of a spin-off, security-specific considerations include the size of the spin-off entity relative to the parent, the difference in industry classification between the spin-off and the parent, and the difference in key business model and valuation drivers. In addition, if we identify a large shareholder of the parent who is likely to sell the spin-off shares due to nonfundamental portfolio considerations, we may be in a position to anticipate or explain weakness in the stock price. Similarly, if we conclude that the management team of the spun-off entity may be limiting communications with the investment community to keep the stock price low until management's stock options are struck, we may have a basis for explaining an artificially low stock price.

What Is the Margin of Safety?

The difference between intrinsic value and the market price typically represents the focus of our analysis into any equity security, including an event-driven investment. Generally, the greater the discount to intrinsic value, the wider the margin of safety. In the case of highly leveraged equities, the margin of safety may be more fragile, as changes in the value of the enterprise or the assets on the balance sheet cause disproportionately large changes in the fair value of the equity. A similar dynamic may apply in the case of low-margin businesses, as relatively small absolute margin erosion may cause a significant drop in earnings and equity value. Finally, in situations in which a large portion of value depends on one customer or one regulator, an apparently large margin of safety could diminish quickly, assuming adverse external action.

Each type of special situation may require a different approach to the mechanics of value appraisal, but the general principle of adopting an owner mind-set applies to all equities. When we reason from first principles, we worry less about the bucket into which a particular situation may belong. Instead, we focus on what we get for the cash we give up. This approach provides significant advantages, not least because some special situations do not fit neatly into any one bucket. If we try to force a security into a category to enable ourselves to apply the valuation process appropriate for that particular category, we may misjudge the components of value.

When we analyze an equity from first principles, we obviously know with certainty how much cash we give up and at what time we do so. The focus therefore falls on what we get and, if possible to estimate intelligently, *when* we might get it. The benefits we expect to derive in the future typically amount to cash in our home currency or in a foreign currency, but we may also receive value in the form of securities or, more rarely, other assets.

In the case of an announced but not yet completed spin-off, we may give up cash to buy a share of parent company stock. In exchange, we will retain ownership of that share of stock and receive some amount of stock in the spin-off entity. To appraise the value we receive for the cash we invest, we may appraise the value of the post-spin-off share of the parent entity, plus the value of the equity we expect to receive in the spin-off entity. To do so, we separately value the parent and the spin-off entity, and we then calculate the value of our stake based on our actual or expected percentage ownership of each entity.

It helps to consider the value that accrues to us at a specific point in time. If we consider the value we get today, we could appraise just the parent entity as it has existed until today, that is, including the entity to be spun off. If, on the other hand, we decide to consider value as of a date immediately following completion of the spin-off, we appraise the two entities separately while making sure we do not double-count the value of the spin-off entity by including the financial data related to the spin-off in our appraisal of the parent. Choosing a post-spin-off date may be most appropriate when investing in a pre-spin-off parent, as the rationale for doing the spin-off typically includes the argument that the two entities should be valued based on different parameters.

What Is the Path to Value Creation?

Special-situation timelines typically play an important role in determining expected annualized return, necessitating some awareness of the steps to value realization. Even in the case of completed events, timing may play a role in the analysis. For example, if we accept the view that spin-offs may underperform during their first year in the public market, as holders of the parent company sell the spin-off shares, we may use the effective date of a spin-off as an input in our purchase timing decision. Timing plays a greater role in situations in which the absolute expected return is quite small but in which the short timeline yields a large annualized return. If the timeline stretches beyond expectations, the annualized return may decline to such an extent that the investment no longer makes sense from a risk-reward standpoint.

Another reason for paying attention to the path toward value creation has less to do with the impact of timing on annualized return and more to do with insights gained from the resulting feedback loop. For example, if we invest in a distressed equity because we expect asset sales to generate cash to recapitalize the balance sheet in a way that avoids equity dilution, we may benefit from tracking the progress of asset sales versus our expectations. If such sales need to occur prior to certain financial covenants being triggered or principal payments becoming due, then an indication of a delay in asset sales could be important to the investment thesis. By developing a clear view of the milestones toward value creation, we avoid a situation in which hope prevails over reality. If an event-driven investment fails to meet a key milestone, we may be in a position to exit the investment without much impairment, especially if we have set the milestones independently instead of relying on the market consensus.

When we consider the ways an event-driven investment may play out, it helps to assess the incentives of the key players

involved. This is particularly true in complex situations in which
multiple scenarios are plausible and potentially opposing interests
are at play. In a distressed situation in which a company needs
to be recapitalized, for instance, it would be impossible to attach
probabilities and payoffs to various scenarios without considering
the interests involved. A chief executive who holds a large equity
stake in the company will generally exhaust all other options
before resigning himself to major dilution or a wipeout of the
equity.

The key hurdles to successful completion of a special situation
also figure prominently in our analysis. As the investment thesis
overcomes each successive hurdle, we reevaluate the probabilities
and payoffs involved, probably accreting some value even as completion of the overall event remains pending. For example, in certain announced mergers, expiration of the Hart-Scott-Rodino period
removes the last serious impediment to deal closing. As a result, the
merger arbitrage spread may narrow materially following this date.
Other event-driven investments face their own particular hurdles.
The greater the hurdles perceived by the market, the greater the
payoff might be for investors who correctly appraise the probabilities of those hurdles being overcome.

Key Takeaways

Here are our top 10 takeaways from this chapter:

1. Special situations encompass equities whose near- to medium-
   term stock price performance is largely independent of the
   performance of equity markets.
2. The flood of talent and capital has taken some areas of special-
   situation investing from obscurity to popularity, reducing prospective investment returns.
3. The more obscure a market niche, the higher the likelihood
   that diligent investors will generate market-beating returns.
4. In markets that exhibit informational inefficiency, rewards may
   accrue to those who make the effort to obtain timely, accurate,
   and relevant information.
5. Analytical inefficiencies may play an even greater role in driving outperformance in special situations. While information is

generally available to investors willing to dig for it, many market participants struggle to overcome analytical hurdles.

6. Investing rules, as distinct from laws, need to be broken occasionally in the pursuit of investment excellence. In this context, rules include the financial formulas we have memorized along the way.

7. Some insights can be gained only if we launch the process of inquiry at the relevant point in time. If we do so, we may enrich the process with new insights at a later date, but if we fail to launch the process, we may never capture the available insights.

8. Special situations are one of the few investment areas in which it makes sense to pay at least as much attention to the time component of annualized return as to the absolute return expected in a particular situation.

9. Special situations crystallize the meaning of value. In a liquidation, value is determined solely by when and how much cash we will receive in exchange for the cash we give up today. When no terminal value remains, we cannot base the investment thesis on what other investors might pay for a business.

10. In the absence of identifiable drivers of inefficiency, the probability may be higher that our appraisal of value contains an oversight or flaw. If we can identify a non-fundamental factor that explains the low valuation, we gain confidence in an estimate of value that differs from the market price.

Notes

1. *The Manual of Ideas*, August 2010, 9.
2. *The Manual of Ideas*, July 2011, 106.
3. *The Manual of Ideas*, January 2012, 9.
4. Ericsson (2004), http://edianas.com/portfolio/proj_EricssonInterview/articles/2004_Academic_Medicine_Vol_10,_S70-S81.pdf.
5. *The Manual of Ideas*, October 2011, 16.
6. *The Manual of Ideas*, October 2011, 12.

CHAPTER 9

Equity Stubs

Investing (or Speculating?) in Leveraged Companies

If you've ever made 10 times your money on anything, you'll know that it releases a certain chemical in your body—and you want that chemical released again.

—Bill Browder

Proceed with caution. That may be the only sensible advice to anyone seeking to profit from investing in highly leveraged companies. Warns Tim McElvaine: "The single biggest mistake I've made is having companies that have too much leverage. . . ."[1] Adds Jake Rosser: "Whether it be AIG or Long-Term Capital Management, most of history's largest investment wipe-outs have been accompanied by leverage. Once you take on leverage, you no longer have control over your destiny. The use of leverage entails binary outcomes with a huge payday at one end and the permanent impairment of capital at the other end."[2]

Investing in equity stubs may shake up your portfolio and your confidence. Nonetheless, money can be made in this portion of the public company universe. If selected properly, equity stubs can be one of the most rewarding pieces of a portfolio. Table 9.1 shows the effect of balance sheet leverage on the returns of an equity investor. In scenario 1, we assume that the market's estimate of enterprise value increases by 50 percent, and in scenario 2 we assume that enterprise value decreases by 20 percent. These

TABLE 9.1 The Rewards and Perils of Leveraged Equities

	With Leverage	With No Leverage	With Net Cash
Market's initial estimate of enterprise value	100	100	100
Net cash/(debt)	−80	0	80
Market's initial estimate of equity value	20	100	180
Scenario 1: The power of leverage			
Market's subsequent estimate of enterprise value	150	150	150
Net cash/(debt)	−80	0	80
Market's subsequent estimate of equity value	70	150	230
Change in enterprise value	50%	50%	50%
Return to equity holders	250%	50%	28%
Scenario 2: The peril of leverage			
Market's subsequent estimate of enterprise value	80	80	80
Net cash/(debt)	−80	0	80
Market's subsequent estimate of equity value	0	80	160
Change in enterprise value	−20%	−20%	−20%
Return to equity holders	−100%	−20%	−11%

changes in enterprise value have a disproportionately large effect on equity value if a company employs financial leverage.

The term *equity stub* illustrates quite well the nature of opportunities in this category. In prebarcode days, when you went to a concert or ballgame, an attendant would tear up your ticket at the door, leaving you with the stub. The stub typically amounted to just a small piece of the ticket, leaving you with something to remember the event. If we think of the capital structure of a company as the ticket, the equity is the stub. When a company has modest debt, the stub is quite large and does not fit the ticket analogy.

However, when a company is heavily indebted, the equity stub becomes a small piece of the overall funding pie. In this case, the analogy applies quite well. No specific limit exists with regard to the maximum equity ratio for a stock to be considered an equity stub. Rather, each investor is free to label an equity a stub if leverage starts predominating the analysis.

The Approach: Why It Works

We have not seen conclusive proof that passive investing in equity stubs outperforms. The famous Fama-French time series studies showed that equities with low price-to-book ratios outperformed other equities over long periods of time. Equity stubs fall disproportionately into the low price-to-book category, as their valuations may be depressed due to a perception of distress. Still, the Fama-French data include the full spectrum of leverage ratios, making it impossible to isolate equity stubs.

David Swensen, chief investment officer of Yale University, has persuasively argued that the rewards to active management increase in asset classes in which a wide performance gap exists between top-quartile and bottom-quartile performers. In government bonds, this gap has been narrow historically, while in venture capital it has been wide. A second-tier venture capitalist may generate little value for investors, while Andreessen Horowitz looks likely to earn outsize returns over time. In his published analysis, Swensen did not break out equity stubs as a separate asset class. If he had done so, we might have seen very wide dispersion of returns.

Passive returns to investing in leveraged equities reveal little about the merits of such an approach. On the other hand, the all-but-certain wide dispersion of the returns likely to be earned by market participants strikes us as crucial. We may succeed or fail spectacularly in this area, depending on factors that are only partly known. No one has cracked this approach entirely; otherwise, we would see the investor moving up the various *Forbes* rich lists rather quickly. One does not need a perfect batting average to earn handsome, albeit lumpy, returns in this category. At the very least, the wide range of potential returns supports the notion that an enterprising investor may want to accept the intellectual challenge posed by equity stubs.

When we consider what might distinguish top-quartile from bottom-quartile performers, we reflect on Michael Mauboussin's take on top-performing investors: "First, they focus on process and not outcomes. In other words, they make the best decisions they can with the information they have, and then let the outcomes take care of themselves. Second, they always seek to have the odds in their favor. Finally, they understand the role of time. You can do the right thing for some time and it won't show up in results. You have to be able to manage money to see another day—that is, preserve options for future play—and take a long-term view."[3]

It may make sense to start with a de minimis capital allocation or even just a no-money practice portfolio. Should you conclude over time that you probably possess above-average judgment with regard to leveraged equities, you retain the option of increasing your allocation. This chapter shares a number of observations gained largely from our experience while publishing the periodical edition of *The Manual of Ideas* and investing capital in this area.

Uses and Misuses of Investing in Equity Stubs

It would be difficult to overstate the importance of judgment in this area. Even if all investors possessed comprehensive data on equity stub securities, their investment decisions—and outcomes—would differ materially. We use the word *judgment* to highlight the lack of a specific recipe. George Soros once observed that he always invested on the basis of hypotheses he formed about markets or securities. He constantly tested those investment cases against market reality, creating a process for improving his theses and honing his judgment. A similarly iterative approach is crucial in this area. States James Montier:

> *The longer I've spent in this industry the more I have come to realize that common sense just isn't so common when it comes to investing. Good judgment really seems to come hand in hand with experience. For instance, there was a great research paper written by Stefan Nagel and Robin Greenwood, which showed that it was the younger fund managers who really bought into the TMT bubble, while the old grey beards were much more skeptical. People only really seem to learn when they themselves have made the mistake and accepted it as such.*[4]

Avoiding Biases

We need to be careful not to overreach when our judgment turns out to have been correct. The payoffs in equity stubs may exert an intoxicating effect on the successful investor. Warns Mark O'Friel: "Research has shown that the single biggest error is overconfidence. Investing is hard, with elements of skill, hard work and luck. An investor who attributes every success to skill is susceptible to over-reaching."[5] Adds James Montier:

> *The best rule of thumb is that if you feel confident you are probably overconfident. I have regular debates with one of my colleagues on this subject. He is a great believer in having confidence behind an idea. I am much more skeptical. The evidence is overwhelming; we are generally massively over-confident, so erring on the side of caution makes sense to me. That said, investing is a very fine balance between humility and arrogance. You need a certain amount of arrogance to be willing to take positions that are contrary to everyone else, but you must also have the humility to keep looking for the evidence that shows you are wrong in your arrogance.[6]*

Michael Mauboussin, chief investment strategist of Legg Mason Capital Management and chairman of the Santa Fe Institute, advises us to "maintain the discipline to consider every situation probabilistically and keep an investment journal so as to track your thinking and give yourself honest feedback."[7] If we use a journal not only to record our investment theses but also to track investment outcomes, we should recognize that it may take a long time before we can infer conclusions from the hard data with any confidence. Due to the lopsided payoff in leveraged equities, the probability of winning on any one investment may be well under 50 percent. The low batting average increases the size of the sample required to estimate the ex ante likelihood of success.

Probabilistic evaluation of potential outcomes addresses the question of risk versus reward, a consideration that should lie at the heart of any investment decision. Nick Kirrage, fund manager of Specialist Value UK Equities at Schroders, laments that many investors "are very focused on either risk or reward, and that to us seems like a bit of an abdication of our responsibility. Are you invested in banking? 'No, there's too much risk.' Well, the first question is, at what price are you compensated for that risk? Or, 'that stock's very attractive; it's got 300% upside.' Okay, but how much risk is there that's giving you that? That is the entire job, and we're constantly trying to work through the accounts to try and quantify, what is the risk and what is the reward?"[8]

Consider the case of an airline that is believed likely to file for bankruptcy. Many investors would say, "This airline will go bankrupt and shareholders will get wiped out. I don't want to own the stock." A more enlightened investor might say, "There is a 90 percent chance the airline goes bankrupt and the stock is worthless. If the airline doesn't go bankrupt, though, the stock should be worth at least $10." If the stock can be bought materially below $1, it may be a favorable speculation, even though we expect the company to go bankrupt. If the company fails, it does not mean that allocating a small amount of capital to it was a bad decision. As former U.S. Treasury Secretary Robert Rubin points out, "Even a large and painful loss didn't mean that we [his arbitrage team at Goldman] had misjudged anything."[9] One outcome simply isn't enough to judge. Tens or even hundreds of similar situations would need to be tallied up to decide whether an investor has a good grasp of the probabilities and payoffs involved. Even so, evaluating probabilistic judgments can be tricky.

It helps to commit our investment theses to paper—and then test and refine them over time. In leveraged equities, experience is an investor's key asset, if interpreted properly. We add this qualification because the danger exists that we overlearn. We should not strive toward a checklist that will eliminate wipeouts, as individual losses should be expected. Rather, we should strive toward an approach that maximizes overall expected returns while avoiding debilitating portfolio-level losses when our judgment turns out to have been wrong or when we suffer bad luck.

The tendency of investors to think about the likely outcome rather than the range of possible outcomes represents a key stumbling block to success in leveraged equities. According to Mauboussin, "The biggest mistake is a failure to distinguish between fundamentals and expectations. Using a metaphor from the racetrack, the idea is that you make money only when you find a discrepancy between a horse's chances and the betting odds. What's important is that almost everyone thinks that they are doing this, but very few actually do."[10] If we decided to invest only in ideas we could not kill in a pessimistic scenario, we would have little to do in equity stubs. If a situation offers a highly positive expected return, the decision may be not so much whether to allocate capital, but rather how much. James Montier agrees: "It is perfectly legitimate to kill an idea and then conclude it is a good risk-reward, it just needs to be sized appropriately."[11]

Massimo Fuggetta embraces the notion:

My basic idea is that people are prone to make major mistakes in assessing probabilities. So I look for situations where I think prices reflect some sort of probability misjudgment, which creates an opportunity as the market eventually corrects the misperception. I actually see this as the root of all value investing, underlying many different "strategies." The market can attach high probabilities to events or scenarios that in fact have low probabilities; or, vice versa, give low probabilities to outcomes that have really high probabilities. The typical example is extrapolation of past performance. Of course, the problem is that low-probability events do occur sometimes, the post-Lehman crisis being the perfect example: a highly improbable outcome (in my opinion!) that rapidly became inevitable. . . .[12]

Fuggetta also warns of the human tendency to "use too little information to reach too strong conclusions."[13]

Loss aversion is another bias that affects investor activity in the area of equity stubs. Academics Amos Tversky and Daniel Kahneman have demonstrated an existence of loss aversion, as distinct from risk aversion. According to related studies, the joy most humans experience from financial gains is not proportional to the emotional pain we suffer from losses. In fact, the latter may be twice as powerful psychologically, skewing many investment decisions toward avoidance of loss, even if the probability-weighted return is favorable. We are used to buying insurance, not writing it, even if we could do so for small-incidence, independent risks appropriate for the size of our investment portfolio. In the context of investing, risk aversion is rational; loss aversion is not. Anyone hoping to succeed in leveraged equities must overcome loss aversion.

Who Owns the Debt?

Assuming we wish to wade into treacherous but potentially rewarding equity stubs, one of the key considerations is the ownership of
the debt on a company's books. Debt is often described as fixed
income because the contractually agreed payoff to debt holders is
fixed: They typically receive interest, followed by repayment of principal. The value upside of an enterprise is supposed to accrue to the
shareholders, as they also stand first in line to suffer the downside.

From a debt holder's perspective, the prospect of eliminating
the existing equity may look quite attractive in a distressed situation.
After all, the creditors of heavily indebted enterprises may object to
the asymmetry of their reward. If the enterprise fails, they may suffer a suspension of interest and principal payments. If the enterprise
succeeds, their upside is capped by the terms of the debt agreement.

Many institutional debt holders nonetheless stick to their traditional role, hoping that the equity holders will figure out a way to
satisfy their obligations. Such creditors frequently agree to extend
maturities or otherwise modify the terms of debt agreements to
allow the equity holders to keep performing on the debt. Many
debt underwriting officers or fixed-income managers may preserve
their own bonuses if their debtors do not default.

When principal-agent conflicts do not drive creditor actions,
and when creditors are both sophisticated and aggressive, they may
view a distressed equity situation as an opportunity rather than a
misfortune. Consider the following thought process of Howard
Marks, chairman of Oaktree Capital Management:

> The question is, number one, is this a company that you
> would like to control? And number two, is this a company
> where the creditors will get control? And then number three,
> which creditors? Because usually there is something called the
> fulcrum security, which is the first impaired class. The unim-
> paired will get their money. The first impaired class may get
> the company, and the lower impaired classes may get noth-
> ing. So it is the fulcrum, the one in the middle there, we try to
> identify that. We try to figure out if it will get control and how
> much it will have to pay for control. If it gets control at that
> price, will that be a successful investment? It is a very inter-
> esting area—of course, more moving parts to go wrong. The

investments are by definition less liquid. I would say it's the difference between dating and getting married. When you are a distressed debt investor, you are dating; but when you try for distressed-for-control, you get married. You have to live with the consequences, for better or for worse, richer or poorer. But, it can produce some good outcomes.[14]

Marks's distressed-for-control alternative reflects a strategy debt holders may pursue in a leveraged equity situation. To some investors, distressed-for-control represents more than simply a fallback option if a fixed-income investment goes sour. They may search the investment landscape for potential distressed-for-control opportunities, buying debt only if the possibility exists to squeeze out the shareholders. The rationale for debt holders can be quite compelling.

As investors come to regard an equity as distressed, they may drive down the share price to a level that implies an enterprise value well below the likely fair value of the enterprise. In this case, shareholders may reap significant rewards from deleveraging at the corporate level. However, if debt holders take control before such deleveraging occurs, they may wrest away the enterprise from the equity holders, ending up with a bargain price for the business. The attractiveness of the deal may increase due to the likelihood that the debt itself trades at a discount to face value. Whereas prospective investors in the equity must assume repayment of debt at face value when building their investment case, distressed-for-control debt investors face a lower hurdle due to the twin assumptions of discounted debt and generally worthless equity.

In theory, equity holders remain in the driver's seat even in a distressed situation because they are entitled to retain ownership if they pay off the debt holders in full. Therefore, if a large shareholder perceives a favorable investment case assuming full repayment of debt, the shareholder may assist the company in paying off some debt while refinancing the remainder. For example, a company may raise equity in a rights offering, deleveraging the balance sheet and regaining creditworthiness. The reason such a scenario materializes less often than may seem appropriate lies in sophisticated investors' ability to become distressed-for-control investors themselves. Why would a fund manager build a case on repayment of debt when he can purchase debt at a discount, thereby creating the equity at a lower implied price? Such an up-front preference for the equity may exist only if the investor is already a large shareholder or, less likely, if the jockeying for position among the debt holders becomes so fierce that the fight moves to the pre-restructuring equity.

A stub analysis sometimes lulls an equity investor into concluding that management can work through financial distress by communicating forthrightly with debt holders and deleveraging the balance sheet over time. Boards of directors have a fiduciary duty to the shareholders rather than the creditors, putting them on the side of the equity, at least in theory. The investor relations of the executives of highly indebted companies may also give equity investors a false sense of confidence. Optimistic CEOs may be deluded into thinking that the common equity is in a stronger position than it may be in reality. CEOs may view public posturing as important to influencing the course of events by giving creditors confidence in the operations of the company. The hope is to make debt holders more amenable to debt amendments that afford the company financial flexibility.

Despite the brave face a CEO may put on the shareholders' predicament, sophisticated and aggressive debt holders typically have the upper hand. Debt agreements are notoriously complicated and give creditors increasingly onerous recourse against the equity as a company slides down the slope of distress. This recourse may cascade into progressively greater distress for the common stock, raising the specter of a self-fulfilling prophecy once a perception of distress takes hold in the investment community. Most debt agreements contain covenants that threaten the position of the equity well before the company loses its ability to satisfy financial obligations. Covenant breaches, if not waived by the creditors, give the latter a clear path toward implementing a distressed-for-control strategy. In addition, fairly standard cross-default provisions make it difficult for a company to shake off an aggressive creditor holding a piece of company debt.

As a company strains to remain in compliance with covenants, control-minded creditors might be pressuring management behind the scenes. By pointing to the guillotine of increasingly burdensome covenants, aggressive debt holders might offer an alternative to management: Let us take control of the equity through a board-sanctioned debt-for-equity swap, and you get to keep your jobs in a financially healthier company. Suddenly, management's duty to shareholders starts to conflict with the personal interests of key executives. If the CEO takes a strong stance against the creditors, he remains in charge of a heavily leveraged entity in an escalating fight for control. If he loses the fight, the CEO loses the job. If, on the other hand, he works with the debt holders, he secures his job and returns the company to a more normal operating environment.

When the Stars Align

If we have not turned you off to equity stubs yet, let us consider why they occasionally generate eye-popping returns. The basic financial calculus is clear: By layering debt on top of the equity, a company leverages the return to the equity. Leverage famously cuts both ways—and it does occasionally cut to the upside. When this occurs, equity value accretion can be swift.

During the financial crisis of 2008, the stock prices of companies in many industries fell precipitously, creating equity stubs across multiple industries. Had the world as we knew it come to an end in early 2009, debt investors would have reigned supreme. In fact, many of the most sophisticated hedge fund investors shifted their portfolios away from equities toward debt securities at the time, arguing that bonds offered double-digit returns with less risk. They missed the insight that while the future was indeed uncertain for equities, many of them offered triple-digit returns in a return to a more normal market environment. According to Rahul Saraogi, managing director of Atyant Capital Advisors, "It would have been stupid to do 20% annualized risk-arbitrage trades in early 2009 with four- to five-month horizons, when there were potential multi-baggers. . . ."[15] Due to the absence of interest and principal payments on equities, even sophisticated investors made the mistake of switching into more cash-like securities precisely when equities were at their cheapest.

When equities did rebound starting in March 2009, investors who had dared to commit more capital to selected equity stubs benefited to a greater extent than did the creditors of the same companies. In just one extreme example, the equity market value of mattress company Select Comfort fell to a low of roughly $10 million, only to rebound to $1.5 billion a few years later. The number of shares outstanding did not increase markedly over the period, implying an investment return of more than 100x for those who purchased a stake in the equity stub close to the lows reached in 2009. It is hard to imagine that the ex ante distribution of possible outcomes justified the real possibility of such a large payoff. This kind of return can offset quite a few strikeouts that are inevitable in leveraged equities.

The existence of Select Comfort–style returns in common stocks cannot be fully explained unless we consider the impact of fear. Raw and debilitating, fear compels many investors to avoid specific investments at any price, effectively causing the pricing mechanism of markets to break down. Ciccio Azzollini, chief executive officer of Cattolica Partecipazioni, seeks to take advantage of fearful situations. "We consider ourselves bottoms-up stock pickers and, as a general rule, we follow Buffett's timeless principle of be 'fearful when others are greedy and greedy when others are fearful.' I look at areas of maximum pessimism because of the resulting distressed prices. We try to take advantage of panicky and short-sighted investors."[16] In situations in which fear prevails, even rational investors may find few concrete reasons to invest. When price becomes the only reason to make an investment, the point of maximum pessimism may be reached. At such a junction, the rewards to heeding Buffett's advice may be impressive.

One mental model that may receive too little attention by investors echoes Herbert Stein's statement that "if something cannot go on, it will stop." It is hard to say why this simple statement has come to be seen as so remarkable. It might be because the assertion ignores the reason something will stop. As investors, we usually feel that if we cannot pinpoint a reason, our thesis has no basis. Those of us who felt that the housing bubble would end badly failed to profit from the collapse at least in part because we could not identify the specific reason for the inevitable bursting of the bubble. Similarly, most rational investors might have agreed in early 2013 that long-term U.S. Treasury bonds traded in bubble territory. Stein's admonition that the bond bubble would stop if it could not go on moved relatively few investors to action because they were unsure what would stop the bubble—and when.

The same logic that applies to bubbles also applies to companies in distress. If the distressed state cannot go on, it will end. Of course, it could end in a total loss for equity holders. How might we augment Herbert Stein's law to avoid this undesirable outcome? One approach might be to keep looking for companies that cannot go on along their current trajectory *and* that have both a willingness and an ability to turn around their predicament. For example, a technology company hurtling toward bankruptcy due to excessive spending on R&D likely has an ability to curtail R&D spending, at least in the short term. The company may not have the willingness to do so if the CEO owns little stock and may therefore prefer outcomes that involve equity dilution or even bankruptcy. On the other hand, if the CEO owns a large stake in the equity, he will likely do the right thing before it is too late—even if he was foolish enough to exhaust all the inferior alternatives first.

John Lambert hints at the importance of companies possessing the means to turn things around when no other option remains: "We look for investments in areas that for one reason or other are seeing particularly depressed sentiment or are simply out of favor. Within this framework, we also like stocks with a particularly strong internal dynamic, meaning they are to a greater-than-normal extent in control of their own destiny. This usually leads us to recovery or turnaround situations where the company is undertaking a number of different actions to rehabilitate itself following a period of often dramatic underperformance."[17] Rehabilitation may be impossible in situations in which a company is not in control of its destiny, for instance, if it relies on outside funding or operates in a business dependent entirely on the continued confidence of customers.

Screening for Equity Stubs

We distinguish between two types of equity stubs for screening purposes: First, we look for companies that have been designed as equity stubs, namely, private equity-type investments available in the public market. Second, we target companies that have become equity stubs due to some kind of stumble.

Private Equity in Public Markets

When companies decide to part with a business unit, they sometimes seek to unload not only the unit itself but also a chunk of parent company debt. While the amount of debt to be put on the balance sheet of the separate entity may be limited by the debt agreements in place, corporations frequently succeed in unburdening themselves quite nicely in this way. Alternatively, the parent may decide to saddle the unit to be spun off with debt owed to the parent. Such an action reflects the parent company's deliberate choice to create an equity stub. The more indebted the entity to be spun off becomes, the lower the valuation the market may place on the equity of the new entity. In this sense, the parent company may not create economic value by imposing a debt burden on the business unit, but it may create a more predictable stream of cash back to the parent. Occasionally, the enterprise valuation of the spin-off entity may increase if the supply of new equity is de facto constrained through the issuance of debt rather than additional equity. Finally, management of the spin-off may favor a leveraged capital structure, as it amplifies the potential upside.

Screening for spin-offs represents one way of identifying private equity-style stubs. Most spin-offs carry only a modest amount of debt, necessitating examination of the pro forma balance sheets of the spin-off entities. Once we identify a leveraged situation, it makes sense to scrutinize the composition of the management team. Ideally, future wealth creation for the new team is tied closely to long-term increases in the stock price. Especially interesting are situations in which key executives not only receive stock and options from the company but also commit personal funds to an equity stake in the new entity.

Certain other types of initial public offerings also provide a potential source of private equity-style opportunities. For example, companies emerging from bankruptcy protection typically retain some balance sheet leverage. Some bankrupt companies barely emerge as public companies, making them candidates for what is sometimes cynically referred to as Chapter 22—a second Chapter 11 filing after a fairly short time as a public company. Such situations carry obvious risks, but they also promise large rewards if the balance sheet can be deleveraged over time. Another type of initial public offering involves companies that were previously acquired by a private equity sponsor. Firms like the Blackstone Group or the Carlyle Group may take a struggling public company private, turn it around, and take it public again. In all of these situations, it pays to examine both the financial situation of the company and the incentives of the management team.

Distressed Equities

More often than not, a highly leveraged company will exhibit some signs of distress. The following equities may yield promising equity stub opportunities:

- Companies with a debt-to-equity ratio of more than two or three
- Companies with net debt to market value of more than two or three
- Companies with high debt to EBITDA
- Companies with low interest coverage
- Companies that have experienced a large stock price decline

We find the ratio of net debt to equity market value to be one of the most reliable ways of identifying distressed equities. When the net debt of a company exceeds market value, market participants implicitly view debt as a real threat to the equity. Exceptions exist in industries in which leverage may be integral to the business model. That said, the use of market value rather than book value eliminates many exceptions.

Beyond Screening: An Ambulance-Chasing Approach

Many terms have been coined for investors who embrace bad news as opportunity. Unusual as it may seem to most market participants, a minority of investors find it hard to resist catching a falling knife. After all, Buffett's admonition to be greedy when others are fearful seems in perfect agreement with this temptation. The phrasing of metaphors may affect their adoption by investors, as no one literally wants to catch a falling knife. If we wish to cast instances of extreme market pessimism as opportunities, we may prefer the notion of a give-up day—a trading session when fearful investors dump a stock without regard for price. Point of maximum pessimism also reflects a paradoxically optimistic description of a fearful situation. Finally, the notion of blood in the streets may cut both ways—some of us may be terrified while those who appreciate schadenfreude may detect a glimmer of opportunity.

Whatever the wording, headline-grabbing situations may offer a worthwhile non-quantitative starting point for identifying distressed equity ideas. When a deluge of negative headlines hit the solar power industry in 2011–2012, the stock prices of most industry participants imploded. In the stampede toward the exits, investors may have overlooked the nature of the balance sheet leverage of at least one company—MEMC Electronic Materials, a semiconductor firm that develops solar panel technology and operates a solar power business. Most of the debt of MEMC was nonrecourse, implying that the financial situation was less dire than perhaps assumed by the market. Investors' gloomy outlook was best reflected by a decline in the share price of MEMC from $14 per share in February 2011 to less than $2 per share in July 2012. Shawn Kravetz, president of Boston-based Esplanade Capital, sized up the situation as follows: "Wall Street . . . does see balance sheet risk. It was not long ago that cash at the corporate level roughly equaled debt at the corporate level. The majority of the debt is non-recourse . . . and it is backed by extremely valuable, high-quality projects—these are the types of projects that, for example, Berkshire Hathaway's MidAmerican just bought. . . . We are not overly concerned with the balance sheet of the company. Today, in many respects, the stock is trading as if it is a true credit risk, and I think we'll be rewarded for taking that risk."[18] MEMC rebounded off the lows by 135 percent in six months as investors appeared to reconsider the severity of the company's financial situation.

One of the crucial judgments regarding a company whose stock price has plummeted due to bad news involves the nature of the crisis—is it temporary or permanent? When fear clouds our judgment—and it does it to all of us—we tend to view the negatives as permanent. Even if they recede over time, we reason, the damage done to the equity will be such that a rebound will fail to materialize. In hindsight, most such misjudgments seem obvious, but they are anything but obvious in the heat of the moment.

When the Deepwater Horizon accident spilled nearly 5 million barrels of oil into the Gulf of Mexico in 2010, BP shares plummeted due to the fear that the spill might bankrupt the giant oil and gas company. Such fears seem overblown in hindsight, but most of us found it exceedingly difficult at the time to conduct a rational scenario analysis. Whitney Tilson, managing partner of Kase Capital, encountered many vocal naysayers when he made the case for BP at the height of the Macondo oil spill fiasco. Reflects Nick Kirrage:

> *The cash flow generation of BP was not being impinged in the way that many people were thinking it would be. Politically, it was being constrained from paying its dividend in the short term, but in the long term the potential to pay a dividend was as strong as ever. Actually, when you looked at that balance sheet, many people were saying, "This business can be in real solvency trouble given the potential fine." Actually, that was something where as the fear grows it becomes this vicious circle. Suddenly, nobody is doing the numbers, and everyone is just becoming increasingly hyperbolic over the market. When we did the numbers and came up with some scenarios we thought were extremely egregious—gross misconduct, enormous fines—we couldn't really put the hole in the BP balance sheet that people were talking about. In fact, we thought the assets were quite undervalued.*[19]

Examples abound of temporary crises that were misperceived as quasi-permanent by the investment community. Warren Buffett's early successes often featured a low purchase price caused by temporary dislocation. He famously invested a large portion of his investment partnership into shares of American Express during the salad oil scandal of 1963. The scandal caused a collapse in the stock price of American Express, which suffered a financial loss but hardly a long-term reputational impact. When in 2012 investors sold off shares of Chesapeake Energy due to corporate governance concerns, they may have misperceived the magnitude and permanence of the risk. In response to an investor outcry, including by large institutional holders, Chesapeake strengthened corporate governance. The company paid no bonus to founder Aubrey McClendon for 2012, reflecting the positive change. Meanwhile, the controversy had no impact on the natural gas and oil assets owned by Chesapeake.

The list of companies that at one time or another were misperceived as permanently impaired is so long that economic reality could not possibly conform to the frequency of investor fears. The fact that some shunned companies do indeed go bankrupt does not seem to offset the equity value created by abandoned stocks that recover over time. Consider the following list of companies, each of which was left for dead or almost dead by Mr. Market: American Express, Bank of America, Barclay's, BP, Citigroup, Dell, First Solar, General Growth Properties, Morgan Stanley, Nokia, Pier 1 Imports, Research In Motion, Select Comfort, Tempur-Pedic, Sony, Zynga—and, yes, Apple. A few of these companies remain out of favor, so their inclusion as companies that will survive in the long term may be disputed by some. For example, Japanese consumer electronics giant Sony traded at $10 per ADR in late 2012, a quotation that appeared to ignore the company's sum-of-the-parts value. In 2013, most for-profit education companies, ocean shippers, and natural gas exploration companies traded at valuations that implied permanent value impairment.

Our experience suggests that industry-wide sell-offs represent better hunting grounds for potential opportunities than do company-specific crises. A single company may stumble in a way that makes recovery of value impossible, but entire industries disappear quite rarely. Will natural gas producers go out of business because the price of natural gas will forever remain below a level that provides a satisfactory return on investment? Will for-profit education companies disappear because the current administration in Washington, D.C., has expressed hostility toward the industry? Will ocean shipping companies remain shunned forever because the supply of shipping capacity has exceeded demand for several years? We might have asked similar questions following the financial crisis of 2008. Many investors incorrectly believed that the credit rating firms were destined to disappear following their disastrous role in the buildup to the subprime mortgage collapse.

New Zealand's Chandler brothers turned family assets of roughly $10 million into billions in net worth, at least in part by investing in undervalued national champions, companies that were unlikely to disappear but that occasionally traded at rock-bottom prices. Consider the status of Bank of America, Citigroup, or American Express in the United States, BP or Vodafone in the United Kingdom, Deutsche Bank or Daimler Group in Germany, UBS or Credit Suisse in Switzerland, Nokia in Finland, Ericsson in Sweden, Mitsubishi UFJ Financial or Sony in Japan, France Telecom or BNP Paribas in France—the list goes on. While the mere survival of these companies does not guarantee that the equity will escape major dilution, regulators usually prefer to avoid becoming the major shareholders of troubled companies.

Without the benefit of hindsight, it may be exceedingly difficult to disentangle the nature of issues facing a company. Which problems should be considered core to the business, and which are tangential? For example, in the case of for-profit education companies, does increased regulatory scrutiny threaten the survival of the core business, or does it diminish profitability while having little impact on the raison d'être of such companies? In our view, regulatory pressure alone is unlikely to drive education providers out of business—as long as those companies add value to the students. We might be more concerned if emerging educational models, such as those pioneered by the Khan Academy, manage to provide quality educational alternatives at lower cost.

Asking the Right Questions of Equity Stubs

The level of distress varies widely across leveraged equities. Some equity stubs exhibit little distress, having been designed to carry significant debt, as might be the case with some spin-offs. At the other extreme, companies become distressed equities due to poor operating performance or debt-financed acquisitions turned sour. The focus of our questioning varies depending on the situation. Generally, however, the more distressed the equity, the more probing should be the inquiry. For example, if a company is fighting to stave off bankruptcy, the details of the firm's debt agreements become a key consideration.

How Vested Is Management in the Common Stock?

Shareholders tend to be wide-exposed in leveraged equities, as the threat of dilution seems ever present. A board of directors might find it easy to justify an injection of equity capital, strengthening the balance sheet while diluting the equity. Dilution can be particularly pernicious in distressed situations, as the perceived position of weakness may invite low-ball offers. Hedge fund investors may look to buy shares at a material discount to the market price, perhaps insisting on preferred instead of common stock. In particularly egregious cases, the preferred stock would become convertible into the common stock at the option of the holder at a discount to the stock price preceding the conversion.

Toxic securities impose no limit on the dilution inflicted on existing shareholders, establishing a circular relationship between equity value and the market price. In this perverse case of George Soros's reflexivity, a declining share price becomes a self-fulfilling proposition as the pro forma number of shares outstanding increases proportionately to any decrease in the stock price. The fate of shareholders following a toxic financing hinges on the relative determination and power of the common versus the preferred shareholders: If holders of the common are willing and able to accumulate as many shares as it takes to keep the stock price at or above a minimum price, then it becomes possible to calculate maximum dilution, providing a basis for valuing the common.

If, on the other hand, the newly preferred shareholders have their way, short-selling of the common stock might increase, driving down the stock price. Such a strategy by the preferred holders may seem risky due to the associated accumulation of a large short position, but if you consider that conversion of the preferred stock at a low price would create a large number of shares that could be used to cover the short position, the rationale of aggressive shorting becomes quite compelling. We observe this dynamic occasionally in public markets when a company has an outstanding security convertible into common stock. By buying the convertible security and selling common shares, some investors create a profitable trade that is independent of stock price movements.

As shareholders, we want to be as sure as possible that the board will not accept the kind of dilutive capital that would result in permanent loss of capital for holders of the common stock. While certainty is impossible, the probability of responsible management action increases greatly when management has a large vested interest in the common stock. Stock options add little in this regard, as they are likely to be deeply underwater. Ideally, the chairman and chief executive will own a large direct stake in the common stock, measured both in terms of percentage ownership and absolute value. A stake that remains valuable even at a depressed market price will rank highly on the chief executive's list of priorities, strengthened in part by the memory of the likely greater past market value of that equity stake. An owner-operator would be highly motivated to see the market value of stock return to more prosperous levels. Meanwhile, a large ownership stake in percentage terms gives the chief executive influence over any shareholder vote that might be required to approve a recapitalization.

Normally, we might look for the CEO to own shares of stock valued at no less than six or seven times annual compensation. In a distressed situation, this requirement increases as the CEO becomes a potential recipient of inducement awards in a recapitalization. A hedge fund investor staring at the prospect of majority equity ownership of a poorly financed but valuable business would hardly hesitate to reward the CEO for delivering this prize. Inducements may include a promise of continued employment, additional awards of equity securities, and cash.

Given the substantial value the CEO might capture in a shareholder-unfriendly transaction, CEO stock ownership alone may be insufficient for preventing a dilutive outcome. The attitude of the CEO toward the interests of the shareholders, as demonstrated through past statements and actions, becomes critical. Some chief executives own large equity stakes or even have de facto control, but they treat their companies like personal fiefdoms. Whenever such an attitude prevails in normal times, outside shareholders can be quite sure that in a crisis situation, the only concern on the mind of the CEO will be narrow personal interest.

One commitment we would look for in a distressed equity situation regards the type of financing a company would undertake if equity issuance becomes unavoidable. A rights offering provides the fairest way for troubled companies to add to the equity base. Fairness is enhanced in offerings in which the rights become tradable, as shareholders who cannot commit more capital may monetize the value of the rights. No legal restriction prevents a CEO from declaring that a rights offering would be the first choice, should additional equity capital become needed. If a company has a large outside shareholder, it may help to inquire into the willingness of such a shareholder to participate in and, if necessary, to backstop a rights offering. The commitment of a major shareholder to subscribe to shares associated with unexercised rights eliminates any reason for management to look elsewhere for equity capital.

When a leveraged equity finds itself on the less distressed end of the financial spectrum, we may focus slightly more on the upside rather than the downside implicit in management incentives. For example, in the case of a public company spun off from a larger parent, the management team frequently receives a major equity incentive package following the commencement of trading. The price at which the option component of the package is struck may become an anchor for management's thinking about value creation. Expect insiders to do little to boost the stock price in the period leading up to the date of the options award, as a low strike price improves management's prospects for maximizing personal wealth. The insiders' interest in a low options strike price provides an entry timing guide for prospective shareholders. Ideally, we would wait until the strike price is set and then establish a position at roughly the same price.

Are Business Fundamentals Improving or Getting Worse?

When a company is on the ropes, near-term business performance could mean the difference between permanent equity impairment and a chance to preserve equity value. The covenants customary in debt agreements require companies to maintain certain levels of cash flow and equity capital. Typically, highly leveraged companies will release data on their ongoing compliance with covenants, giving investors a view into the wiggle room available to management. When a company breaches a covenant, the process of obtaining a waiver can be treacherous, as management may become distracted at a time when the core business likely requires full attention. The company may have to give up value in exchange for the waiver, which is likely to be only short term in nature. If a waiver cannot be obtained, the company may be pushed into bankruptcy or dilutive recapitalization. As a result, the nature and ownership of debt matter greatly in case of a covenant breach.

A distressed equity with stable or improving fundamentals offers the prospect of value creation. Growth is not necessary in this context, as stable cash flows may suffice for reducing leverage over time. As creditors gain comfort that a company can meet ongoing financial obligations, refinancing of debt on acceptable terms becomes a possibility. Whenever a company can push major debt maturities at least three years into the future, management gains breathing room. The cyclically weak performance of an economy, an industry, or a company may take a few years to revert toward the mean. As a result, the mere act of rescheduling debt maturities further into the future may boost equity value, as it lengthens the expiration date of the optionality inherent in an equity stub.

What Is the Nature of the Leverage?

In normal times, we may view net debt as just a number. While the features of financial leverage may be worthwhile to examine in any situation, their impact on the equity investment thesis grows exponentially as a company becomes more highly leveraged. Whether the credit lines of the Coca-Cola Company mature in one or two years matters little, given the company's strong financial position. Most of us would never even bother to examine the term structure of the Coca-Coca Company's debt—and probably rightfully so. Analogous thinking applies to other companies whose credit is rated highly by Standard & Poor's and Moody's. That said, the credit rating bureaus lost much credibility in the financial crisis of 2008, suggesting that we may prefer to decide for ourselves which companies possess a rock-solid financial position.

When a company becomes overly leveraged, whether due to a strategic event or deterioration in business performance, the role of debt changes from little more than a number to a multidimensional factor. Suddenly, the features of debt, including the term structure, the interest payment requirements, and the covenants, gain significance. If those features are too onerous, the capital structure may become negotiable, with potentially devastating effects for equity holders. Near-term debt maturities can cause equity dilution, even if a high likelihood exists that the company will be able to meet financial obligations in the long term. We distinguish between a liquidity crisis and a solvency crisis, as the fact that a company remains solvent does not preclude it from encountering a shortage of liquidity. Without an ability to keep meeting short-term financial obligations, an otherwise solvent company may be at the mercy of creditors.

Investors in certain industries do in fact carefully consider the nature of debt even in normal times, as some companies utilize various types of leverage as a core component of their business models. For example, retail store operators may show little debt while maintaining large operating lease obligations. Accounting for the latter may be instructive for analyzing the returns on capital of a retail business. In the case of retailers experiencing declines in comparable store sales, the terms of store leases may affect the profitability of a retailer as it seeks to close underperforming stores. In the real estate investment industry, companies utilize mortgage debt in the normal course of operations to generate acceptable returns on equity. Mortgage lenders may have recourse only to the properties to which specific tranches of debt apply. Nonrecourse debt improves the risk profile of a real estate operating business, as a loss limit effectively exists on underperforming properties.

Zeke Ashton explains the benefits of nonrecourse leverage from the standpoint of a portfolio manager:

> *There are two flavors of leverage, and one is vastly superior to the other. One can take recourse leverage by going on margin to buy a stock, but the downside is that with enough leverage, even a moderate and temporary decline in the stock price can produce a very significant loss, and a significant decline can wipe you out. The other kind is non-recourse leverage, where you get the benefits of the leverage if the stock goes up, but at some point the losses become non-recourse to you in the event the stock declines significantly. The way to get non-recourse leverage relatively cheaply is through in-the-money call options. . . .* [20]

Investors sometimes ignore the nonrecourse nature of a company's debt, perceiving the equity as riskier than it actually is. This creates opportunity for research-oriented investors. As real estate turned down in 2007, Marty Whitman held an investment in real estate operating company Forest City Enterprises. Forest City's stock price had plummeted from $70 in May 2007 to less than $4 per share in March 2009. Investors either overlooked or deliberately ignored the nonrecourse nature of Forest City's leverage. A Third Avenue Funds fact sheet touched on some of the rationale behind the firm's holdings in Brookfield Asset Management and Forest City: "When these companies employ leverage, the terms tend to be conservative, such as non-recourse debt with well-laddered maturities." Forest City shares rebounded to $19 per share by April 2011.

As we consider investment in equity stubs, the nature of debt at the company level becomes critically important. We already made the case that ownership of debt by aggressive investors exposes the shareholders to increased risk. We rank the key features of debt in terms of their risk to shareholders as follows: The biggest risk flows from the maturity schedule, as near-term principal payments impose a tangible cash commitment. When a company's inability to meet upcoming debt maturities becomes widely perceived, debt refinancing may become possible only on disadvantageous terms.

Second in impact on the equity risk profile rank the covenants of a debt agreement. Paradoxically, covenants are meant to protect creditors from deterioration in a company's financial and operating position, yet they may serve to accelerate demise or even precipitate bankruptcy in the case of a solvent company. Unless creditors wish to own the equity, it may make little sense for them to impose strict covenants. When a company breaches a covenant, the lender can declare it in default or waive the covenant breach. As default is typically not in the best interest of lenders, covenants frequently serve to extract value from equity holders. If a creditor declines to waive a covenant breach despite concessions, cross-default provisions may kick in, making all of the company's debt due immediately. We rank covenants second to the maturity profile largely because waiver of a covenant breach does not deprive the lender of an expected cash inflow. Many lenders will declare a company in default only if an expected cash payment is not forthcoming.

Kevin Murphy, fund manager of Specialist Value UK Equities at Schroders, illuminates the issue of covenant waivers by reflecting on the example of jeweler Signet:

> *Having looked at a number of retailers in the past and having looked at a number of distressed equity companies in the past, you get a feel for what banks are looking for, what they're willing to extend to companies that are going through these temporary issues, and how onerous some of the terms will be. We could see . . . that [the business] had a fixed charge [coverage ratio covenant], but . . . they had a lot of inventory—they had gold, jewelry, watches—that could easily be liquidated to appease the banks. Yes, they were going to have to have a waiver of their covenants, but that was going to come at a small fine. It wasn't going to result in warrants being given to banks. It wasn't going to involve an equity issuance.*[21]

Finally, we note the risk associated with interest payments. While interest typically represents a cash inflow for the lender and may therefore be more important than a covenant, most distressed companies find it easier to meet interest obligations than to satisfy covenants. An unprofitable company may improve working capital efficiency or sell a noncore asset to meet an upcoming interest payment, but it may have no wiggle room when it comes to a covenant. Not all interest obligations are created equal either. A company may have the right to delay an interest payment or pay in shares rather than cash, though this is more common in the case of preferred stock than debt. We generally view fixed-rate interest obligations as less risky than variable-rate obligations, even though the latter often result in a lower effective interest rate. However, when a company is in distress, it helps to have a fixed commitment rather than one that could spike due to factors outside the company's control.

Key Takeaways

Here are our top 10 takeaways from this chapter:

1. Passive returns to investing in leveraged equities reveal little about the merits of such an approach. On the other hand, the all-but-certain wide dispersion of returns strikes us as crucial.
2. It would be difficult to overstate the importance of judgment in this area. Even if all investors possessed comprehensive data on equity stubs, their investment decisions—and outcomes— would differ materially.
3. We need to be careful not to overreach when our judgment turns out to have been correct. The payoffs in equity stubs may exert an intoxicating effect on the successful investor.
4. Due to the lopsided payoff in leveraged equities, the probability of winning on any one investment may be well under 50 percent. The low batting average increases the size of the sample required to estimate the ex ante likelihood of success with any confidence.
5. It helps to commit our investment theses to paper—and then test and refine them over time. In leveraged equities, experience can be an investor's key asset, if interpreted properly.

We add this qualification because a danger exists that we overlearn.

6. The tendency of investors to think about the likely outcome rather than the range of possible outcomes represents a key stumbling block to success in leveraged equities.

7. Assuming we wish to wade into treacherous but potentially rewarding equity stubs, one of the key considerations in each situation is the ownership of the debt on a company's books.

8. We distinguish between two types of equity stubs for screening purposes: First, we look for companies that have been designed as equity stubs, namely, private equity-type investments available in the public market. Second, we target companies that have become equity stubs due to some kind of stumble.

9. Our experience suggests that industry-wide sell-offs represent better hunting grounds for potential opportunities than do company-specific crises. A single company may stumble in a way that makes recovery of value impossible, but entire industries disappear rarely.

10. The market sometimes ignores the nonrecourse nature of a company's debt, perceiving the equity as riskier than it actually is. This creates opportunity for research-oriented investors.

Notes

1. *The Manual of Ideas*, January 2013, 15.
2. *The Manual of Ideas*, January 2012, 11.
3. *The Manual of Ideas*, October 2011, 14.
4. *The Manual of Ideas*, October 2011, 18.
5. *The Manual of Ideas*, May 2011, 16.
6. *The Manual of Ideas*, October 2011, 17.
7. *The Manual of Ideas*, October 2011, 13.
8. *The Manual of Ideas* interview with Kevin Murphy and Nick Kirrage, Schroders, London, 2012.
9. Rubin and Weisberg: inside cover (2003).
10. *The Manual of Ideas*, October 2011, 15.
11. *The Manual of Ideas*, October 2011, 18.
12. *The Manual of Ideas*, January 31, 2011, 134.
13. *The Manual of Ideas* interview with Massimo Fuggetta, February 2012.
14. *The Manual of Ideas*, December 2012, 14.

15. *The Manual of Ideas*, January 31, 2011, 156.
16. *The Manual of Ideas*, September 2010, 13.
17. *The Manual of Ideas*, March 2012, 7.
18. *The Manual of Ideas* interview with Shawn Kravetz, July 2012, www
    .youtube.com/watch?v=im0IcRxrKAg.
19. *The Manual of Ideas* interview with Kevin Murphy and Nick Kirrage,
    Schroders, London, 2012.
20. *The Manual of Ideas*, May 2009, 31.
21. *The Manual of Ideas* interview with Kevin Murphy and Nick Kirrage,
    Schroders, London, 2012.

CHAPTER 10

International Value Investments

Searching for Value beyond Home Country Borders

See the investment world as an ocean and buy where you get the most value for your money.

—Sir John Templeton

Yogi Berra once presciently observed that "the future ain't what it used to be." The future of international equities, both in perception and reality, has evolved tremendously over the past few decades. In many ways, investors seem to have adopted a more realistic view of international investments, shaped by a surge of information available on markets around the world, lower transaction costs, the bursting of several bubbles, emergence from several crises, and a realization that economies and markets are more interconnected than ever.

Most of the discussion in this book applies globally. However, sufficient peculiarities exist in local markets around the world to warrant closer examination of the rewards and pitfalls of crossborder investing, the associated currency issues, the unique risks involved, and some practical ways in which investors can add international equities to their investment process.

In the interviews we conducted with leading investment managers around the globe, most of them expressed a view that the commonalities outweigh the differences. According to one of Japan's leading fund managers, Scott Callon, CEO of Ichigo Asset Management, "the fundamental principles of sound investing apply the same in Japan as they do anywhere else in the world."[1] The investment activities of Berkshire Hathaway in recent years echo Callon's view, as Buffett has increasingly looked beyond U.S. borders for investment opportunities that meet his criteria. He has found value in several markets around the world, most notably in Europe, Israel, Korea, and even in China.

The world of equity investing should be seen as "borderless," according to Guy Spier. "I think this is a better way to see things. I am not too concerned as to where a company is based. I am more concerned to find the business qualities that I need to find in order to make an investment. While it is easier in the United States, I think that an investor is crazy to stop the search for great investments at the borders of the country they happen to be living in."[2]

The physical domicile and stock exchange listing of a global corporation often provide little insight into the breadth of geographic presence. Tom Gayner relates the following anecdote:

> One question I usually ask people when they ask me about our global investment approach is to mention two companies to them. I say that both companies make engines and move things from one place to another. One of them is Caterpillar and one of them is Honda. Which one is the international company and which one is the domestic firm? Depending on my mood, I give the person either an A or F on that exam. While Caterpillar is headquartered in Peoria, Illinois, it does more of its business outside the United States than inside. While Honda is headquartered in Japan, I believe the United States is still its largest market. Your brokerage statements or pie chart presentations will probably show CAT as a U.S. company and Honda as an international company. I think that is a superficial difference and not a good guide to know if you are investing internationally or not.[3]

If we examine the underlying philosophy of successful investors around the globe, it becomes quite clear that one of the key drivers of success has nothing to do with geography. States Nick Kirrage, fund manager of Specialist Value UK Equities at Schroders: "Value investing is a set of rules that quantify something that is actually much more fundamentally simple than that—and that is human behavior. At its heart, it's a behavioral methodology. Low P/E, or whatever metric you use, is looking to capture a psychological effect of fear and greed. That exists in the U.K. market in the same way it exists in the U.S., European, and Asian markets."[4]

The Approach: Why It Works

Numerous studies confirm that adding international equities to a portfolio improves the risk-reward profile, either by boosting expected returns for a given level of volatility or by lowering the volatility associated with a given level of return. Of course, individual experiences vary widely, depending on the geographies involved, timing, transaction costs, turnover, and other factors. Global investments are not a panacea, nor should they be avoided. Rather, going global offers us an opportunity to find more of what we look for in the first place. If our investment approach is based on finding great businesses trading at reasonable prices, our range of choices will increase if we do not constrain the search to national borders. Wonderful businesses exist in most countries, but perhaps especially in places like Germany, Israel, Switzerland, and the United Kingdom. Even in Japan, many companies possess strong global franchises, achieving returns on equity well above the Japanese average.

As with all investing, the prices paid for international equities will drive investment results. Tim McElvaine stresses the importance of a bargain purchase price: "Since I've worked with Peter [Cundill] or since I had my own fund I've always invested in and out of Japan—quite different culture, its own peculiarities but we've always had a very good experience there. Mostly because we were disciplined about the price we were paying."[5]

A Different Animal

Many investors appear to make the mistake of expecting foreign markets to mirror their domestic market in every material way. This may be particularly true in the area of corporate governance. Unfortunately, governance practices change only slowly and may be impossible to influence from the outside. We therefore have a choice: abandon investing in certain countries altogether or calibrate the approach by using price as a key lever. The valuation we are willing to ascribe to a business represents one of the few areas of complete control in our investment process. If a security fails to meet our required price, we may simply keep our capital allocation to that security at zero.

We avoid much trouble in international investing when we accept that some levers, such as corporate governance, are harder to pull than others, such as the price we are willing to pay. According to McElvaine,

> *The initial mistake I made perhaps is one that other people make as well—they assume that the Japanese are doing it wrong and they'll figure it out and they'll do it the North American way, the American way. Or you just need to tell them enough times how you think they should do it and they'll do it. And I don't think that approach works in Japan. So if you want to make a corporate governance bet in Japan, you might orient your portfolio a little bit differently than I do. I have been a little bit more accepting of, "alright this is what they do and I'm just going to make sure that's factored into the price I pay."*[6]

The Value of Choice

When we go global in the search for investments, we give ourselves a free option to pay a lower price than might be possible in our home market. While no two equities are the same, similar equities frequently trade at materially different valuations across geographies. When entire countries move out of favor, many investors sell all of their investments or stop considering new investments in those countries. Whether Argentina or Greece, some countries acquire a stigma that makes it difficult for investors to look through to the specific businesses on sale. Soo Chuen Tan presented a Greek company case study at a ValueConferences event in 2012, a time when many investors had written off Greece. The company highlighted by Tan possessed durable assets with annuity-like cash flows that were little affected by the financial crisis in Greece. As other investors dared step back into Greece, the assets were revalued closer to their intrinsic worth, resulting in strong gains for those willing to analyze the underlying business at a time of fear.

Also in 2012, a large portion of the Ben Graham–style net current asset value bargains were located in Japan, a country shunned by most investors after two decades of underperformance. Exhaustion sets in even among devoted value investors, as years and years of underperformance erode client assets and personal confidence in the adopted investment approach. How else might one explain the large disparity in the number of net net opportunities in the United States and Japan?

The disparity becomes even starker when we consider that the average company trading at a discount to net current asset value in Japan appeared to be of higher quality than the average net net in the United States. Most of the latter had money-losing operations, but the former remained profitable and cash-generative. Stated Mohnish Pabrai in late 2012: "Japan is the cheapest market in the world, and if you were to specifically do screens which are Ben Graham screens, it is the 'net net' capital of the world. And there's nothing wrong with these businesses. The only thing that's going on here is human psychology. The Nikkei was very overvalued in the late 1980s and early 1990s, and it is extremely undervalued today and therein lies the opportunity."

Pabrai highlighted the example of Japanese company Nakakita Seisakusho at Japan Investing Summit 2012:

> *This is a company that has a $98 million market cap, it's been around since 1930. They're basically in the "extremely sexy" business of manufacturing and selling valves and remote controllers for ships and power plants, and the company has more than $100 million of cash on its balance sheet. . . . From 1979 to today, the company has never lost money. . . . It made money in 2008, in 2007, in 2009, throughout all the different recessions, all earning money . . . $10 million to $15 million a year in free cash flow, and revenue is about $270 million. They're actually pushing a decent amount of the cash out, so the dividend yield on the stock is about 5 percent. . . .*[7]

Another example of the expanded choices available when we venture outside the borders of our home country is Australian holding company Vealls. It not only owns a collection of assets that make it unique but has also historically offered investors an opportunity to purchase those assets at a discount to their stated values. Christopher Swasbrook traces the company's public existence to a 1951 listing by influential Australian businessman Sir Ian Potter. In the 1980s, Vealls moved beyond its roots as an electrical appliance company, reinvesting capital into Australian farmland. They added a ski field in New Zealand and an oak forest in France to the asset base over the years, all the while accumulating a material net cash position. According to Swasbrook, the top executives running Vealls "have been very, very good stewards of capital. They don't pay themselves egregiously. They don't do any of the things that these family-owned enterprises can fall victim to."[8]

Uses and Misuses of Investing in International Equities

Buffett's concept of "circle of competence," while typically used in the context of different industries, also has some applicability to investing in different countries. Due to the many unifying features of global equity investing, we may falsely assume that our competence extends to investing in all geographies. Eric Khrom, managing partner of Khrom Capital Management, frames the issue in the context of avoiding a situation in which he might be one of the least informed parties. He cites Venezuela as an example of a country in which he would be unlikely to invest: "The problem with Venezuela is it would probably violate one of my rules of the investment process, which is, make sure you are never the patsy at the table. It would probably take me a very long time— years—before I become as smart as one of the major shareholders of a Venezuelan company . . . and that by itself is enough for me to avoid the country and not to look at it."[9]

Don't Assume You Know Who You Are Dealing With

Even if we accept that the core principles of investing apply globally, we may wish to adjust our focus of inquiry based on the peculiarities of each market. Guy Spier advises us

> not to take the conditions that exist in the home investing country and assume that the same conditions exist in the

country where the investment is being made. I have seen that going both ways. From the United States investing out, there are assumptions that investors have made about how the managers of the foreign company will allocate capital. There are also assumptions about what kind of standard managers hold themselves to. Not all managers of companies want to be remembered for being the best capital allocators. In some countries, being rapacious and greedy is considered a normal standard. Russia might be an example of that. At the same time, there are some countries, such as Switzerland, where I would argue the ethics of drawing a modest salary and really acting in the best interest of the shareholders are possibly even higher than the very high standards that already exist in the United States.[10]

Spier's insight has several implications for the investment process of globally active investors. First, it pays to develop a distinct baseline for analysis of companies in each country or region. When we analyze a Russian equity, we may assume a higher degree of corporate governance risk than in a typical Swiss company. By placing the burden of proof on the Russian equity, we sharpen the focus of our analysis. Unless the company possesses attributes that set apart its corporate governance from that of the Russian corporate average, we may wish to pass on the investment or require a wider-than-normal discount to estimated value.

Second, we should be careful not to punish investment candidates unduly if they differ from domestic market investments in a way that does not detract materially from the core thesis. For example, if we reject Japanese equities trading at Graham-style bargain prices because their managers fail to embrace U.S.-style capital allocation policies, we may miss some exceptional opportunities. In the case of a net net, cash-generative operations, a decent dividend payout, and honest management may suffice for a strong investment case. The U.S.-style capital allocation would be a bonus, but it should be neither required nor expected if the purchase price is sufficiently low.

Finally, Spier's insight may be extended beyond management-related expectations to other areas, including the regulatory environment, the transparency of financial reporting, and the key features of a company's business model. Even if a foreign company operates in the same industry as a U.S. firm, the model might be materially different. For example, the cash flows of a U.S. for-profit education provider might bear little resemblance to those of a similar provider in Singapore. The business franchise of a company providing nontradable services in a country where such services are cheap and plentiful may be quite a bit weaker than the franchise of a similar business in a country like Switzerland, where even basic nontradable services, such as dry cleaning or gardening, command premium prices.

The Pitfalls of Chasing Growth in Emerging Markets

One of the biggest drivers of disappointment for investors who venture globally might be unrealistic expectations of the rewards of emerging markets. Simply mentioning the size of the Chinese market—1 billion people—has a mouthwatering effect on many investors. No wonder Chinese fraudsters succeeded in duping many U.S. investors through reverse-merger IPO schemes. When unbridled optimism sets in, rational risk assessment becomes virtually impossible.

Sell-side investment banks hold culpability in feeding investor enthusiasm for promising but treacherous markets. The term BRICs invariably elevated the status—and market valuations—of companies in Brazil, Russia, India, and China, four large emerging-growth markets. Russia had sorely disappointed Western equity investors by 2012, with many smart investors also betting that the huge imbalances in China would cause another collapse.

In the rush toward growth, some investors readily ignore the return-on-capital prospects of fast-growing but highly competitive and capital-intensive industries. Rahul Saraogi shares a poignant observation of the presence of foreign investors in his home market:

> Since I am currently focused on India, let's take some Indian examples. I find it strange that investors fall all over each other to invest large sums of money in businesses like telecom, infrastructure, etc. India has six full-service telecom operators that have their entire pan-India networks built out. In telecom, all the investment happens upfront and the marginal cost of delivering a call is virtually zero. Also, in order to stay alive, telecom companies have to continuously spend

on expanding and upgrading their networks. As a result, telecom companies never generate any free cash and then eventually get crushed by their debt burdens. However, you'll see the smartest analysts and the smartest fund managers talk about subscriber additions, market penetration, average revenue per user, accounting earnings, advertising campaigns, brands, etc. The bottom line is that telecom companies will never be able to compound the money that investors allocate to them in aggregate and most of the invested capital will get destroyed. However, in the testosterone rush of high "growth" and subscriber additions/network expansion, the stocks of telecom companies do well and they raise capital at every opportunity (justified, of course, by the need to capitalize on the fantastic available growth opportunities).[11]

In an increasingly interconnected world, it becomes exceedingly difficult for countries like India and China to sustain strong growth rates when key Western markets enter recession. China kept growing throughout the financial crisis of 2008–2009, despite the associated drop-off in U.S. consumer demand for Chinese goods. It appears the Chinese government encouraged real estate investment with questionable returns on capital to offset the impact of U.S.-related weakness. When an emerging market growth story starts defying the odds of an integrated global market, investors may wish to reexamine their optimistic assumptions.

Making Money amid Challenging Demographic Conditions

Investors based in the United States sometimes fail to appreciate the fact that their home demographics rank among the most favorable in the developed world. While the average U.S. household size has declined from 3.7 in 1930 to 2.6 in 2010, household size has remained roughly flat over the past two decades and may even have ticked up recently.[12] This compares to 2.2 in France and 2.0 in Germany.[13] More significant than household size, which may be skewed by cultural factors, may be the rate of population growth and the shape of the population pyramid. The U.S. population grew 0.96 percent in 2011, outpacing 0.50 percent growth in France, –0.21 percent in Germany, and –0.28 percent in Japan.[14] The U.S.

population pyramid is less top-heavy than is the case in most other developed economies, giving the United States a relatively more favorable outlook. That said, virtually all developed economies face serious issues around their obligations to an aging population.

Few developed economies have faced the kind of worrisome population trend seen in Japan. Perhaps surprisingly, the overall Japanese population size reached a near record of 127 million people in 2012. However, declines have been prevented only by the aging of the Japanese populace. The percentage of people age 65+ reached 23 percent in 2010, up from 20 percent in 2005 and 10 percent in 1985.[15] As a result, while the overall population size has remained roughly flat over the past decade, the number of people in certain key consumer categories has declined precipitously.

Persistent declines in the number of potential customers challenge our ability to value a business. What multiple of current-period earnings should an investor be willing to pay for a company whose customer base may keep eroding over time? Should we model future corporate tax increases that might be needed to help the government meet its obligations to an aging population? Do we consider the possibility that Japan may, despite cultural reservations, invite immigration to offset declines in the workforce? These and other difficult questions have kept many foreign investors from deploying capital in Japan, perhaps so much so that Japanese equities have become undervalued after more than two decades of declining stock prices. The Nikkei 225 index declined from a peak of 38,957 in 1989 to 10,900 in 2013, an astounding loss in light of the increase in most other developed-country market indices during the same period.[16]

The issue of challenging demographics confirms the importance of calibrating fundamentals versus expectations, a concept explained in Alfred Rappaport and Michael Mauboussin's *Expectations Investing*. When the expectations implied in stock prices fall materially short of the likely fundamentals, a buying opportunity may be at hand. Scott Callon argues that such a dynamic may be at work in Japan:

> *If the population is shrinking, then retail sales are also likely to shrink. We own a couple of great retailers, and we have forecast very little in the way of future growth from them. However, if you have a market cap that is 60 to 70 percent made up of cash holdings, a dominant market position which*

translates into significant positive cash flow, and a price-to-book ratio well below one, you can build in a large amount of macro deterioration and still be confident of generating a reasonable return. In fact, what we tend to find is that the negative demographic headwinds have been overly priced in, that the negative scenarios baked into certain companies' stock prices are wildly more extreme than what is actually happening.[17]

Agrees Howard Smith: "It's a cheap market with a lot of cash generating companies and a lot of liquid assets on the balance sheets of companies. We think that provides a lot of opportunities to find interesting value ideas."[18]

Practical Trading Considerations

Impediments to foreigners investing directly in local stock markets around the world have been steadily removed, largely due to electronic trading, the global presence of large banks and brokerage firms, and increasing homogenization of the rules of key stock markets globally. According to Guy Spier, "Transaction costs in international markets have been going down over time, so I don't think they should be a big concern. I have been a buy-and-hold investor, and my average holding period is in excess of three years. To the extent that the transaction costs are a bit higher, it has not been a deterrent for me."[19]

As Spier points out, the longer an investor's time horizon, the easier it may be to overcome any practical shortcomings of local stock markets. The relative importance of illiquidity and higher transaction costs diminishes as the investment horizon lengthens due to the higher gross return anticipated over a long time period. This raises the analytical hurdle somewhat, as we want to avoid changing our minds shortly after investing in an illiquid foreign security. If we judge the margin of safety to be wide enough to justify an investment even if bad news emerges in the near term, then an investment with above-average trading costs might make sense.

The question of currency hedging seems ever present in international investing. On a short time horizon, a decline in the value of the currency in which a foreign equity is quoted may erase any increase in the foreign currency stock price, resulting in an unsatisfactory outcome. While a currency translation loss represents a risk to a short-term investor, viewing currency as an additional layer of risk appears misguided. Rather, currency represents both a layer of risk and a layer of reward. The greater variability of outcomes to a foreign investor may affect position sizing, but it should have little impact on the merits of an investment.

Currency hedging becomes especially immaterial—and perhaps even too costly—when we adopt a long-term time horizon. Currency exchange rates and local stock prices may behave independently in the short term. Over long periods, however, the two variables correlate inversely, with local currency stock prices increasing in response to a declining currency—and vice versa.

Currency risk may also exist at the company level as distinct from the portfolio management level. Such risk does not represent a trading consideration but rather affects the fundamentals of an equity investment instead. According to Caglar Somek, portfolio manager of Caravel Fund, "We just want to make sure that we don't have too much of a risk in terms of balance sheet mismatch—a business that is dependent on importing a raw material that you pay in dollars and yet you get local currency cash flows."[20] In addition, if a company has debt, a mismatch could exist between the currency in which the debt is serviced and in which company sales are denominated.

Clarity through Extremist Thinking

The extremism described here has nothing to do with how the term is commonly used in society. In our context, extremist thinking can be one of the more useful tools for analyzing complex interactions between economic and financial variables. Often, the causal relationship between variables is difficult to judge. We illuminate a relationship by pushing one or more variables to an extreme.

Let us explore the connection between currency devaluation and the prices of American Depository Receipts. Consider this question: What happens to the price of an ADR if the foreign company's home currency is devalued by 20 percent versus the U.S. dollar? Since ADRs are quoted in dollar terms, we may conclude that the ADR price should also decline by 20 percent. This may indeed occur, assuming the company's home currency stock price remains the same. But is this assumption realistic? Since a sharp currency devaluation and investor pessimism regarding a country's economic prospects go hand in hand, investors may sell the locally listed shares as well. The decline in the foreign stock price, coupled with 20 percent currency devaluation, of course, implies that the ADR price may fall by more than 20 percent. So far, this scenario sounds logical and, indeed, may occur in reality.

But what if the local currency were devalued not by 20 percent but by 95 percent? Would the ADR price drop by 95 percent as well? Or, as we have seen, could the ADR price drop by even more than 95 percent? Might a foreign company that is the number-one telecom firm in its country, has a strong balance sheet, and was valued at $5 billion only a few days ago suddenly be worth $250 million or less simply because its government wasn't able to defend the currency?

If a $250 million valuation for such a company does not strike you as odd, let's take one more step in our extremist thinking. Imagine a different foreign company that owns 10 percent of the real estate of an entire country—let's say Argentina—has no debt, and is profitable. If the home country's currency is devalued by 99.99999 percent, should the market value of the company decline from $10 billion to $1,000? Put differently, would you buy 10 percent of Argentina's land for $1,000, even if the currency was worthless and there is a risk of expropriation? The following must be true to prevent us from buying 10 percent of Argentina for $1,000: The Argentine company's local currency stock price must *soar* postdevaluation rather than decline, as we might have assumed initially.

Extremist thinking has just helped us debunk a common stock market misconception—that currency devaluation should result in a similar or even greater decline in the U.S. dollar stock price. So next time we hear of a major currency devaluation, we may wish to look at how the ADRs of relevant companies respond. If their prices drop more than the change in the currency exchange rate, and if the companies own real assets—raw materials, land, or industrial equipment—and have a healthy balance sheet, we may consider buying. Such an opportunity existed in late 2002 when the ADR price of Cresud, an Argentine agricultural company with large land holdings, was cut in half due to the devaluation of the Argentine peso. Cresud had a solid balance sheet and was trading significantly below tangible book value, suggesting that investors had overreacted. A year later, the price had increased from $5 to $15 per ADR.

Screening for International Equities

Most equity databases still focus on companies listed on U.S. stock exchanges, including American Depository Receipts and some foreign companies traded over the counter. For those without a costly Bloomberg or Capital IQ subscription, screening for locally listed equities requires greater effort. As of the publication date of this book, the *Financial Times* made available a comprehensive no-cost screening tool for global equities at markets.ft.com (click on "Screener").

Go Anywhere or Stick to Investable Markets?

The global equity screener of the *Financial Times* enables investors to focus their search by country or region. We generally find it useful to search by country, especially if we wish to obtain a fairly long list of investment candidates for further research. By contrast, if we wish to pinpoint a small number of companies meeting stringent performance or valuation criteria, we may screen without regard for geography. We find it instructive to devote chunks of time to specific geographic markets, as each market comes with a set of peculiarities, including the way companies disclose financial information. What's more, we may prefer certain geographies to others due to political, regulatory, and economic factors, making it cumbersome to recalibrate the valuation analysis as we move from one equity to the next. That said, we sometimes learn more from slicing up the equity universe by industry rather than country. For example, we may want to consider the relative valuations of the incumbent telecom services carriers around the world. The disparity in valuations we are likely to encounter may point us toward worthwhile opportunities.

Worldwide screening makes it quite easy to identify countries shunned by the investment community. For example, if we screened for Graham-style net nets in early 2013, we were likely to see a list dominated by Japanese equities. By identifying a fearful country and then screening for all equities in that country, we may encounter some exceptional companies that, while still not dirt cheap, trade at a material discount to similarly strong businesses in other countries. Tim McElvaine lets market headlines and low valuations steer his search for international investments: "I prefer to go into areas where there's turmoil and find something that you'd like to do in it. I'm always torn when you're in an area of turmoil between paying an okay price for probably the better company or paying a really cheap price for the not so good company—that's a conflict I have even to this day."[21]

Screening for neglect provides an alternative to screening for turmoil. Low valuations may be found in both types of markets, so the preference for turmoil versus neglect may be driven by the psychological constitution of each investor. Some of us thrive at buying securities other investors are actively dumping; others prefer buying securities others seem to have forgotten altogether. Howard Smith makes the case for investing in Japan by highlighting investor neglect of this once-popular market:

Japan is a very inefficient market overall. It's a market that has generally been going down for the last 23 years since the bubble burst at the end of 1989. It's generating less attention as the years go by. Even five years ago, Japan still had a stand-alone presence as an asset class. There was still a bucket for Japan equities in people's portfolios. Increasingly now, Japan is just a part of a broader Asian approach to equity investing, and even then, Japan seems to find it hard to compete with the interest levels people pay to China or India or the ASEAN markets. Japan is an overlooked market that gets less analytical attention than it deserves.[22]

Sebastien Lemonnier explains his interest in neglected equities by citing the example of Baron de Ley:

This company is not far from having everything investors currently don't want: Spanish exposure, low stock liquidity, no emerging markets exposure, limited operating leverage, no acquisition strategy, limited investor relations. In reality, this Rioja wine producer's fundamentals are strong. The company has two strong brands (El Coto and Baron de Ley). It is a differentiated player with no young wine production, contributing to a robust margin track record. It has scale and a good organization. It is signing exclusive distribution agreements with leading local distributors. It has a strong balance sheet, with solid tangible assets and no debt; solid and stable free cash flow; and quality management. The fundamental picture is much stronger than the top-down market perception. Finally, the valuation provides enough margin of safety for an investor like me who does not like to pay up—it trades at 1x book value despite 13 percent ROCE and 7x EBIT 2011, which is a roughly 40 percent discount to its historical level.[23]

We may sometimes exclude certain markets from consideration entirely due to their lack of alignment with our key investment criteria. Investors who require a shareholder-friendly attitude by management to commit capital to a company may find little to do in Russia. We recall an anecdote told by a value investor who had met with a Russian management team at their headquarters. The investor quizzed them on why the company, given its low stock price, had raised expensive equity capital when cheaper debt financing would have been available. "What do you mean?" wondered the CEO in disbelief. "Equity capital is free. We never have to pay it back!" While perhaps unique in the sincerity with which it was communicated, this view seemed rather prevalent among Russian executives.

Another reason to exclude a country from consideration might be the political and economic system in place. For example, investors who view government steering of an economy as destructive may regard China as destined for collapse. Observes Rahul Saraogi,

India will definitely outperform China over a long period of time. China's model is completely top-down and driven by gross misallocation of capital. I don't know whether the come-uppance will be in 2012 or 2022, but when it does happen, the damage will be devastating. The reason the free market (for all its flaws and shortcomings) works better than any other system is because it is driven by the daily, small and incremental decisions made by millions of market participants. No single individual or authority has enough knowledge, experience and understanding to take benevolent decisions for hundreds of millions of people. It can work for a time (or appear to work), but the system has no automatic stabilizers and is institutionally bankrupt. If anything breaks or stops working, the system has to go into free-fall—there is no other possible outcome.[24]

Excluding a country from consideration without regard for valuation may seem like an irrational decision for investors who subscribe to the view that there is a price for everything. However, the decision becomes more sensible if the importance an investor places on a factor like corporate governance differs materially from the importance placed on the same factor by other investors. If most investors cared little about corporate governance in Russia, the likelihood would be high that the valuations prevailing in Russia would be out of reach for an investor who demands a large discount for bad governance. As a result, in a time- and resource-constrained world, it may make sense to pass on certain countries altogether.

On the flip side, we may choose to direct our search toward specific countries that may not have the biggest or most liquid markets but that do possess the right climate for equity investment. Kaushal Majmudar, chief investment officer of the Ridgewood Group, learned about one such country in the book *Startup Nation:* "It tells the amazing story of how the entire country of Israel has become wealthy and productive under seemingly harsh circumstances due mainly to the determination and moxy of its entrepreneurs, many of whom are ex-military. Besides being a great read, the book conveys a lot of lessons about success, culture, and how committed people find a way to win. I'm in awe of what Israel has accomplished in a relatively short time and its relevance to many, many aspects of business and investing."[25]

Beyond Screening: Riding the Coattails of Regional Experts

A superinvestor-following cottage industry has sprung up in the United States, with many market participants scrutinizing the moves of great investors like Warren Buffett, Bill Ackman, and Mohnish Pabrai. Similarly successful fund managers tend to be quite a bit less prominent in other countries. Most investors would be hard-pressed to name even one great investor in countries like France, Germany, the United Kingdom, India, or Japan.

Such global superinvestors do exist. And given the relatively smaller size of their home markets, they generally possess deep local market knowledge and strong business relationships within their home countries. Knowing which companies such investors embrace, and which they shun, can improve our probability of success. It still makes tremendous sense to conduct independent research and arrive at an investment thesis built on the fundamentals of the business rather than the shareholder structure. However, a list of international companies owned by great investors in their respective local markets may serve as an excellent starting point.

Two layers of difficulty enter the picture: First, building a list of investors whose portfolios have signal value as opposed to noise is no small feat. Published rankings of the world's largest asset management firms or hedge funds reveal little about the truly great investors. Many of the best investors operate under the radar and may be known only by a small group of family offices and funds of funds. For example, the public prominence of New Zealand's Chandler brothers ranks far below their deserved prominence as two of the most successful global investors of the past few decades. Have you ever heard of these great investors: Tito Tettamanti of Switzerland, François Badelon of France, and Daniel Gladiš of the Czech Republic?

Second, reporting requirements differ around the world. In many countries, investors need not release portfolio-level information. Reporting requirements kick in only if an investor acquires a certain percentage of the common stock of a specific company—typically 3 percent or 5 percent. This makes it more challenging to track the moves of fund managers who focus their activities outside the United States.

The example of Daniel Gladiš, chief executive officer of Vltava Fund, shows quite convincingly why we may benefit from tracking the investment activity of global superinvestors. Not only has Gladiš ranked as one of the best-performing global fund managers for several years but also his firm does the kind of in-depth analysis for which most of us lack the requisite time and resources. States Gladiš regarding his analysis of the copper mining industry:

> We've analyzed all projects in copper that are being developed, maybe 60 or 70 of them that comprise about 95 percent of what is being drilled. I've calculated in each of them what the average long-term price of copper has to be in order for that project to make enough return on capital, say 15 percent to 20 percent depending on where the company is based.

For example, for copper it comes to about $2.50 or $2.70 [per pound]. Now if copper is $2.70, we'll probably worry about that quite a bit. The valuation of copper companies also reflects that. If copper gets way below the average or below $2, then we might be interested, because then copper companies will be decimated with those prices. Some of them will make it; some of them won't make it. But eventually, copper prices have to get to the average at least, otherwise the project will not be developed. . . .[26]

The depth of Gladiš's research into copper mining makes us quite interested in the copper-mining companies he owns at a given point in time.

François Badelon's investment firm Amiral Gestion has successfully applied value investing techniques in France and beyond for many years. As Badelon modestly explains, "We're just trying to do the Warren Buffett way with our own personality, our own background, our own edge. . . . Trying to do things we understand is probably the most difficult part because you think you understand, but you don't . . . a very important part of the philosophy we took from those [value investing] books is concentration. I have very few good ideas, so when I find one, I'm trying to invest quite a lot. Another important part of the philosophy is to have an open mind and invest anywhere."[27] While Badelon keeps an open mind to investments wherever they might be, his firm's location makes it somewhat of a champion of value investing in France. As a result, whenever we consider an equity in France, we like to know whether Badelon's firm owns it and why.

Table 10.1 lists 50 international investors who may be considered value investing thought leaders in their respective countries.

Asking the Right Questions of International Equities

The questions we pose to international investment candidates flow both from an overarching investment philosophy and the specifics of the investment under consideration. The goal remains the same across the globe—to identify equities trading at wide discounts to fair value.

TABLE 10.1 Selected International Value Investors (outside North America)

Investor(s)	Company	Country
Kerr Neilson	Platinum	Australia
Allan Gray, William Gray	Orbis	Bermuda
Bruno Rocha	Dynamo	Brazil
Daniel Gladiš	Vltava Fund	Czech Republic
Emmanuel Daugeras	Amdamax	France
François Badelon	Amiral Gestion	France
Max Otte	PI Global Value Fund	Germany
Frank Fischer, Reiner Sachs	Shareholder Value	Germany
Peder Prahl, Florian Schuhbauer	Triton Partners	Germany
Richard Lawrence	Overlook	Hong Kong
V-Nee Yeh, Cheng Hye Cheah	Value Partners	Hong Kong
Rahul Saraogi	Atyant	India
Sidd Mehta	Beaconsfield	India
Amitabh Singhi	Surefin	India
David Coyne, Paul McNulty	Setanta	Ireland
Ori Eyal	EVCM	Israel
Ciccio Azzollini	Cattolica Partecipazioni	Italy
Robert Macrae, Mark Pearson, Peter Tasker	Arcus	Japan
Scott Callon	Ichigo	Japan
Alexander Kinmont	Milestone	Japan
Shuhei Abe	SPARX Group	Japan
David Baran	Symphony	Japan
Jiro Yasu	Varecs	Japan
Chan Lee, Albert Yong	Petra	Korea
Juan Matienzo	Mercor	Mexico
Georg Krijgh	Guardian Fund	Netherlands
Chris Swasbrook	Elevation	New Zealand
Jochen Wermuth, Sergey Ezimov	Wermuth	Russia
Ngiek Lian Teng	Target	Singapore

TABLE 10.1 Selected International Value Investors (outside North America) (*Continued*)

Investor(s)	Company	Country
Richard Chandler	Richard Chandler	Singapore
Francis Daniels	Africa Opportunity	South Africa
Simon Marais, William Gray	Allan Gray	South Africa
Pablo González López	Abaco	Spain
F. G. Paramés, A. G. de Lázaro Mateos	Bestinver	Spain
Lars Förberg, Christer Gardell	Cevian	Sweden
Guy Spier	Aquamarine	Switzerland
Philip Best, Marc Saint John Webb	Argos	Switzerland
Jean-Pascal Rolandez	L.T. Funds	Switzerland
Felix Zulauf	Zulauf	Switzerland
Massimo Fuggetta	Bayes Fund	United Kingdom
Jeroen Bos	Church House	United Kingdom
James Findlay, Charles Park	Findlay Park	United Kingdom
Andrew Green, John Lambert	GAM	United Kingdom
Simon Denison-Smith, Jonathan Mills	Metropolis	United Kingdom
Thorsten Polleit, Matthias Riechert	Polleit & Riechert	United Kingdom
Hugo Capel Cure, Rupen Patel, Mark Wallace	Rothschild	United Kingdom
Ian Lance, Nick Purves	RWC	United Kingdom
Stephen Butt	Silchester	United Kingdom
Christopher Hohn	Children's	United Kingdom
Dominic Fisher	Thistledown	United Kingdom

Source: The Manual of Ideas.

A Question for Europe: How Global Is the Business?

In Europe, we face a multitude of distinct areas of potential opportunity under one unifying umbrella. Europe's leading academic in the field of value investing, Max Otte, founder of the IFVE Institut für Vermögensentwicklung in Köln, Germany, contrasts Europe and the United States: "Europe simply is 'more messy and complicated'—if you don't have a truly global player, you really have to go country by country. That's 10 times the market research you do for a U.S. company. This is a reason why many U.S. investors don't look here much, which in my view is a big mistake. The legal system is as reliable as in the United States (fewer liability suits), and the business culture is generally one of more trust than in the United States. The firms are generally more global than U.S. firms. . . ."[28]

When European equities move out of favor due to macroeconomic concerns, investors may find rewards in identifying companies that generate most of their profits outside the continent. Not only may such European companies trade at lower multiples than similar companies based in North America or Asia but also they may benefit from potential weakening of the euro. For example, when the euro depreciated versus the dollar as concerns about the European debt crisis escalated in 2011, business picked up for many German exporters as their products became more price-competitive.

A Question for India: What's the Right Concentration?

In India, an investor may not get to ask many crucial questions of prospective investment candidates due to the barriers of distance and language. As a result, foreign investors may have few alternatives to focusing on Indian companies listed in New York or London, which adhere to higher transparency and reporting standards. Observes Amitabh Singhi, managing director of Surefin Investments:

> I would do one of three things depending on how active one
> wants to be. Either average into an index over the next five
> years with a simple formula which dictates putting more
> money when valuations are cheap versus expensive. But do
> it mathematically and consistently. This is great if you don't
> want to be active. If you do not want to have a physical base
> in India but are an active investor, then diversify into various

statistically cheap "Graham-type" stocks and rebalance the portfolio occasionally. Again, discipline and consistency would be important. Ideally, you want to have a physical base in India—or in an area close to the Indian time zone so you can travel frequently—if you want to concentrate your investments.[29]

Singhi alludes to the issue of portfolio concentration in foreign markets, suggesting that an ability to concentrate may go hand in hand with an ability to kick the tires. Absent a high degree of confidence in a specific investment, it makes sense to reduce risk through a smaller allocation of capital. Buffett famously invested in Graham-style bargains in Korea several years ago after reportedly flipping through profiles of Korean public companies. His view that the equities as a group were likely to outperform, coupled with an absence of conviction in any one of those equities, necessitated a basket approach involving a relatively small allocation of capital to each security.

A Question for Japan: What's an ROE?

In Japan, many foreign investors have lamented the low returns on equity of Japanese companies. Yet, by focusing solely on the final return on equity number, investors may be missing a key question: Why? Scott Callon shares this perspective:

Japan's ROE challenge is really about the E, not the R. Japanese companies' returns are very similar to those of peers in the United States and Europe, so the R part of the equation is fine. The driver of low ROEs is thus the denominator, E: Japanese firms frequently have very large amounts of retained earnings, often in the form of cash, so the returns are diluted across a massive equity base. On the one hand, this is enormously comforting: Japanese balance sheets are about as bullet-proof as they come, and cash has real value. However, the large equity bases do dramatically reduce ROEs, so from a shareholder's perspective, this is a negative.[30]

Echoing Callon's observation, we may ask ourselves which of the following two hypothetical companies we would prefer:

Company A has shareholders' equity of $100 million and generates $20 million of net income. Company B has shareholders' equity of $200 million and generates $20 million of net income. Most of us might prefer Company A in a going-concern scenario, as an ROE of 20 percent suggests a higher-quality business than does an ROE of 10 percent. We might even conclude that Company A is likely to experience faster growth, as it reinvests capital at rates closer to 20 percent than 10 percent.

Our analysis of these two hypothetical companies might change if we find out that Company B is actually Company A, with one difference: In scenario B, the company has an additional $100 million of cash in the bank. In other words, the operating business generates $20 million of net income on $100 million of equity employed in each scenario. In scenario B, the company also has $100 million in cash earning essentially no return, due to the low interest rates prevailing in Japan. Would we still prefer Company A? Most likely not. To the extent Callon is correct, might Western investors incorrectly perceive Japanese businesses as inferior simply because they hold large excess assets? If foreign investors revised their view of Japanese equities to conform more to Callon's view, material revaluation of those equities would seem unavoidable.

When we approach an investment candidate, we therefore disaggregate the components of return on equity. Does the company have noncore assets that, if separated from the calculation of ROE, would reveal a high-quality business attached to a bunch of excess assets? Perhaps more so than in any other equity market, it might make sense to approach Japanese companies as sum-of-the-parts opportunities rather than efficiently run monoliths.

Once we start viewing Japanese companies as comprised of several types of assets, the question of strategic action acquires significance. If a company takes the steps needed to force potentially ignorant investors to view it as a sum of valuable parts rather than as one inferior business, the perception of value might improve materially. Japan-based investment manager Mark O'Friel reveals the existence of situations in which management is taking the requisite strategic actions: "There are fund managers who have complemented their success in Japan by behaving in an activist fashion, that is, working with management to implement change. These shareholders might not be noisy, but they have frequent and meaningful meetings with managers and directors of corpo-rates. . . . *Gaiastu* is a well recognized term in Japanese vocabu-lary that describes using the threat of foreign pressure to implement change. The improvements in balance sheets of corporate Japan over the last decade can be attributed to some degree to share-holder pressure."[31]

Key Takeaways

Here are our top 10 takeaways from this chapter:

1. Investors seem to have adopted a more realistic view of inter-national investments, shaped by a surge of information, lower transaction costs, the bursting of several bubbles, emergence from several crises, and a realization that economies and mar-kets are more interconnected than ever.
2. In the interviews we conducted with leading investment man-agers around the globe, most of them expressed a view that the commonalities of international markets outweigh the differences.
3. Numerous studies confirm that adding international equities to a portfolio improves the risk-reward profile, either by boosting expected returns for a given level of volatility or by lowering the volatility for a given level of return.
4. Many investors appear to make the mistake of expecting for-eign markets to mirror their domestic market in every mate-rial way. This may be particularly true in the area of corporate governance. Unfortunately, governance practices change only slowly and may be impossible to influence from the outside.
5. We avoid much trouble in international investing when we accept that some levers, such as corporate governance, are harder to pull than others, such as the price we are willing to pay.
6. When we go global in the search for investments, we give our-selves a free option to pay a lower price than might be pos-sible in our home market. While no two equities are the same, similar companies frequently trade at materially different valua-tions across geographies.

7. Buffett's concept of circle of competence, while typically used in the context of different industries, may also have applicability to different countries. Due to the many unifying features of global equity investing, we may falsely assume that our competence extends to investing in all geographies.

8. One of the biggest drivers of disappointment for investors who venture globally might be an unrealistic view of the promise of emerging markets. In the rush toward growth, many investors readily ignore the return-on-capital prospects of fast-growing but highly competitive and capital-intensive industries.

9. The issue of challenging demographic trends confirms the importance of calibrating fundamentals versus expectations, perhaps best explained in Alfred Rappaport and Michael Mauboussin's *Expectations Investing*. When the expectations implied in stock prices fall materially short of the likely fundamentals, a buying opportunity may be at hand.

10. Excluding a country from consideration without regard for valuation may seem like an irrational decision for investors who subscribe to the view that there is a price for everything. However, the decision becomes more sensible if the importance an investor places on a factor like corporate governance differs materially from the importance placed on the same factor by other investors.

Notes

1. *The Manual of Ideas*, May 2011, 10.
2. *The Manual of Ideas*, July 2009, 17.
3. *The Manual of Ideas*, March 2009.
4. *The Manual of Ideas* interview with Kevin Murphy and Nick Kirrage, Schroders, London, 2012.
5. *The Manual of Ideas*, January 2013, 6.
6. *The Manual of Ideas*, January 2013, 9–10.
7. Mohnish Pabrai, Q&A session transcript, Japan Investing Summit 2012, November 7–8, 2012.
8. *The Manual of Ideas* interview with Christopher Swasbrook, Omaha, Nebraska, May 2012.
9. *The Manual of Ideas* interview with Eric Khrom, New York, 2012.
10. *The Manual of Ideas*, July 2009, 17.

11. *The Manual of Ideas*, March 2011, 19.
12. http://usatoday30.usatoday.com/news/nation/census/2011-05-04-Census-Households-Demographics_n.htm.
13. http://appsso.eurostat.ec.europa.eu/nui/show.do?dataset=ilc_lvph 01&lang=en.
14. http://en.wikipedia.org/wiki/List_of_countries_by_population_growth_rate.
15. http://en.wikipedia.org/wiki/Demographics_of_Japan.
16. http://en.wikipedia.org/wiki/Nikkei_225.
17. *The Manual of Ideas*, May 2011, 9–10.
18. *The Manual of Ideas*, November 2012, 10.
19. *The Manual of Ideas*, July 2009, 17.
20. *The Manual of Ideas* interview with Caglar Somek, New York, 2012.
21. *The Manual of Ideas*, January 2013, 15.
22. *The Manual of Ideas*, November 2012, 9.
23. *The Manual of Ideas*, January 31, 2011, 142–143.
24. *The Manual of Ideas*, March 2011, 20.
25. *The Manual of Ideas*, January 31, 2011, 144.
26. *The Manual of Ideas* interview with Daniel Gladiš, Zurich, Switzerland, February 2012.
27. *The Manual of Ideas* interview with Daniel Gladiš, Klosters, Switzerland, February 2012.
28. *The Manual of Ideas*, October 2009, 99.
29. *The Manual of Ideas*, June 2011, 9.
30. *The Manual of Ideas*, May 2011, 11.
31. *The Manual of Ideas*, May 2011, 14.

References

Andreessen, Marc. 2011. "Why Software Is Eating the World." *Wall Street Journal*, August 20.

Berkshire Hathaway. 2010. Definitive Notice and Proxy Statement, filed with the Securities and Exchange Commission (March 11), 7.

Bogle, John C. 2005. "Individual Stockholder, R.I.P." *Wall Street Journal*, October 3, A16.

Brooks, John. 1969. *Once in Golconda: A True Drama of Wall Street, 1920–1938*, 272. New York: Harper & Row.

Brown, Stephen J., and William N. Goetzmann. 1995. "Performance Persistence." *Journal of Finance* 50 (2): 679–698.

Buffett, Warren E. 2007. Letter to Shareholders of Berkshire Hathaway (February), 21.

Buffett, Warren E. 2009. Letter to Shareholders of Berkshire Hathaway (February), 5.

Carhart, Mark M. 1997. "On Persistence in Mutual Fund Performance." *Journal of Finance* 52 (1): 57–82.

CNN/Money online edition. 2002. (April 16), http://money.cnn.com/2002/04/16/news/deals/hp_deutsche/.

Coffee, John C., Jr., Louis Lowenstein, and Susan Rose-Ackerman. 1988. *Knights, Raiders, and Targets*. New York: Oxford University Press, 15–16.

Einhorn, David. 2010. Greenlight Capital Q4 2009 Letter (January), accessed online at www.marketfolly.com/2010/01/david-einhorns-greenlight-capital.html.

Ericsson, K. Anders. 2004. "Deliberate Practice and the Acquisition and Maintenance of Expert Performance in Medicine and Related Domains." *Academic Medicine* 79 (10): S70–81.

Fama, Eugene F., and Michael C. Jensen. 1983. "Separation of Ownership and Control." *Journal of Law and Economics* 26 (2): 301–325.

Ferri, Richard A. 2003. *Protecting Your Wealth in Good Times and Bad*. New York: McGraw-Hill, 61–63.

French, Kenneth. Data Library, accessed online at http://mba.tuck.dartmouth.edu/pages/faculty/ken.french/data_library.html.

Grantham, Jeremy. 2005. "Everything I Think I Know about the Market in 20 Minutes." Market Commentary Document. Grantham, Mayo, Van Otterloo & Co., accessed online at www.siliconinvestor.com/readmsgs.aspx?subjectid=51347&msgnum=27570&batchsize=10&batchtype=Previous.

GreatInvestors TV. 2012. "The Importance of Business Cycles, with Simon Caufield, Managing Director of SIM Limited." (July 6), accessed online at http://greatinvestors.tv.

Hagstrom, Robert G. 2005. *The Warren Buffett Way*, 2nd ed. Hoboken, NJ: John Wiley & Sons.

Khorana, Ajay, and Edward Nelling. 1997. "The Performance, Risk, and Diversification of Sector Funds." *Financial Analysts Journal* 53 (3): 62–74.

Klarman, Seth A. 1991. *Margin of Safety: Risk-Averse Value Investing Strategies for the Thoughtful Investor*. New York: HarperCollins.

Malkiel, Burton G. 1995. "Returns from Investing in Equity Mutual Funds 1971 to 1991." *Journal of Finance* 50 (2): 549–572.

The Manual of Ideas. 2008. "The Magic Formula 100," November.

The Manual of Ideas. 2009. "Top Ideas Based on Four Different Qualitative Screens," February.

The Manual of Ideas. 2009. "Ben Graham–Style Investing: The Deep Value Report," April 27.

The Manual of Ideas. 2009. "The Superinvestor Issue," May 28.

The Manual of Ideas. 2009. "Companies with Hidden Real Estate Value," June 19.

The Manual of Ideas. 2009. "Businesses with Pricing Power and Low Capital Intensity," July 31.

The Manual of Ideas. 2009. "The Superinvestor Issue," August 21.

The Manual of Ideas. 2009. "The Magic Formula Issue," September 29.

The Manual of Ideas. 2009. "The European Value Issue," October 27.

The Manual of Ideas. 2009. "The Superinvestor Issue," November 20.

The Manual of Ideas. 2009. "2009 Losers, 2010 Winners?" December 31.

The Manual of Ideas. 2010. "Best Ideas for 2010," January 21.

The Manual of Ideas. 2010. "The Superinvestor Issue," February 18.

The Manual of Ideas. 2010. "The Brand Value Issue," March 25.

The Manual of Ideas. 2010. "The Deep Value Report," April 21.

The Manual of Ideas. 2010. "The Superinvestor Report," May 24.

The Manual of Ideas. 2010. "The Magic Formula Issue," June 30.

The Manual of Ideas. 2010. "The Downside Protection Issue," July 29.

The Manual of Ideas. 2010. "The Superinvestor Report," August 27.

The Manual of Ideas. 2010. "The European Value Issue," September 30.

The Manual of Ideas. 2010. "Value Opportunities in Banks?" October 29.

The Manual of Ideas. 2010. "2010 Losers, 2011 Winners?" December 27.

The Manual of Ideas. 2011. "Large Cap Stocks: How Cheap Are They?," January 31.

The Manual of Ideas. 2011. "The Superinvestor Issue," February 28.
The Manual of Ideas. 2011. "Small- and Micro-Cap Value," March 31.
The Manual of Ideas. 2011. "The Japan Issue," May 2.
The Manual of Ideas. 2011. "The Superinvestor Issue," June 1.
The Manual of Ideas. 2011. "The Magic Formula Issue," July 1.
The Manual of Ideas. 2011. "Underappreciated Balance Sheet Values," August 1.
The Manual of Ideas. 2011. "The Superinvestor Issue," September 2.
The Manual of Ideas. 2011. "The Model Portfolio Issue," October 1.
The Manual of Ideas. 2011. "The Fear Issue," November.
The Manual of Ideas. 2011. "The Superinvestor Issue," December.
The Manual of Ideas. 2012. "Great Companies, on Sale," January.
The Manual of Ideas. 2012. "The Small-Cap Value Issue," February.
The Manual of Ideas. 2012. "The Superinvestor Issue," March.
The Manual of Ideas. 2012. "Value in Emerging Markets," April.
The Manual of Ideas. 2012. "Deep Value Issue," May.
The Manual of Ideas. 2012. "The Superinvestor Issue," June.
The Manual of Ideas. 2012. "Wide-Moat Companies," July.
The Manual of Ideas. 2012. "The Equity Income Issue," August.
The Manual of Ideas. 2012. "The Superinvestor Issue," September.
The Manual of Ideas. 2012. "The European Value Issue," October.
The Manual of Ideas. 2012. "The Japan Value Issue," November.
The Manual of Ideas. 2012. "The Superinvestor Issue," December.
The Manual of Ideas. 2013. "Best Ideas 2013," January.
The Manual of Ideas. 2013. "Small-Cap Value," February.
The Manual of Ideas. 2013. "The Superinvestor Issue," March.
The Manual of Ideas Interview. "Alon Bochman, Managing Member, Stepwise Capital," accessed online at www.youtube.com/watch?v=4H2n6RGXCoc.
The Manual of Ideas Interview. "Andrew Williamson of Hawkwood Deep Value Fund," accessed online at www.youtube.com/watch?v=Gki52YyOSRc.
The Manual of Ideas Interview. "Ben Graham's Deep Value Approach, Refined and Globalized—VS Capital Advisors," accessed online at www.youtube.com/watch?v=4fkfjIlAdUM.
The Manual of Ideas Interview. "Brad Hathaway, Managing Partner, Far View Capital," accessed online at www.youtube.com/watch?v=F8tRr1p7cxo.
The Manual of Ideas Interview. "Brian Bares, Chief Investment Officer, Bares Capital," accessed online at www.youtube.com/watch?v=8uSOYtRe7VA.
The Manual of Ideas Interview. "Caglar Somek, Global Portfolio Manager, Caravel Management," accessed online at www.youtube.com/watch?v=5Lj3-U1zlfA.
The Manual of Ideas Interview. "Contrarian Investing, with Randall Abramson of Trapeze Capital," accessed online at www.youtube.com/watch?v=T3b3129LQG8.

The Manual of Ideas Interview. "Dan Sheehan, General Partner, Sheehan Associates," accessed online at www.youtube.com/watch?v=UgwBZ26R274.

The Manual of Ideas Interview. "Dave Sather, President, Sather Financial," accessed online at www.youtube.com/watch?v=az6Zl4PKm7k.

The Manual of Ideas Interview. "David Coyne of Setanta Asset Management on His Approach to Value Investing," accessed online at www.youtube .com/watch?v=8-_cqvv2OS8.

The Manual of Ideas Interview. "David Nierenberg and Cara Jacobsen, The D3 Family Funds," accessed online at www.youtube.com/user/ manualofideas/videos?view=0.

The Manual of Ideas Interview. "Dominic Fisher, Director, Thistledown Investment Management," accessed online at www.youtube.com/ watch?v=l1Soea4mgWI.

The Manual of Ideas Interview. "Emmanuel Daugeras, Founder Partner, Amdamax," accessed online at www.youtube.com/watch?v=ReFOu5LrEiY.

The Manual of Ideas Interview. "Eric DeLamarter, Portfolio Manager, Half Moon Capital," accessed online at www.youtube.com/watch?v=l8DRkYvHT7w.

The Manual of Ideas Interview. "European Small-Cap Value Investing, with Philip Best and Marc Saint John Webb," accessed online at www .youtube.com/watch?v=saVXcBM7Elk.

The Manual of Ideas Interview. "Exclusive Interview with Pier-Alberto Furno on Opportunities in Europe and Japan," accessed online at www .youtube.com/watch?v=hDP5mVojQXk.

The Manual of Ideas Interview. "Global Value Opportunities with Charles Heenan of Kennox Strategic Value Fund," accessed online at www .youtube.com/watch?v=QvxuijDZZuw.

The Manual of Ideas Interview. "Guy Spier on European Credit Crisis and Investment Opportunities," accessed online at www.youtube.com/ watch?v=YSkJzBoAGC4.

The Manual of Ideas Interview. "Hasbro Ex-CEO Alan Hassenfeld on Toy Industry, Global Risks, Philanthropy," accessed online at www.youtube .com/watch?v=X54KHXW3tOo.

The Manual of Ideas Interview. "How to Achieve Abnormal Returns in the Stock Market, with Tadas Viskanta," accessed online at www.youtube .com/watch?v=1hUVOX1S5xo.

The Manual of Ideas Interview. "How to Analyze an Insurance Company and More, with Amir Avitzur," accessed online at www.youtube.com/ watch?v=MKrW53GDpdM.

The Manual of Ideas Interview. "How to Become a Better Investor, with Greg Speicher," accessed online at www.youtube.com/watch?v=biitcLoZsIQ.

The Manual of Ideas Interview. "Howard Marks, Chairman, Oaktree Capital Management," accessed online at www.youtube.com/watch?v= HXQhKJkgo88.

The Manual of Ideas Interview. "Insights from Global Value Investor Ori Eyal," accessed online at www.youtube.com/watch?v=RbHFq5wY7vg.

The Manual of Ideas Interview. "Investing in Great Businesses Globally, with Daniel Gladis of Vltava Fund," accessed online at www.youtube.com/watch?v=fO8MNy-kwSI.

The Manual of Ideas Interview. "Investing Insights: Simon Denison-Smith and Jonathan Mills of Metropolis Capital," accessed online at www.youtube.com/watch?v=kHy2h_CmpOo.

The Manual of Ideas Interview. "James Montier: Applying the Seven Immutable Laws," accessed online at www.youtube.com/watch?v=xYV7-VGoqFM.

The Manual of Ideas Interview. "Josh Tarasoff, General Partner, Greenlea Lane Capital," accessed online at www.youtube.com/watch?v=XAubRoZbI9U.

The Manual of Ideas Interview. "Lauren Templeton and Scott Phillips," accessed online at www.youtube.com/watch?v=Npl8rNM9jvE.

The Manual of Ideas Interview. "Lisa Rapuano, Portfolio Manager, Lane Five Capital Management," accessed online at www.youtube.com/watch?v=Uy2h-lT9FmE.

The Manual of Ideas Interview. "Metals and Mining Investing, with Alex Tsukernik of Syntella Partners," accessed online at www.youtube.com/watch?v=hlbV48hoX7U.

The Manual of Ideas Interview. "Mike Onghai, President, AppAddictive," accessed online at www.youtube.com/watch?v=IN8pzeJVZk0.

The Manual of Ideas Interview. "Pat Dorsey on Moats," accessed online at www.youtube.com/watch?v=LHx19-BZVwQ.

The Manual of Ideas Interview. "Paul Sonkin, Portfolio Manager, Hummingbird Management," accessed online at www.youtube.com/watch?v=hOOCG8lEyLU.

The Manual of Ideas Interview. "Pitfalls of Financial Ratios in Value Investing, with Robert Leitz of Iolite Capital," accessed online at www.youtube.com/watch?v=Xk7j8dqcNRE.

The Manual of Ideas Interview. "Protect Your Assets and Profit from the European Debt Crisis, by Prof. Dr. Max Otte," accessed online at www.youtube.com/watch?v=PP_DpgwgpH8.

The Manual of Ideas Interview. "Robert Robotti, President, Robotti & Company," accessed online at www.youtube.com/watch?v=N1MVgz6dJd0.

The Manual of Ideas Interview. "Sean Riskowitz, General Partner, Riskowitz Capital Management," accessed online at www.youtube.com/watch?v=hnVRI6XLfi8.

The Manual of Ideas Interview. "Shawn Kravetz of Esplanade Capital on Value Investing, Solar Stocks and More," accessed online at www.youtube.com/watch?v=im0IcRxrKAg.

The Manual of Ideas Interview. "Simon Caufield, Managing Director, SIM Limited," accessed online at www.youtube.com/watch?v=oZ-SA_3NSjk.

The Manual of Ideas Interview. "Stephen Roseman Discusses His Investment Approach," accessed online at www.youtube.com/watch?v=PlL4opd1m-8.

The Manual of Ideas Interview. "The Economic Sell Rule and More on Investing, with David Merkel," accessed online at www.youtube.com/watch?v=wubEyyAtXuE.

The Manual of Ideas Interview. "Three Gs of Investing: Pavel Begun and Cory Bailey," accessed online at www.youtube.com/watch?v=fXHWIo5X2vg.

The Manual of Ideas Interview. "Tom Russo of Gardner Russo & Gardner," accessed online at www.youtube.com/watch?v=asduGUY09NY.

The Manual of Ideas Interview. "UK Deep Value Investing, with Jeroen Bos of Church House Deep Value Fund," accessed online at www.youtube.com/watch?v=wyK_cVSQTCA.

The Manual of Ideas Interview. "Value Investing in France and Beyond, with François Badelon of Amiral Gestion," accessed online at www.youtube.com/watch?v=RbUsidNzM48.

The Manual of Ideas Interview. "Value Investing in India, with Rahul Saraogi, Atyant Capital Advisors," accessed online at www.youtube.com/watch?v=kZBWZd_zB8w.

The Manual of Ideas Interview. "Value Investing in Smaller Companies, with Jeff Bronchick of Cove Street Capital," accessed online at www.youtube.com/watch?v=zPKxdumf3ro.

The Manual of Ideas Interview. "Value Investing Wisdom and Ideas, with Glenn Surowiec," accessed online at www.youtube.com/watch?v=kXzSOBT8Evo.

The Manual of Ideas Interview. "What All Investors Can Learn from the Great Investors, with Stephen Weiss," accessed online at www.youtube.com/watch?v=64gnCfh1Lgs.

The Manual of Ideas Interview. "Why Reading International Is Misunderstood, with Andrew Shapiro of Lawndale," accessed online at www.youtube.com/watch?v=VmJWbQJCxko.

The Manual of Ideas Interview. "Yusuf Samad on Long-Term Investing," accessed online at www.youtube.com/watch?v=SHgj8ZJqkDY.

The Manual of Ideas Interview. Eric Khrom, New York, 2012.

McDonald, Ian. 2005. "Heard on the Street: The Energy Conundrum: To Own or Ignore?" *Wall Street Journal*, October 7, C1, C4.

Mihaljevic, John. "The Manual of Ideas on Business Leader Henry Singleton, Founder of Teledyne," accessed online at www.youtube.com/watch?v=3BeqIrpnmT8.

Morgenson, Gretchen. 2004. "Jackpot Du Jour: It Pays to Quit." *New York Times*, October 31 (Section 3), 1, 6.

Oldfield, Richard. 2007. *Simple But Not Easy*. London, England: Doddington, 94–96.

O'Shaughnessy, James P. 2012. *What Works on Wall Street: The Classic Guide to the Best-Performing Investment Strategies of All Time*, 4th ed. New York: McGraw-Hill, 71.

Pabrai, Mohnish. 2002–2004. *Mosaic: Perspectives on Investing*. Lake Forest, CA: Grammer Buff, 33–35.

Pabrai, Mohnish, and Guy Spier. 2012. Exclusive Q&A Transcript. Japan Investing Summit 2012 (November 7–8).

Paulson, John. 2012. Presentation on Hartford Financial Services Group (March 9), accessed at www.marketfolly.com/2012/03/john-paulsons-presentation-on-why.html.

Porter, Michael E. 1998. *On Competition*. Cambridge, MA: Harvard Business School Publishing, 164–165.

Rubin, Robert E., and Jacob Weisberg. *In an Uncertain World: Tough Choices from Wall Street to Washington*. New York: Random House.

Schwed, Fred, Jr. 1995. *Where Are the Customers' Yachts?* Hoboken, NJ: John Wiley & Sons, 62.

Stone, Amey. 1999. "Homespun Wisdom from the 'Oracle of Omaha.'" *BusinessWeek* (June), accessed online at www.businessweek.com/bwdaily/dnflash/june1999/sw90625.htm.

Tweedy Browne. *What Has Worked In Investing*, accessed online at http://www.tweedy.com/resources/library_docs/papers/WhatHasWorkedFundVersionWeb.pdf.

YouTube. "Marty Whitman on Moving beyond Graham & Dodd Investing," accessed online at www.youtube.com/watch?v=39qDeG5Foko.

About the Author

John **Mihaljevic**, CFA, is a Managing Editor of *The Manual of Ideas*, the monthly idea-oriented research publication for value-oriented investors, and a Managing Director of ValueConferences, the series of fully online investment conferences for value-oriented investors. He has also served as Managing Partner of investment firm Mihaljevic Capital Management LLC since 2005. He is a member of Value Investors Club, an exclusive community of top money managers, and has won the club's prize for best investment idea. John is a trained capital allocator, having studied under Yale University Chief Investment Officer David Swensen, and served as research assistant to Nobel Laureate James Tobin. John holds a BA in Economics, summa cum laude, from Yale and is a CFA charterholder. He resides in Zurich, Switzerland, with his wife, two boys, and a girl.

Index